JUST BETWEEN US

The Southwest Center Series
Joseph C. Wilder, Editor

Just Between Us

An Ethnography of Male Identity and Intimacy in Rural Communities of Northern Mexico

GUILLERMO NÚÑEZ NORIEGA

THE UNIVERSITY OF
ARIZONA PRESS

TUCSON

The University of Arizona Press
© 2014 The Arizona Board of Regents
All rights reserved

www.uapress.arizona.edu

Library of Congress Cataloging-in-Publication Data
Núñez Noriega, Guillermo.
    Just between us : an ethnography of male identity and intimacy in rural communities
of Northern Mexico / Guillermo Núñez Noriega.
        pages cm. — (Southwest center series)
    Includes bibliographical references and index.
    ISBN 978-0-8165-3094-6 (paperback)
    1. Men—Mexico, North—Identity.   2. Masculinity—Mexico,
North.   3. Patriarchy—Mexico, North.   4. Intimacy (Psychology)   5. Sex role—
Mexico, North.   I. Title.
    HQ1090.7.M6N85 2014
    305.310972—dc23   2013039497

Originally published in Spanish as *Masculinidad e intimidad: Identidad, sexualidad y sida*
by Miguel Ángel Porrúa, El Colegio de Sonora y Universidad Nacional Autónoma de
Mexico 2007.

Publication of this book is made possible in part by a grant from the Southwest Center of
the University of Arizona.

Manufactured in the United States of America on acid-free, archival-quality paper
containing a minimum of 30% post-consumer waste and processed chlorine free.

19   18   17   16   15   14   6   5   4   3   2   1

With enormous gratitude and admiration to Maribel Álvarez: for her intelligence, support, and friendship.

And to the memory of Jorge Madrid Valencia, who taught me through his friendship the skills to do ethnographic work among Serrano people.

Contents

JUST BETWEEN US

Introduction

*There is something I am very much interested in nowadays; it is the issue
of friendship. Through the centuries that followed Antiquity, friendship
was a very important relationship: a relationship where individuals had a
certain freedom . . . which allowed them to have very intense affective
relations. . . . One of my hypotheses . . . is that homosexuality (by which I
understand the existence of sexual relations among men) became a
problem since the 18th century. . . . As much as friendship was considered
something important, as much as it was socially accepted, nobody was
aware that men had sexual relations then . . . that they made love or
kissed each other had no importance . . . the disappearance of friendship
as a social relation and the fact that homosexuality was declared a social,
political, and medical problem, are part of the same process.[1]*

FOUCAULT 2001, 1563–4

Questions Around a Photographic Image

According to a popular proverb, "an image speaks louder than a thousand
words." How convenient everything would be if this were true. If that were
the case, then the scholarly need to "know things" and the anthropologist's
anguish over the desire to express in words the ethnographic experience
(those details that Malinowski [1922] called "the imponderables of everyday life") would be so much easier to resolve. If images could speak, then
by exhibiting or introducing the right image, presumably one could sum-
marize into simple, powerful arguments those aspects of another's life that
are otherwise obscure to us.

Unfortunately, this is not how it works. Images do not speak by themselves. It is true that images are ubiquitous, but most of the time they function as registers of actions performed in very specific moments and framed
by specific contexts. Images derive their meanings from the cultural and
historical realities in which they are embedded, and those realities in turn
frame their production and interpretation. Those cultural and temporal
specificities can in some instances become barriers for interpretation for
those coming from another time or cultural context; they can represent
hard-to-bridge gaps between the image and its observers. Sometimes, these

3

gaps can even lead to deception: they induce us to see only what seems obvious. However, as another common proverb admonishes, we cannot forget that "not all that shines is gold."

The image on the following page of José Pedro and Francisco tenderly holding hands seems to speak louder than words.[2] After all, one could argue, it is evident that they are holding hands. Why should there be any difficulty involved in simply naming that which is plain to the eye? This naïve belief in the capacity to name "reality" and to represent it truthfully is precisely what the philosopher and linguist Derrida (1976) calls, cryptically and critically, "the metaphysics of presence." But as Derrida himself points out, the meaning of an action is hardly ever as transparent as it seems, and finding the right words to name what is happening can often be quite difficult. For instance, are we sure that we can know why these two men are holding hands? What was the meaning of this gesture to them? What was the social significance at the time this photo was taken of two men holding hands? Is it possible to attribute a "sexual" meaning to the gesture captured in this photograph? And if that were the case, what do we mean by sexual in this instance? What cultural contexts made possible the production of this image? What personal, familial, or social consequences followed from the circulation of this image at the time of its production? More than speaking louder than a thousand words, the image seems to provoke a thousand questions. In fact, assaulted by these interrogations, the image seems quite silent—incapable of providing answers by itself.

Nonetheless, a belief in the transparency of the meaning of that which is "seen" is very common. For many, it is taken for granted. A brief exercise I conducted during fieldwork demonstrates this point. The exercise consisted of presenting the photo above to a random group of young people not familiar with anthropological methods or theories in the cities of Hermosillo, Sonora, and Tucson, Arizona. Most respondents expressed surprise at the fact that "old photographs of gay people" or of "two lovers" existed. The responses were uniform, regardless of which side of the US/Mexico border they were collected. Some gay[3] men in Hermosillo to whom I showed the image commented in jest, "I wonder who is the fairy (*joto*) and who is the trade (*mayate*)."[4] "Maybe they both enjoyed having fun (*cotorreo*)?" Others commented on what they perceived to be a "contrast" between the men's "masculine appearance" represented by the hats, boots, clothing, muscled bodies, big hands, and their origin in the countryside and their "homosexual appearance" symbolized by the action of holding hands discreetly. A young transvestite remarked in emphatic camp style, "Look at that, and they seem so manly, that's the way it is sometimes,

you find guys that strut their manhood but that in the end are more feminine than me." Other men tended to remark on the age or antiquity of the photograph. Others asked, "Who are they?" Upon noticing that the men were holding hands lightly, one man said, "Geez, what is up with that?" and another man said, "How interesting . . . no? Was that common back then?"

A quick analysis of the responses of these men suggests that for them the meaning of the image can be interpreted in relation to the play of various signifiers: gay, homosexual, *mayate, joto*, lovers, feminine, and so forth. These words are presumed to carry transparent meanings that are in turn applied transparently or "obviously" to the image. Even though the men interviewed varied in their reading of these signifiers, their comments reveal some points in common: first, the image of two men dressed in cowboy attire and holding hands seemed "strange" to almost everyone. Second, this sense of the strange in almost all cases is understood furthermore as an "oddity" (in Spanish, a *rareza*, which can be related to the English word *queer*). In this context, the term *queer* (*raro*) is intended to communicate sexual and gender dissidence.

Commonsense interpretations of the transparency of these signifiers begins to crumble when we learn that this photo of José Pedro and Francisco was framed and hung on the living room wall of a family home in a small town in the country side of Sonora, visible to the wife, children, relatives, neighbors, and visitors for decades. Commonsense interpretations shatter even further when we learn, after more than three years of anthropological fieldwork deep in the sierra of Sonora, that José Pedro and Francisco's image is not unique, that similar photographs can be found in select homes in the region. As a matter of fact, one of the men interviewed in the short exercise mentioned above commented that his own mother kept a similar photo in their family home depicting his grandfather "in that way, holding the hand of his friend, his compadre."

Hence, the more or less "familiar" or everyday character of this type of image during a particular historical period renders as inadequate the current commonsense interpretations that tend to point toward the homosexual or gay nature of the holding of hands between the men in the photo, or of the men themselves as homosexuals. Yet, understandably so, this sexual reading of the image fits the contemporary social milieu in Mexico. In today's Mexican society, especially in rural communities, the concept of homosexuality hardly offers the range of permissive possibilities represented by the public display of the image in question.[5] What can be made then of the incompatibility of these two readings? Would it be correct to say that in Mexico, and in northern Mexico in particular, homosexuality was more amply permitted and socially sanctioned scarcely two generations ago than it is today in urban centers such as Hermosillo and Mexico City? Such a conclusion is unlikely.

An explanation about the discrepancy of meanings of homosexuality must be explored through other means. What should be clear at this juncture, however, is that applying commonsense notions of the present to the historical reality represented in a photo of the past is tricky and makes for inadequate social analysis. We are left to inquire: what has happened in Mexican (or in Sonoran) society in the last few decades that makes coming to terms with an image like that of José Pedro and Francisco difficult and equivocal?

We thus come face-to-face with one of those quintessential paradoxes of anthropology: an action that is so obvious, so transparent by virtue of the fact that is publicly enacted, so "plain to the eye" of common sense, appears at the same time to have a meaning so elusive that it actually results in being something strange and foreign to our experience. The only thing that is plain to the eye is that our conceptual resources fall short in accounting for what we see. The paradox becomes yet more disorienting when I informed the young respondents to my survey that the men in the photo were inhabitants of the same region in which "we" live; in other words, the men in the photo could have been one of my informant's grandfathers. How is it possible that something could be so foreign in its meaning to "us" when it is at the same time so familiar in terms of time and geography?

Fortunately, anthropology has the disciplinary habit of bringing forth paradoxes in order to subject them to a kind of analysis—a systematic way of asking questions and engendering knowledge—that can come very close to "explaining" things and hence to assuage our anxieties about not knowing. In doing so, and also quite fortunately, anthropological methods shed light into the cultural and historical nature—and therefore the relative or artificial character—of the ways in which human beings formulate meanings about things and the world.

When I presented the above image of José Pedro and Francisco to my friends and acquaintances, the photo not only confused the obvious signifiers described above, it also revealed even more entangled paradoxes. In a tone of voice resembling that of a complaint (*queja*), a nineteen-year-old gay man from Hermosillo expressed: "So you mean to tell me that back then men could hold hands and not be homosexuals? And how come it is not like that now? Ahh, that's funny, today things should be as they were then." This comment would seem to call into question the commonsense notions about modernity and urban life prevalent in Mexico and other countries. Under such terms, the past (as rurality) is a marker of "tradition" and hence of the premodern—of backwardness (*atraso*), secrecy (*oscurantismo*), and lack of personal freedom—whereas the present is a time/space above those limitations, a "forward" time in the ascendant path toward reason and liberty.

Various authors have argued that nationalist and regionalist movements of different sorts attach themselves to discourses about the past to reconfigure a sense of tradition that supports their individual political projects (Alonso 1995; Anderson 1983; Corrigan and Sayer 1993). However, we must also recognize that in their efforts to suggest that "everything was better in the past," cultural resistance efforts against processes of modernization can similarly mobilize visions about the past that are no less artificial than the hegemonic ones. Hence, both what is thought of as traditional and what is considered the past could serve as justification for diverse political agendas. The notion of the traditional in Sonoran regionalist discourse is no exemption (Núñez 1995). And such a discourse, inflected as it is with sexist and racist ideologies, does not include in any sense of the word a greater sense of freedom and intimacy in the past, as the comment by the young man above suggests.

How is it possible to explain, then, a field of personal freedom[6] in the past that does not exist in the present? To answer this question, I find that the work of the philosopher and historian Michel Foucault on the "history of sexuality" offers the best theoretical grounds (Foucault 1976). Foucault demonstrates that the history of sex, far from being the history of a desire that advances historically from repression to liberation, can be better understood as the history of a "mode of speaking" about sex, of understanding it socially and politically, and of the ways in which the erotic desire is defined socially. The very notion of sexuality as an inner "truth of the self" (such as when one speaks of "my sexuality" or of "women's sexuality") that permeates the whole being is a cultural and political modern invention. Each one of those modes of speaking exists also as a "discursive regime" that incites or limits certain actions; in other words, as a regime of power and freedom.

This book seeks to insert itself within these theoretical lines of inquiry— with the help of the paradoxical effect of an image—to demonstrate the existence in contemporary Mexico of an invisible regime of power that constructs and regulates the field of possibilities for the social actions of men, especially those acts of friendship, affection, and eroticism with other men. This work is therefore an investigation of modes of speaking about being a man, being gay, homosexual, masculine, trade, fairy, or having sexual relations with another man that construct possibilities for intimacy in general, but affective and erotic intimacy among men in particular.

The image of José Pedro and Francisco and other similar photos of the time thus stand as mirrors. They serve as heuristic devices that both invite and provoke reflection to make us aware of the fact that we have, in the present, particular ways of understanding and signifying people's conceptions of their bodies and sex differences, their sexual and reproductive practices, their femininity and masculinity, their affective and erotic behaviors, and the social distinctions and power relations that cross all these dimensions. That is, we inhabit a particular historically and socially constructed sexual/gender regime.[7]

In this general theoretical framework, several questions emerge prominently: What exactly makes up the power regime of which I speak? What are the conceptions and modes of speaking about being a man, about men's sexuality and diverse forms of intimacy between males, that are invisibly constructing the possibilities of acting, understanding, being, and relating sexually and affectively? How are the meanings attributed to bodies, sexual experiences, demonstrations of affection, attractions, and masculinity and femininity, conditioning the relations of power and pleasure exerted over and between male subjects? How do sexual and gender categories and meanings take part in this sexual/gender regime that frames the possibilities of men's intimacy with other men?

I believe that the image of José Pedro and Francisco can do more than simply help us become aware of the present dominant discourse in which we are living. It can also stand as a sui-generis mirror that assumes a surrealist character and makes a proposal for what is not present. This proposal is a call for exploration and awareness of a subsumed reality: "another" reality that remains occult and denied within the sex/gender regime and its taxonomy of identity categories.

The ethnographic work I conducted, as well as my own practices of gender and sexual dissidence, has brought me face-to-face with a reality more ambiguous and contradictory than that which is contained in the dominant discourses of what currently counts as being a man, heterosexual, gay, or *joto* (fairy). I am referring to certain subjects' behaviors, relationships, and forms of signification that are constantly subverting the borders of identities as prescribed by the dominant gender and sexual discourses and through which the same subjects sustain complex relations of subversion, resistance, and/or accommodation.

The contributions of postmodern feminism (Butler 1990, 1993) have put into evidence the unstable, incoherent, and heterogeneous character of sexual and gender identities (especially the identity "woman"). As such, they have countered the patriarchal pretensions that hold up various systems of dominant homologies (for instance, the formula man = masculine = heterosexual; that is, the idea that masculinity derives naturally from the male body and predicts heterosexuality). This book stirs the theoretical grounds tilled by those contributions in order to reexamine the identity "man," and particularly "the Mexican man," by analyzing a reality of affective/erotic expressions, of intimacy among males that escapes the disciplinary and regulatory discourses we may be accustomed to. In this process I try to answer a series of questions that have intrigued me:

Are there other loving and erotic realities among men today that escape the conventional conceptions evoked by the terms *gay, homosexual, trade, fairy (joto, mayate), men, masculinity*, and the like? Of what do those other realities consist? And what relationship do those alternative erotic realities have with the dominant categories of the discursive regime that frames the possibilities for intimacy among males?

How is it that this discursive regime, this system of dominant representations about men—their gender identities and their sexualities—becomes incapable of understanding different realities that do not conform to its preponderant meanings, both in the past, as in the image of José Pedro and Francisco, and in the present?

What is the nature of the relationship between the possibilities for affective and/or erotic intimacy between males and the dominant discourses and categories about homoerotic practices and notions of being a man?

These questions have figured prominently among my research interests for a long time. They have structured and guided my ethnographic investigations in the sierra of Sonora as well as in Hermosillo, capital city of the same state, from 1997 to 2002. In the chapters that follow, I try to provide answers to these questions.

Male Intimacy and the Discourses on and Categories of Homoerotic Relations in Mexico

Sexual practices and the categories that designate them are of central importance to my arguments in this work. In this regard, I should say first of all, that the choice of the term *male intimacy* in the title of this book is intended to mark a particular theoretical position in a debate concerning the use of the modern sexual category homosexual or gay to refer to erotic and/or affectionate practices and relationships among human males in a given culture or through time. In this debate, my argument is that sexual categories are inextricably embedded in sexual and gender systems and convey meanings, ways of understanding actions and people, and ways of creating social distinctions and power relations. Sexual categories and their meanings are neither universal nor neutral descriptors, but cultural ways of understanding and acting. They reflect the way a society has constructed its sexual values and distinctions in a particular moment. They change historically and from culture to culture, along with many other social, political, economic, and cultural changes. They are part of colonial and globalization processes too. Insofar as sexual meaning and categories are relevant to people in their daily lives in every society, they should be relevant to researchers and their accounts.

For those reasons, instead of using the modern sexual category of gay or homosexual to name and understand all erotic relationships among males, I use the concept of male intimacy to function as a methodological device to open some analytical possibilities to get to know the complex array of meanings and categories that frame the understanding of male homo-erotic practices and relations in a given society. As I hope to demonstrate in the following chapters, the Mexican sexual/gender system contains multiple ways of understanding and multiple categories related to male-to-male erotic relations, including, but not limited to, modern discourses and identities such as homosexual, gay, and even queer. Other traditional categories are used such as those of *joto* (fairy) and *mayate* (trade) as part of a Mediterranean gender and sexual culture. In as much as we are trying to understand the relationship of those meanings, categories, and practices to gender identities, power relations, and resistances, I believe it is preferable to make those categories objects of study instead of deploying them as analytical tools in and of themselves.

The ethnographic data in this book show us that Mexican homoerotic reality cannot be characterized by any single discourse, be it one framed by dominant traditional sexual categories and meanings (e.g., *joto*, *mayate*, etc.) of Spanish Mediterranean origin or by modern ones (e.g., gay)[8] of American origin. Many men have sex and love relations with other men at the margins of those typologies and meanings; they have them simply as men, as the ethnographic account in this book clearly demonstrates. Most of these men do not conceive of themselves as having a sexuality in the modern sense of the word, as an inner truth that gives meaning to all of their being. Therefore, in Mexico, concepts such as homosexual subjectivity, gay world, or homosexual discourse of resistance can hardly account for all subjects or groups of people engaged in same-sex male erotic and affective relations, their subjectivities, their subject positions in the sexual/gender field, or their cultural practices and life-styles.

The study of this social reality helps us point to a different understanding of homoerotic relations than those elaborated by authors in Europe, such as Didier Eribon (1999), which tend to characterize such relations only in terms of something that happens in modern times with a single, stable, and spreading gay identity, subjectivity, and culture, created as a *discourse en retour* against a dominant homophobic culture. Homoerotic relations among males in Mexico (and, I dare to say, anywhere) do not conform to and are not exhausted by this narrative.

Cultural and political forces, even in modernity, are complex and contradictory; and the tensions generated by such contradictions can be detected in sexual and gender power relations as well as in practices that involve homophobia *and* resistance or accommodation to it. Gay discourse and identity has not been the only means people have invented, known, or adopted in their daily lives to express dissident forms of sexuality and desire. In many regions around the world gay discourse and identity is not known or familiar. Furthermore, even when gay discourse is well known, it does not always offer a comfortable fit with class and ethnic experiences or other vernacular ways of understanding sexuality and gender (Núñez 2009). Nevertheless, even outside the framework of gay identity, men and women resist compulsions of heteronormativity and try to live out their affections, desires, and pleasures as best they can. This book explores precisely these divergent histories and practices through ethnography in communities of northern Mexico and, by doing so, tries to reveal the complexities of the social and cultural process of modernity.

The perspective on homophobia sustained in this book is different in two ways. First, I strive to understand homophobia as a historical and cultural phenomenon. As a historical phenomenon, homophobia changes in relation to many other social dimensions. As a cultural phenomenon, it is an integral part of sexual/gender systems—their ideologies, relations, and identities. Thus, instead of assuming a timeless and structural homophobia, I suggest the need to study how a particular sexual/gender system may promote an array of violence in relation to those culturally defined (by the same system) as sexual/gender "deviants."

Second, I focus on the role of homophobia in the process of masculinization of all men, and the importance of gender identities (effeminacy and masculinity) in the construction of their vulnerabilities in the face of homophobia. In Mexico and according to literature in many other countries as well, homophobia is something that structures not only homosexual subjectivities but also men's subjectivities and masculine identity dynamics, because all men are subject to homophobic violence as part of their masculinization process. At the same time, there is a specific and discretional violence toward those men (particularly when they are children and boys) who are "less masculine," "effeminate" or "not masculine enough" according to social standards, and not necessarily toward those men who happen to have affectionate or sexual bonds with other men. Gender comportment (manners, attitudes, and gestures) is of tremendous importance in the shaping of the homophobic experience, which in turn shapes very differently the subjectivities and subject positions of those men having love or sexual relations with other men. At the same time, other aspects such as age, class, marital status, and sexual preference and behavior (be it nonexclusive homosexual preference or the specific sexual acts), as we shall see in chapter 4, shape in definitive ways men's experiences with homophobia as well as their ways of living their homoerotic relations.

This book tries to demonstrate that there are multiple heterogeneous ways of living homoerotic relations among men in Mexico; these ways are as varied as the perceptions, values, meanings, contexts, gender identities, and sexual practices that accompany them. Some of these differences have been captured and described by literature on gay or homosexual identities, and some others by literature focused on the traditional Mexican sexual system that stresses gender differences as the macho/*joto* dichotomy. Yet these classifications are insufficient in covering all the homoerotic realities and, most of the times, are even subverted and resignified.

The social process of making men out of biological males, or masculinization, is not homogeneous, as I try to show in chapters 1 and 2. One important pedagogical element, homophobia, which seems integral in this process, takes many different forms. Discourses on manhood or masculinity are historical and social forces. They change; they are diverse, relational, contradictory, and contested in daily lives. Men are socialized in those contradictory discursive spaces—and therefore the subjectification process—and the subjectivities and subjections that result from those processes are far from homogeneous, unitary, and stable.

As shown in chapters 2 and 3, men negotiate these unstable and contradictory meanings and those unstable and contradictory politics and subjectivities (their own and others') not only to negotiate their own subject
positions and identities as men, true men, and so on, but also—and very
important to our subject of study—to negotiate their own intimate relationships: emotional communications, love confessions, friendships, and
erotic relationships, which could be considered unacceptable by dominant discourses of manhood. The Mexican expressions *rajarse* and *acá
entre nos* ("open oneself to others," and "just between you and me" or "just
between us") that we explore in chapter 3 are most often used to engage in
a resubjectification process. This is a complex process of resistance to the
dominant ideological process of masculinity, which tends to lead men to
silence, self-restraint, emotional distance, and homoerotic repression.

In this book we argue that masculinity or manhood is not, therefore, the
stable and homogeneous subject position and identity of patriarchal
power. As gender studies on men and masculinities have shown, men are
not all equal. Even if in an androcentric culture they share a gain of symbolic power (which in its turn gets translated to other powers: economic,
political, social, etc.), there are deep internal differences and power relations by class, ethnicity, sexual orientation, gender identity (more or less
masculine, more or less effeminate), educational status, occupation, rural/
urban origins, among other elements. Many men get oppressed, discrimi-
nated against, by other men and women, and deprived of their share not
only of privilege but even of human dignity. Classist, racist, homophobic,
and gender, or age discourses function to classify men according to their
share of the symbols of power. As I show in this book though ethnographic
data from rural communities of northern Mexico, dominant discourses on
manhood sometimes deny or dispute the identity of man to some human
males.

Men who experience special affective or erotic bonds with other men
have to deal with this power machinery. For many men, there is no alternative but to resist in multiple ways. These resistances do not necessarily
take the already described known path of gay or fairy (*joto*) identity formation and strategies of resistances, but instead, other complex, ambiguous,
and contradictory paths. They are effective for these men in many different ways, as in the following: (1) by enlarging the very concept of what
counts as being a man, resignifying their affective and homoerotic relations in gender terms (as a masculine issue), and resisting other dominant
categories; (2) by framing those relationships in terms of friendship, comradeship, or just having fun together, thus enlarging the meanings and

practices of homosociality; (3) by engaging in silence; (4) by pretending or living in the unconsciousness of drunkenness so as to enable them to manage their feelings and pleasures; and (5) by signifying the experience not only as something that goes beyond the search for pleasure but also as a way of obtaining economic gratification or a favor.

This issue takes us to the broader subject of dominant discourses of manhood (and its homophobic consequences) and the resistance to those discourses and consequences. But more important, it also directs us to the problem of how to conceptualize power and resistance in the first place. We understand power as a social relation, not as something one either has or lacks. As a social relationship, power is expressed as a process through which subjectivities are being constructed and, in this way, subjected to a relation of power (Laclau and Mouffé 1982). This process is never finished and it is open to instabilities and contradictions. That is, the subject is never completely trapped in a relation of power and domination, and there are always possibilities of resistance. Resistance is also a social relationship that involves a subject already immersed in a power relationship at the level of one's subjectivity. By resistance we mean a subject that is already aware of dominant discourses that in some way or another have had an impact on one's structures of perception, thought, and feeling, and on one's possibilities for action. All forms of resistance involve an opposition to dominant discourses and bring about a process of resubjectification, of reinventing oneself through the new meanings we give to our identity or our actions.

The issue of men resisting homophobic power through silenced transgressive practices or through the tactical uses of masculine enunciations[9] disputes a dominant ideological concept of gay liberation, but equally appropriated by the heterosexist power, as Sedgwick already has demonstrated (1990): "the closet." As there are some scholars and activists who consider that studying homoerotic relations of those who suspend or resist for themselves the term of *gay* or *homosexual* are not "gay studies" but "men studies," there may also be some others who consider that what I describe as resistances are in fact examples of the closet.

I do not intend to write an apology of masculinity or of silence. This is not a moral project. However, I think the category closet should be revised in light of contemporary theories of power, subjectivity, and resistance. As we know, the closet is a metaphor integrated into the modern notion of sexuality as a true desire living inside oneself, and giving sense to all our being and acts. As Foucault (1976) says, one of the characteristics of this modern technology of sexuality is not only the system of "prohibitions" but also the obligation to speak, to say the truth about oneself. Confessing oneself as indicated in the out-of-the-closet metaphor can also be conceived as a type of governance. In this regard Foucault says: "How did a type of government of men take shape, one in which they are not simply required to obey, but to express, by telling that what one is?" (1990, 35).[10]

For many men who have sex with other men, the "assigned identity" from where resubjectification takes place is not homosexual or gay, or fairy (*joto*) but man, and from that identity starts their process of "reinventing themselves" to allow their homoerotic and/or love relations take place. These forms of resubjectification take many forms, such as pictures, confessions, jokes, key words, ways of reasoning, conceptions, silences, and excuses, according to what takes more or less time and effort. In as much as the identity and the subjectivity from where these men start their resubjectification process is not the same in all cases, and it is not the same to those who get to identify themselves as gay or fairies, the concept of the closet is not adequate.

The homoerotic experience is not inscribed in the privileges of the dominant ideological project of manhood (Herzfeld 1985), and it is always somehow heterodox in the sexual/gender field. We are in the presence of other paths for resubjectification for confronting homophobia, not in the face of hypocrisy or way of masculine privilege. These men who engage in homoerotic relations do so by opposing dominant ideologies and resisting in a greater or lesser degree (depending on many social factors such as class, cultural capital, rural/urban living). We are presented with men struggling to become "subjects of their own" (*sujet d'eux mêmes*, as Eribon says [1999, 116]) regarding their homoerotic experiences and desires, by engaging in a reflection over issues of manhood and masculinity and their emotional and erotic capabilities. As I show throughout this book, many times these reflections involve an awareness of masculine identity as an artifice, a construction, a performance, a masquerade, that ends up in the strategic use of its instabilities, ambiguities, contradictions, in order to resist or to create a *discourse en retour*.

Polymorphous and Perverse: Sexuality, Desire, Male Intimacy, and Homosociality

Once confronted with the heterosexist question of the origin of homosexuality, Foucault refused to give any explanation about it. I agree with this refusal and its political dimension. Foucault also rejected, as Eribon does later (1999), the militant and Freudian-based conception of original bisexuality as a political statement intending to get acceptance. My conception regarding this issue is similar to Foucault and Eribon's; I also reject the vindication of bisexuality as an ideological subterfuge in favor of a political purpose. Nevertheless, I accept the Freudian conception of Eros as polymorphous and perverse.[11] To my understanding, it is necessary to regain the radicalism of this theoretical position to account for the diversity of homoerotic experience and the oppressive character of dominant sexual and gender discourses. To say that sexuality and sex are cultural inventions, objects of discourse, does not mean that there is not a reality related to those categories that should be accounted for.

According to Foucault, sexuality does not preexist modern scientific discourse. It is an object of discourse tightly related to a technology of knowledge and power. Nineteenth-century medical discourses gave birth to *scientia sexualis* with its new technologies of confession and hermeneutics like psychotherapy, psychoanalysis, and the medical interview. To Foucault, sex is an artificial unit of different anatomical elements, biological functions, pleasures, sensations, and behaviors. This fictitious unit is naturalized by modern discourse of human sexuality and made a causal principle. The relationship between power and sex is therefore internal, given by the very organization of this artificial unit, and not only a matter of prohibition or repression (Foucault 1976, 187). But sex plays another role in Foucault's analysis: one that is productive.

I believe it is important to have a definition and a theoretical position regarding sex. To me, and following Foucault, sex is a cultural construction, a way of understanding, and the product of a set of disciplinary technologies operating over the body and our libidinal energy, or Eros. Therefore, it sets limits on and possibilities to our pleasures. Culture has to do not only with the particular reading of the body and anatomical and reproductive differences (as Judith Butler [1990] has stressed) but also with a particular shaping of a corporeal and psychic libidinal energy or Eros through the rituals of body socializations, family organization, social norms, social experiences, categories, values, and meanings, and thus creates our sex.

Homosexuality and heterosexuality as well as bisexuality (as a social category of sex) are social products. Eros or libidinal energy is polymorphous and perverse; it may be addressed to any object and it is moved by a pleasurable relief. Certainly, heterosexist society with its norms, institutions, and values tends to foster and accept within people an exclusive "heterosexual desire" (Rich 1980). The homosexual desire, in its turn, emerges in a dialogical relation to heterosexist society as despicable. It becomes therefore the repressed or the productive force for the reinvention of the self in the margin of, but in relation to, heterosexist society.

It is my theoretical position here that the homoerotic desire is therefore always present, even when absent from consciousness. The trajectory of desire is heterogeneous enough in the subject's history to always include a homosexual (and heterosexual) object choice, as Freud said (1962). A binary ideology around sexual preference tends to polarize our understanding of a personal desire that happens to be much more complex, ambiguous, and multiple than dominant sexual discourse leads us to believe, and as social studies have demonstrated (Kinsey 1948).

To acknowledge or propose this intrinsic polymorphous and perverse character of Eros, or this intrinsic instability and multiple character of desire, is not to say that all people are bisexual or that, in an open society respectful of sexual diversity, heterosexual and gay people will become bisexual or even that bisexuality is what is desirable politically. My theoretical argument in debt to Freud does not deny erotic preferences or sexual orientations (including, of course, bisexuality). It does affirm that in an open society—that is, in a society that is not androcentric, heterosexist (with is identity binaries), or homophobic—we may get to have a much more fluent and heterogeneous sexual existence than we tend to think; even hetero and homo desires will have different shapes and meanings.

The political implication of this theoretical approach is not the creation of a bisexual world, but instead the creation of a symbolic space to think or rethink of homoerotic desire as something that is not alien to anybody, as it crosses all cultural formations and social relations. It makes possible a type of thinking that encompasses a wide array of homoerotic practices—which I believe we can cluster under a category simply referred to as intimacy between men (or women).

The concept of male intimacy should be understood within this conception of desire. It refers to a space of affective and/or erotic intimacy, or proximity—which can be created among males—that covers a wide spectrum of possible social configurations of desires and identities. Intimacy goes beyond sexual contact, but involves a closeness of souls and/or bodies in the framework of a special relationship of revelation (Bawin and Dandurand 2003). Male intimacy is not the result of a specific homosexual preference in the theoretical perspective elaborated here and corroborated by research, but it is an expression of a desiring dynamic that has multiple object choices and get its way under certain cultural forms. I am not referring here, therefore, to something that—paraphrasing Adrienne Rich—we may call a "homosexual continuum" that would involve friendship and gay erotic, but to a kind of proximity and revelation that takes place by subverting somehow dominant ideologies of masculinity or sexuality.

I understand friendship as a social relation that may involve intimacy, but this is not always the case, even if it has as its principle a homoerotic desire, although previously oedipalized, as Guy Hocquenghem (1972) once said; that is, sublimated by patriarchal institutions. According to some scholars—such as Katz (2001), Dulac (2003), and others—it seems that, with the increasing heterosexualization of society, and homophobia, friendship has historically tended to "crystallize more around social relations than on intimate relations" (Dulac 2003, 27). As a cultural formation, intimacy has changed over time and in relation to many other social dimensions. Dulac expresses the profound transformation of intimacy in modern times in this way:

> Since [the] 19th century, masculine intimacy, especially as a feature of friendship between men, has been radically transformed. One has assisted not only to a passage from masculine friendship to heterosexual marriage . . . but also to a decline and a reduction of appropriate places for its expression. At the end of 19th century marriage became the place par excellence of intimacy, at the same time that the ideal of masculine friendship was deprived of its characteristic of intimacy and associated with suspected behaviours. Very soon, physical and affective intimacy with another man stopped to be part of acceptable social behaviours, and went along with fear and discredit of homosexuality. (Dulac 2003, 11)

Contrary to this fear of discredit, male virility was not considered endangered by male intimacy before the modern idea of homosexuality and the binary distinction heterosexual–homosexual were present in people's spirits and vocabulary, says Dulac. He explains by quoting Foucault:

> The continuum of intimacy which goes from word to sexuality was applied to people's relations more than to discrete categories (men–women) which could, for instance, to apply today to bisexuals, queer, behaviours. If masculine intimacy is further confined to the heterosexual relations framework within the nuclear family, comradeship and links between men are launched into the public sphere, there where they may be subjected to a visibility and to a cluster of moral dispositives. (Dulac 2003, 11)[12]

It is important to mention that this transformation of social expectation around intimacy, although it has not eliminated male intimacy, has shaped it in such a way as to make it a relationship that demands from men a "set of paradoxical traits regarding traditional (hegemonic) masculinity" (Trobst, Collins, and Embree 1994). Examples of this are the sustaining of affective expression, the "opening" or revelation of the self (*rajarse*), the sharing of emotions and body contacts, including erotic ones, and in many cases its confinement to hidden or marginal places in personal and social life.

Homosociality, as friendship, is not necessarily a space of male intimacy; on the contrary, most of the time it tends to be a space of masculinization or of enactment of masculine tests. As a homosocial group, a peer group of men function as a witness of the performance of masculine identity in daily life of men, and often operates in a manner contrary to any kind of revelation or proximity more typical of our definition of intimacy. Although men's homosexuality may work as a technology of power to reproduce patriarchal ideologies and identities, it is much more contradictory and ambiguous than we tend to think.

The idea that men's homosociality is necessarily linked to the homophobic or sexist system is wrong. There is a long tradition of democratic homosociality among men and among women. Whitman's vindication of "love of comrades" and "adhesive love" (1973) allowed us to discover the existence of a subculture of intimacy among men that does not reproduce or even oppose the puritanical and patriarchal demands of his times, making at the same time a strong defense of democracy. According to Eribon, Edward Carpenter—the famous British sexologist and social reformer inspired by Whitman (and I would add more contemporary intellectuals such as Italian filmmaker Pier Paolo Passolini)—has contributed to a culture of friendship among men (of different classes or ethnic backgrounds) that is coextensive to the idea of social equality and democracy (Eribon 2004, 197). It is worthwhile to remember that many of these men were also important and enthusiastic supporters of feminist movements.

In this book I propose that we should understand men's homosociality as a social organization that, as in any social organization, is not already fixed and forever, but is as unstable, contradictory, and contested as masculine identity itself.

Context: The Traveled Path

The sierra of Sonora is a semiarid and mountainous zone, traversed by three main rivers from north to south that have facilitated the development of small agricultural valleys on their banks. It was originally inhabited by the Opata tribe, an indigenous group that was the main source of local *mestizaje* along with the Spaniards. Jesuit missionaries organized small mission pueblos starting in the seventeenth century until their expulsion in 1765. The dissolution of the mission system yielded the formation of small agro-pastoral communities, largely dedicated to subsistence agriculture. During the nineteenth century this economy coexisted along with waged labor at the local mines and was complemented by artisans and merchants. The permanent war campaigns against the Apaches, in which both indigenous and nonindigenous groups participated, exerted a significant influence on the development of the region. In some areas of the sierra, those wars lasted all the way into the 1920s. The wars against the Apaches, according to anthropologist Ana Alonso, conditioned the ethnic and gender ideologies of the people groups in the area, including their conceptions of honor, virtue, respect, dignity, and autonomy (Alonso 1995). They also engendered an egalitarian ethic among the settlers, partly as a result of the need to join efforts to defend their communities.

The post-Revolutionary state brought with it a gradual expansion of its central institutions, ideologies, and regulations throughout the course of the twentieth century. Nonetheless, subsistence agriculture continued to coexist throughout the century, supplemented by temporary wage labor in the mines and by migrant laborers or *braceros* that moved back and forth to the United States. The 1960s brought access to domestic comforts and "modern" services such as electricity, potable water, roads, telephones, health clinics, as well as a full integration to a market economy through the cattle and forage industries. The 1980s brought to the sierra widespread access to television and most recently cable TV. All these changes have resulted in a kind of modernization process that has not always been efficient; such unevenness has resulted in what has been called a "broken" or defective modernity (Simonelli 1987). During the 1990s, the export assembly plants known as *maquiladoras* turned to the sierra as a means of reducing production costs. Maquiladoras can be described as either the "crown jewel" or the "last drop" of the transformation of sierra society, depending on one's point of view. Drug trafficking and the expanding presence of the military and the judicial police in the last few years have completed the full cycle of changes in this region. In the last two decades, maquiladoras have been the occasion of a set of discourses regarding their impact on women's reproduction and sexuality, as well as on men and women gender identities, especially in the younger generation (Núñez 1998).

These Serrano communities, most of them with populations less than three thousand, have also served as the main source of migration to the

Sonoran coastal and border cities since the 1950s. But the largest migration has been to the capital city of Hermosillo. Many of these immigrants have integrated themselves successfully into the local labor market, including the automotive and high-tech manufacturing industries. Others find jobs in construction or service occupations. With a population nearing eight hundred thousand according to the 2010 census, the city of Hermosillo nonetheless retains an undeniable "countryside" flavor in spite of the fact that its primary industries are commerce, services, and manufacturing. This distinguishing characteristic owes much to the fact that many first- and second-generation immigrants hold on to the modes of dress, talk, and behavior that they and others call *cheras* (from *vaqueras*, or cowboy-like), de pueblo (small-town feel), or simply serranas. My own family history in some way fits this profile.

The Methodology

The fieldwork for this investigation was realized as part of my duties as a researcher within an academic institution in Hermosillo (CIAD, A.C.) where I began working after completing graduate coursework at the University of Arizona. My responsibilities in this institution allowed me to engage in two primary research projects: the first one examined prevalent conceptions of gender in Serrano communities; the second one investigated sexual and reproductive conceptualizations in three generations of men in the same communities. For purposes of the present work, I am also drawing on research that I conducted in the city of Hermosillo from 1988 to 1992 and from 1997 to 2002.

The tasks involved in the collection of data for this investigation were consistent with the well-known and time-tested practices of the ethnographic method. They included the methodical registry of what is observed, heard, and felt in field notebooks, in the same day if possible. In some instances, when I was too tired at night to record in detail things that I had heard or observed, I always made it a point to do so immediately upon rising the next day. The field notebooks contain analytical and methodological as well as descriptive entries. I also kept a personal journal along with the field notebooks. The journal allowed me the freedom to explore in more extensive and subjective terms my own reactions to the research process. Through my journal writing I was able to "track," so to speak, changes in mood that affected my desire to engage in some topics at different times and not others, or to explain why I tended to seek the

company of some informants more than others, or why I occasionally suffered from nightmares.

The people around me, both in Hermosillo and in the communities in
the sierra, were aware that I was a researcher. I described the investigation
in simple and concise terms: I was conducting a study about differences
between being a man and being a woman, changes about those ideas,
machismo, relationships among couples, and the like. Most people re-
acted positively to the study and commented that it was relevant to them
because the recent expansion of the maquiladora plants had brought about
"many changes" among families in those areas.

The kind of subjects that provide the main source of information for a
study of this kind can hardly be chosen according to statistical sampling.
Sometimes the best informants emerge out of a chance encounter or from
a casual conversation in a setting specific to the kind of topic that is being
investigated. Sometimes one informant leads you to another and then to
another until, as they say, the network and the topics of conversation
snowball. In these instances, the preferred research methods are a peculiar
combination of observation, in-depth interviews, and informal conversations. However, trust, and hence frankness, is extremely important in all
cases. It is what guarantees to the researcher the abundance of enunciation
required to make a nuanced and detailed analysis.

In this investigation, therefore, the primary objects of analysis are those
enunciations that conform the discourse of masculinity—modes of talking
about being a man, being homosexual, having sexual relations with men,
loving men, being gay or fairy (*joto*), and so on, as well as the complex relationship of those verbal statements with the actions and identities of subjects. The elements of discourse that I am describing could not be determined prior to the investigation. Even though I had sketched some notions
and lines of inquiries about the topic at hand, some of the critical discursive evidence in this study appeared gradually as spontaneous expressions
uttered by informants. In other instances, I probed everyday forms of
speech used by informants in order to clarify concepts and terms that up
until then I had taken for granted.

In conclusion, in the process of gathering and analyzing information I
used grounded theory and analytical induction. The information provided
by the interviews was used to generate, compare, and confront hypotheses
during the ethnographic work. Grounded theory does not seek to verify
previous theories or hypotheses, but to discover regularities and irregularities in the collected data in order to develop concepts and interpretations.
Analytical induction as a method involves the constant confrontation of

certain detected regularities with new fieldwork information, especially those that seem to contradict previous analysis. Analytical induction complements grounded theory (see Charmaz 2000; Glaser and Strauss 1967; Turner 1981).

My native fluency in Spanish in general, as well as my extensive knowledge of the dialects and variations in Spanish use peculiar to Sonora, helped me establish quick and fluid connections with the meanings implied in certain words and expressions. My prior experiences researching the sexual field in Sonora (Núñez 1994) and my own personal ventures into various aspects of gender and sexual dissidence, while not authoritative, gave me valuable insights that carried through in the present investigation. Nonetheless, I want to make clear that I never engaged in sexual practices with my informants, men or women. This decision was not the result of a lack of desire, opportunity, or some abstract reverence to objectivity, but rather it was made out of the fear of altering the dynamics of communication between researcher and informants. Neither I nor the discipline of anthropology itself has yet found a satisfying resolution to the ethical and scientific issues raised by crossing such boundaries.

Although my research practices elucidated very personal information from the subjects of study, they were not in any way similar or related to psychoanalysis. I reached conclusions about male intimacy and identities through a cumulative process of analysis that surmised regularities in the discourse out of the accumulation of diverse enunciations by multiple subjects. The primary activities employed to accomplish this kind of analysis were listening and observation—my own "voice" appeared in these exchanges primarily as an interlocutor, never as an interrogator. My goal was to tease out of these conversational contexts those speech acts that constitute "objects of discourse" in the manner in which Foucault (1969) described such processes. In other words, I wanted to appreciate those instances wherein repetition constituted regularity as well as those in which oppositional, alternative, and heterogeneous points of view were manifested vis-à-vis the commonsense perspective. I found particularly interesting those instances in which observed practices seemed to contradict conceptualizations articulated in other moments by the same subjects, what the Mexican scholar Ana Amuchástegui (1998) has called "practice's subjugated discourse." I found that it is precisely in the irregularities of speech and practice, in the contradictions of nonofficial histories, that the alleged normativity of the discursive regime becomes most apparent.

I refer to certain histories as nonofficial because the picture of male intimacy and identity that emerges out of an analytical incursion into those stories is predominantly one that contradicts what I call "the dominant model of apprehension of homoerotic practices in Mexico." That model is in fact a regime of understanding that operates at the level of social discourse by representing itself as common sense or conventional wisdom. It is in every sense of the word, a "regime"—deeply violent and patriarchal—yet likely to be reproduced as easily in the texts of anthropologists and social scientists as it is by social activists who claim to have unique access to the "true" representation of homosexuality in Mexico.

To the extent that I was primarily interested in the total set of expressions of the discursive regime I have described, I found in the messages crafted by gender and sexual activists in Mexico a very productive source of ethnographic information. I found particularly intriguing and fruitful several novel conceptualizations that began to circulate in Mexico and Latin America during the first years of the twenty-first century—namely, those related to notions of homophobia, the appellation "men who have sex with other men" (Núñez 2007a, 2012), and the movement on behalf of "sexual diversity." These new terms have joined the older, existing lexical categories that designated male sexuality and have attempted to account for realities of intimacy and erotic practices that the dominant discursive regime has excluded or ignored (Núñez 2011). Although these efforts have not always been carried out successfully, in this book, I analyze these alternative formulations in light of the ethnographic data I collected and in dialogue with key theoretical points derived from feminist studies in order to elucidate both their explanatory power and their political implications.

Reasons and Uncertainties

The personal reflections that underscore the production of this text are deeply rooted in my own intellectual trajectory and in what I would like to describe as the civic dimension of my life in Mexico (*participacion ciudadana*). These reflections emerge from a deeply rooted interest in understanding the range of affective and sexual possibilities for men in Mexican society, as well as the range of these possibilities among and between men. I find that I am most capable of articulating this deep and restless personal interest through the practice of ethnography and through engagement with a variety of theoretical and methodological contributions to the social sciences, primarily those concerned with studies of masculinity, gender studies, and the field of queer theory. As a result of this multivalent theoretical approach, I believe I am able to offer a kind of analytical immersion into men's subjectivities and into the power dynamics that regulate them, especially their intimacy with other men.

The discovery that emerges out of this process is nothing short of radical: in the struggle over the meaning of being a man, one could also find the hidden possibilities for love, health, pleasure, peace of mind, dignity, happiness, and even of life itself, that are so important to human beings. It is no wonder, then, that the meaning of *ser hombre* constitutes a site of social struggle over the power of signification. These meanings are translated into politics and policies also evident in the social or civic life of men. To peel apart the veil of the commonsense of those policies—their taken-for-granted character and their ideological and material operations—is therefore to confront in large measure the powers themselves that inhibit, limit, shape, and deform the possibilities for love and intimacy that men possess in general but also among themselves.

This book attempts to reveal (or uncover) the politics of meaning that regulates intimacy among men in Mexico. In chapter 1, through an interview with José Pedro and several other random field notes, I try to reveal various elements that could help us understand in more contextual terms the origin and meaning of the photograph on page 5. More important, I attempt to demonstrate something that has long been a benchmark of semiology—that is, the relational character of the meanings of words and concepts. By understanding this relational (and, thus, relative) dynamic at play in verbal and visual representations, we are also able to understand something about the social struggle to represent—or better yet, about having the power to represent—social reality, including representations of the lives of men and their intimate connections. The social struggle implicit in these human processes becomes even more evident in the chapters that follow. In chapter 2, I examine a concept that gained particular currency in the decades following the Mexican Revolution and that has played an important role in the context of the country's aspirations toward modernization; I am referring to notions about the Mexican man (*el hombre Mexicano*). In the chapter, this concept is studied in great detail with the purpose of revealing a multitude of realities under the surface of its apparent transparency—realities that hide diverse and competing modes of representing manhood (*hombria*) and forms of resistance that challenge the dominant interpretations of it.[13] Everyday expressions associated with the idea of manhood, inflected by regional and national common expressions such as *no rajarse* (literally, not to rip oneself apart), can shed light on the exigencies and conventions implicated in constructing a masculine identity in Mexico. At the same time, other popular expressions such as *acá entre nos* (similar in function to the English idiom "between you and me") are effective in demonstrating the construction of alternative social spaces where it becomes possible to contest and resist dominant ideas. Taken together, these two expressions point out two distinct but interrelated aspects of the dynamics through which men become "subjects" and therefore access possibilities for intimacy with other men in Mexico. Chapter 3 explores these ideas in greater detail.

In chapter 4, I examine one of the foundational elements of the dominant form of male identity constructed under the influence of gender ideologies—the notion of homophobia. Far from being simply a mechanism that feeds the desire to overpower the "other," I argue that homophobia is primarily a kind of fear that reveals the incoherent, anxious, and fragmented character of the kind of male subjectivity constructed by the dominant discourses of manhood. In effect, once it has installed itself within an individual, homophobia is expressed as a mechanism of social power, but one that derives its strength from a fear of intimacy that impacts not only the so-called "homosexuals" but also all persons and all forms of romantic relationships. Homophobia in the context of this chapter is also introduced as a theoretical means of linking the various strands of masculinity studies, feminist theory, and queer studies.

In chapter 5, I discuss the characteristics as well as the fallacies of a phenomenon that I term the dominant model for understanding male homoerotic experience in Mexico. This model—insofar as it represents homoerotic experience as a phenomenon exclusively and predominantly sexual in nature (structured, that is, only in relation to anal penetration), and therefore only understandable in terms of dichotomies such as active–passive, macho–*joto*, masculine–feminine—is strongly complicit with the sexual and gender ideologies that sustain a system of patriarchy. The most effective and at the same time most perverse forms of social control over males rest precisely on the control of their affective and sexual possibilities: the possibilities of men reaching meaningful levels of intimacy. In characterizing male-to-male intimacy only in terms of prescribed notions of who is or what practices make someone a fairy (*joto*) or a homosexual, these forms of social control pretend to speak the truth about the only possibilities for men to experience intimacy with one another.

As a final note, I would like to mention that I am not yet aware of the implications of this research or its applicability to the homoerotic relations of women. Although during my research I interviewed many women on issues related to sexuality and reproduction, this was not an easy task. The gender and sexual politics of those communities was a great obstacle to create a more fluent interaction without raising all kinds of mistrust. However, I became aware of the existence in some women of certain knowledge about other women who liked women in the communities, and some categories like *marimachas* (tomboys) and *lesbianas* or just "she likes women" were applied. A similar study would have been easier to do in a city like Hermosillo or by a women researcher working in these communities. The absence of this knowledge continues to be a great failure of Mexican academia, an expression certainly of its sexual and gender constraints.[14]

I should say that in the last twenty years there has been an increasing academic production in Mexico and other Latin American countries on gender and sexuality. This academic production has different emphases, and different theoretical and disciplinary perspectives. It takes part in the general academic field under different names: feminist studies; gender studies; studies on men and masculinities; gender studies on men; lesbian, gay, bisexual, transsexual, transgender, and intersex (LGBTTI) studies; and sexual diversity studies. Although they have apparently different objects of research, they tend to share theories, methodologies, interests, and a strong feminist influence (Núñez 2010).

The academic production on men and masculinities has gone from an initial interest on machismo (see Gutmann 1996) to elaborate analyses on a wide array of issues such as the following: violence (Garda 2007; Ramírez 2005); sports and leisure (Huerta 1999); sexuality, eroticism, and love (Amuchástegui 2007; Guevara 2010; Ponce 2006; Rodríguez y De Keijzer 2002); reproductive health and rights (Figueroa 2006; Gutiérrez 1998); paternity (Jiménez 2003; Salguero 2007); body representations and subjectivity (Muñiz 2002; Parrini 2007); nationalism (Domínguez 2007); risk and mortality (Calvario 2003; De Keijzer 1988; Rivas 2005); class (Gutmann 1996; Hernández 2004); epistemology (Núñez 2004b); migration (Rosas 2007); ethnicity (López 2010); and partnership, marriage, conflicts, and divorce (Núñez 2004a; Zazueta 2008).

The studies on sexual and gender dissidence at the same time have revolved around issues such as the following: structural positions in society and culture (Monsiváis 2010; Núñez 1994); building of identity (Hernández 2002); gay culture and language (Acosta 2003; List 2007; Marquet 2001, 2006, 2011); gay tourism and sexual work (López and Carmona 2012); identity and homophobia (Balbuena 2006); public policies (Salinas 2006); mental health (Granados and Delgado 2007); and indigenous cultures (Cosío 2005; Miano 2002; Núñez 2009), among many other subjects and authors.

Studies on the AIDS epidemics have intersected many of the studies on men, masculinity, and homoerotic relations in different and complex ways, and have made a great contribution to this academic field. Particularly relevant to this book is the epidemiological concept "men who have sex with men" because it came to stimulate a reflection on a traditional model of homosexuality of Mediterranean origin in different Latin American countries (see the articles published in Cáceres, Pecheny, and Tértor 2002)—already described for Mexico more than two decades before by American anthropologists like Carrier (1972, 1976) or Taylor (1978a, 1978b)—as well as a criticism on its limits to understand male homoerotic experience (Núñez 2007a). To this rich and complex field of studies we should add those studies more focused on sexuality or women that also have contributed enormously to the better comprehension of the gender and sexual regime in Mexico, and in the different regions and social sectors.

This book, published originally in Spanish in 2007, and a number of essays I have published in the last ten years have contributed to the making of some of these theoretical debates, themes, and approaches. This English version is almost identical, although shorter, and has benefited from additional comments by anonymous English readers. I am very grateful to all of them.

A Note About the Presentation of Data

In this book, I have made an effort to maintain a fluid and dynamic interchange between the data that support my analysis and the presentation of theoretical material. I have deliberately avoided making the text itself a false "performance" of scientific discoveries. The research process is dense and complex enough by itself without trying to add on any kind of faddish textual innovations. Nonetheless, I am deeply aware that in the final analysis anthropological knowledge is communicated essentially in textual form. For that reason, I have made it a point to insert throughout the academic text the voices, human frailties, and personal twists and turns that made the process of research interesting and consequential. In the end, I hope to affirm through this mode of writing the importance of intertextuality for the construction of knowledge. In fact, I have found that the most useful insights into the human condition are those that emerge out of a critical reflection of the binaries that order social reality; in other words, reflections that emerge out of the persistent contrast between "reality" as an abstract entity and the readings we are always attempting to make of the "real."

Except for the city of Hermosillo, I have changed all the names of all persons and all locations. All the names that appear in the manuscript are fictitious. I have also been particularly careful to avoid sharing details of personal histories that may have betrayed the anonymous identity of my informants. Sometimes this was done at the expense of a better and more contextualized narrative in the manuscript; but it was an important decision given the fact that in many small communities of the sierra it is common for people to have access to much family and personal information about their neighbors, thus making it potentially easier for someone to trace the origins of particular details of my informants' lives.

CHAPTER ONE

The Social Regulation of Male Identity and Intimacy

A Photograph and a Context: The Voice of José Pedro

Field Note, November 17, 1997

I met Don José Pedro as a result of walking past his house every day and exchanging the normal greetings. On many occasions, the greetings have led to long conversations. Our talks have usually revolved around different aspects of his life and his family. I have noticed that Don José Pedro really enjoys our conversations, partly due to the fact he is spends most of the day alone. The other reason might be that he seems to derive a special pleasure from sharing stories about his life; it is the pleasure of remembering a time in his life when he had many projects and was overcome by many emotions. Today, however, the conversation took a special turn. At last I was able to bring up the subject of the photograph that for so long had captured my attention. The conversation unfolded as follows:

"Chico and I were partners [*compañeros*]," says José Pedro, holding in his hand the photograph. "We were always together, since we were kids. We were cut from the same cloth, you know what I mean? There was a slight age difference between us, only months really, but I always looked younger because I had a more happy disposition [laughs] . . . he was a little slow, or he pretended to be. I think mostly he pretended because he was also hard of hearing. That's why people started calling him 'the little deaf one' [*el sordito*], because he seemed like he was innocent and naïve, but, man, he fooled everyone!" says Don José Pedro in a jovial tone.

"Don José Pedro," I ask, "was he *vaquetón*[1] [a tough guy]?"

[He laughs] "Well, I should not say this, but . . . yes, yes, yes, he was," he says while touching his pale forehead with his strong and rough hands. Don José Pedro is eighty-four years old. But in spite of the wrinkles on his face and of the gray that invades not only his hair but also his eyebrows and the shadow of his beard, there is something in his expressions that reminds you of the handsome and debonair man he once must have been. After wiping his forehead with a red handkerchief, he continues: "To tell you the truth, we were both *vaquetónes*, but not in the way it is today. We did not do anything really bad or ugly, like people do today . . . drugs and robberies, none of that. There was no way; in those days there was a whole lot less to go around and people had to lead straight lives to get by. The things we did were kid's stuff, mischievous tricks so to speak, and nothing compared to what goes on today."

"How was a man expected to be and act when you were young, Don José Pedro?"

"Serious. Honorable, especially. A man of his word. A man had to be trustworthy in everything he said, not going around telling lies or engaging in idle talk, none of that. A man had to live by his word; whatever he said, promised, or committed to, he had to carry through. He could not 'break down' [*rajarse*[2]] on his commitment. If you promised to do something, you had to fulfill that promise no matter what it took. That's how things had to be, yes, sir . . . a man had to be trustworthy. There was no chance that if you had a girlfriend you could just leave her hanging, no way; you had to marry her!"

"What is expected of a man who is 'honorable' [serious, or in Spanish *serio*[3]]?"

"Just like I tell you, he is expected to be firm, hardworking, a good breadwinner for his family, responsible . . ." He pauses, and then I echo his last word: "Responsible."

"That his wife and kids do not go lacking, and that he never embarrasses or dishonors his wife; she has her place and you have to respect her. You also have to be a good citizen, have civic consciousness, and civic courage . . . that's what makes a man 'serious' [honorable]."

Don José Pedro pronounces each word intensely, with moral strength — as if the very performance of his words and gestures were an embodiment of what it means to be a man, in his opinion. Then he continues:

"A man of honor, a respectable man, is someone who respects others and that commands respect for himself. He is not wishy-washy, given easily to betray his principles. As I told you, he faces the consequences. He is a good friend. He greets everyone pleasantly. That's how I have tried to be all my life, both because that's how they taught me and because that's the way a man shows his true value to others."

"What is the worst thing that a man can do?" I ask.

"To be lazy [*flojo*], not a hard worker. Ask anyone and they'll tell you the same thing. A lazy man is of no use to anyone. He cannot support a family; he does not command respect. What can he offer to his family? All he would bring upon them is suffering. They would go hungry, and they would feel shame for their condition. That is the lowest one can stoop. Then, it would not be any wonder if his wife goes with another man; he brought it upon himself. He turns into a cuckold [*lo hacen chivo*], as they say. If he does not have means of supporting a family, why should anyone love him? Ahh, and another thing . . . a man who steals, who turns into a thief, that is also not well received by society."

"Which is worse?" I ask.

"Being lazy is worse. At least a man who steals has something to take back to his family, but one who is lazy, he can't even boast of that. So not only does he hurt himself, but also his family."

"Hey, Don José . . . let me ask you this: if a man must be hardworking, then a man who is lazy, is he less of a man or not-man-enough?"

"He is a man in the sense that he has the organ [genitals]! He is a sorry excuse of a man. [¡*Es un hombrecito a güevo!*] He is a man because he has 'that,' but nothing more than that. What is understood as being 'a man'—a 'real man'—no, he would not be."

"Don José," I ask, "do you remember a specific time when you felt that you had finally become a man?" Don José smiles and looks away pensively. I feel he enjoys my question.

"How can I tell you? I think that I first felt that I was a man when my father took me with him to work in the fields, when he donned a sombrero on me, and said, 'Alright, let's go to the cornfield, from now on you will start helping me.' At that moment I felt really proud. Proud to go along with my father; I felt as if I was like him in some way. Even the food my mother cooked tasted better to me, because now I was earning it, so to speak. Because now I was also contributing. I did many different kinds of work. Shortly after working in the cornfields, I was put in charge of the cattle. I worked on the other side [the United States] for a while to save enough for my marriage [helping with the wedding expenses]. I also worked in the mine, the one in Nacozari. Yes, sir, I worked at many different occupations. I was also very hardworking; always busy doing something. Now I am older, and things have changed."

"How did you meet Chico [Francisco]?" I ask.

Don José Pedro smiles. It shows that he enjoys talking about his old friend. Then he says: "My buddy Chico? Well, we should make some coffee. This fine conversation is just getting started . . . is that agreeable to you [the coffee]?"

"Great idea, Don José Pedro."

"Let me boil some water . . . it will be done in just a short while." He gets up from his seat and lights the stove. We are in his house. Today he is alone, he tells me, because his wife is visiting one of their daughters.

He continues: "Chico, may he rest in peace, was from around here. He was from my same circles. Since we were young kids we always got along. We ran around with the same crowd; back then people used to call it the *cuadrilla* [crew or gang]. Like the same troop, if you will. We did the usual kids' things—idle, silly things [*vagancias*]. We used to go to the river to collect figs. Always together! We remained that way for a long time. When he was sent to collect firewood, he used to come for me and we would do it together, keeping each other company. We also worked together a few times. One time when we were already in our teens my dad asked that I deliver a load of beans to the town of Nacozari and he went with me. During that trip we became really close and remained closer friends ever since . . . we even used to kid around that we were compadres."

"Just teasing?"

"Oh, yeah, just something sweet to say, you know? Because we really held each other in high esteem; that's the way it was until his death." Don José Pedro gets quiet for a few moments. He gets up to serve the coffee and resumes talking: "I tell you, a friendship is a beautiful thing. If you have a good friend sometimes you feel closer to him than to your own wife. There's just something different about it. But it makes sense. Who else is going to understand you better than a man who is just like you, a man also?"

"You don't talk about the same kinds of things?" I ask.

"No, not in a million years. One has to always show respect toward the wife. It can never be the same. It's different with a friend. You can tell him almost everything; he shares in all your adventures, he knows the things that happen to you and the things that happen to him while he was with you. That's how you become close friends."

"Did you trust him?"

"Oh, yes, of course I did! We were friends since childhood . . . we did a few mischievous things together." [He laughs, evoking a sense of complicity and mischief.]

"What kinds of mischievous things, Don José? Don't tease me and leave me hanging."

"Well, the same kinds of things kids do today; I don't think that has changed, at least around here. I see the kids ganging up together and heading down to the river—some are young, the older ones are the heavy ones [*caponeros*], the ones that teach them what is normal, only natural when boys' bodies begin to change, when they start to grow into men. Oh, and smoking, that too. The only thing is that all of that is kept a big secret. Nothing shall ever leak out of that place. If somebody ever got a bruise or something because they fell, no one would ever say where it really happened. We would all say that it happened doing a chore [he laughs]. . . . You start becoming a tough guy [*vaquetón*]. What happened was that usually parents were very strict, at least in the past. Today, parents let their children do as they please; they don't watch over them. Consider also that women now work just like men do, in the factories, the *maquilas*."

"And the mischievousness continued when you went to Nacozari?" I ask with a smile.

"You are very right . . . between you and me, I am going to tell you what really lies underneath the surface of how one acts. You see, in that occasion when Chico accompanied me to take the bean sacks to Nacozari, we carried the load on a mule and we rode horses. It was a long trip. Today one can get there quickly because they now have roads. But not back then. Everything took longer, and sometimes you had to stop and rest or even spend the night somewhere midway. That was one reason why it was preferable to bring a friend along. Chico always kept me company when I had to run errands and I did the same for him. When it was not possible, well, we accepted that, but we always managed to find a way to make it possible for us to be together [he laughs]. Along the way, we started to talk to make the time pass faster. We talked about whether he had already been with a woman, or if I had done the same thing, and as it turns out neither one of us had had that experience yet. We only knew the things we had heard from the older boys. But in that time those kinds of conversations were very secret, they were a sin—not like it is today. . . . [Suddenly, from a short distance—Don José Pedro lowers his voice as if he were getting ready to make a confession—a woman standing by a door called us toward her.] Well, the rest is history . . . we forgot about the load, the bean sacks, and the money! We came back to town empty-handed [he laughs]. That's how we carried on when we were young."

"And what excuse did you make up when you returned home?" I ask.

"We said that the river had overflowed and had taken all along its path [he laughs]. You see, that's the kind of tough guys we were in those days."

"And were you really compadres [had become 'godparents' through baptism of one of each other's children]?"

"No, never. We called each other 'compadre'—my 'compa' Chico and I was his 'compa' José Pedro [shortened 'compa' is similar to good old buddy or pal]—but it was not something official. I told him once that as soon as I had a child he would baptize him or her, and the same for me from him, but when my daughter was born he was on the other side [the United States], and it was uncertain when he would return, so we had to go ahead and baptize the baby. That happened too with my second child. And later on, when he had his three children, one right after the other, then it was my turn to be on the other side. I was away for almost six years, hard to believe but true. Then he had another son, but his brother asked to be the godfather and he felt bad saying no to his brother. As you know, the holy sacraments are not something to argue about, and his own brother always had that desire. Nonetheless, we were compadres—that's how we felt."

"And that photo, when did you have it taken?"

"Oh, you mean the portrait. Oh, you see, that's from one time when we went together to Douglas, Arizona. We took some animals over there, and after finishing the job we had some free time. Photography was popular in those days, so I said to Chico, 'Let's go get our photos taken.' Back in that time, photographic equipment was something very different than today. Today there are very small cameras and anyone can carry one. But in those days, there was no hope for owning a camera; cameras were a novelty and everybody went down to the studio to get their portrait done. I had already noticed that one of my cousins had his photo taken posing together with a friend of his. So when we saw the photo outfit over there, it occurred to me to do the same. I told Chico, let's go have our photo taken. I don't remember how much we paid. Let me see. . . uhm . . . no, I can't recall; why pretend otherwise. We went into the shop and a very elegant-looking man, wearing a tight vest, asked us to enter a small room that he had set up, behind a curtain, to take the shots, as they said. We stood up there and he took two photos—the one you see here I have kept all these years and Chico kept the other one. I wrote a dedication on his photo: 'To my friend Francisco, from his friend who holds him in high esteem, José Pedro, in memory of our friendship.'"

"What year was it?" I ask.

"Must have been around 1935 or there about; isn't the date inscribed on the portrait?"

"No."

While I observe the image, I say to him casually, almost inadvertently, and pretending to strain the eyes to distinguish the image correctly [although deep inside I could hardly contain my surprise and excitement]: "You are holding his hand."

"Hey, of course, we were very close friends." He answers me laconically, as if the simple phrase was all that was needed to convey the true meaning of his words.

"Was that the custom in those days?"

"Uhm. . . ." He pauses and I stay quiet. I don't want to interrupt him. Then he resumes: "I saw that my cousin's photo was like that and I wanted the same, so I grabbed his hand."

"And how was Chico with you? Did he hold you in high esteem?" I ask, using the same terms he has used before.

"Yes, very much so; we were close friends. We got along real well. We were both outgoing; we enjoyed going to dances. He was quiet, a lot quieter than I was. To speak truthfully, I was more devilish. He was quiet but he had his own spark. One time he made us laugh a lot—it was Christmas time and he came over to ask that I go with him to his family's house. I had been drinking and was in one of those light moods. Observing the situation, my wife who is very outspoken, said to him: 'No, he is not going with you anywhere.' I figured she thought maybe I would stay overnight, maybe with another woman or something like that. And Chico responded: 'What do you mean he cannot come with me? What are you saying? Don't you know that he is more mine than yours, that I met him first? (*lo conocí primero*)' And then everybody broke out laughing. But he was right, he had met me first. He was always very witty like that."

Don José Pedro gets up one more time to offer me more coffee.

"Don José Pedro, was there ever any conflict, any misunderstanding between you and Chico?"

"No, never. We always got along just fine."

He turns quiet and pensive. Then he adds: "There was this one time, when something happened that made him feel ashamed. I am going to tell you without mentioning the real names, although come to think of it, all the people involved are already dead and I am going to follow soon. But I know that you are interested in these kinds of stories . . . and also as a way of saying that people have always been the same and difficult things have always been part of life. So, you see this one time Chico and I were riding horses in the countryside and suddenly we saw something move behind some bushes. The sun was almost setting. We approached the bushes to take a closer look and we found his brother dressed in women's bride clothes, the brother's wife's clothes, that is—he was wearing his woman's dress."

"And what happened then?" I ask.

"My compadre yelled at him, 'Have you no shame? What is wrong with you? Are you crazy or something?' He got really mad, grabbed a rope, and began to hit him. He ordered him to take the clothes off and to go home to his wife. I did not say a word. What could I say? He was overcome with shame. He did not speak on the way back or for days after that. Then, I said to him: 'Don't worry, compadre, no one in town needs to find out; pretend that I was not even there.' And that's how we handled that situation. That's why I am telling you that there's nothing new in this world; things have always been what they are."

"And what did people call someone who was like Chico's brother?"

"Do you mean what insults they used? Well, people called him *na-huilon*[4] [sissy, effeminate], but they would not say it to his face; it was the word that people would use to insult someone who liked to dress or act like a woman. But this man did not always go around like that. Not at all. He was a regular person, he was married, had a good wife—the poor thing. Who would have ever thought?"

"And nobody ever found out?"

"Well, people sort of knew; it was rumored that he was into that kind of thing, but nothing beyond that. I imagine even his own wife must have known about it in some way."

"And did people talk about whether he had sexual relations with other men?" I ask.

"Mmmm. . . ." Don José Pedro clears his throat. He pauses as if to choose his words carefully. It's clear that this is not a topic that he is used to discussing.

"Well, why would I lie to you? Yes, the fact is, yes . . . it was rumored that a man who was always hanging out with him, that used to fix his car . . . yes, but I never had any firsthand knowledge that that was true, so why would I go around speaking badly about someone . . . I did not see it. I could not be sure."

Don José Pedro becomes pensive again. Then, lowering his voice, he asks me: "Listen, now that we are on the subject, I have been wondering about something. Maybe you can clarify it for me. I think you can because you seem to be a very educated man. What does that little word they use nowadays—"hombresensual" [sensual man]—mean?"

"Do you mean 'homosexual'?" I ask him.

"Ah, that's the one, yes . . . homosexual," he says, trying to pronounce the word correctly. "What does it mean?"

"Someone who, for instance, a man who prefers to have sex with another man."

"Ah, that. . . ," he says with a hint of reflexivity in his voice.

I am not sure I answered his question. He still looks preoccupied about something. Aware that I am coming across as somewhat awkward, I ask him, "Did those kinds of things also go on when you were young?"

"They must have. How can I tell you . . . most likely they happened . . . the tough guys and their games [*vaquetonadas*]; that has always existed."

The Politics of Male Identity and Intimacy: The Relational Character of Signification

The photographic image of Jose and Francisco lightly holding hands moves us. Many reasons possibly account for this reaction. First, we may find dissonant the convergence of conventional markers of masculinity as represented in these two "country" men exhibiting the affective and corporeal act that brings them together in the image. Second, the idea that a register of an emotional and bodily union between two men can circulate publicly and become a personal and family document seems strange within our contemporary frames of reference. Third, we are startled to discover historical evidence about visible bonds and expressions of affection among males in the northern region of Mexico barely two generations ago. In other words, it is difficult to come to terms with the temporal and geographic proximity of something that in many other ways seems rather "foreign." In fact, upon reflecting on the image, we begin to realize that while in today's social context an action similar to the one represented in the photo immediately conjures up notions of homosexual identity that assign to the men involved presumptions about being a gay couple, in the past this same action was invested with other meanings. When Jose and Francisco posed for their photo, the sexual identity we nowadays call gay did not exist and the concept of a homosexual identity was known only to select medical professionals. Of course, there were other terms used then to designate those who transgressed the established canon of male masculinity. In northern Mexico, men who were perceived as effeminate were called *nahuilon* or *marica*.

However, the most surprising and significant realization in trying to understand the meaning of this image is recognizing that the photographic register of two men holding hands to symbolize their affection toward each other was not deemed a transgression of the socially prescribed norms of masculinity or male sexuality prevalent at the time. Even when the photograph was inscribed with a personal and intimate dedication, as in this instance, such an action did not bring upon the participants the kind of social stigma that would eventually lead to the construction of a new identity and a differentiated life-style. The contrast between the meanings of the same act in different historical moments brought forth by the photo of Jose and Francisco leads me to advance two conclusions that I hope to thoroughly substantiate in this chapter:

The meanings attributed to "being a man" are historical constructions. These meanings can change over time and, with them, the gender connotations for what we denominate as masculine or effeminate in relation to men's behaviors, including acts of bodily affection such as holding another man's hand. In other words, connotations of gender that affect the whole experiential range of intimacy for and among men come into question. To the degree that the meanings of these actions change, so do the possible actions and behaviors undertaken by men in their daily lives.[5]

The meanings attributed to being a man and the changes in those meanings throughout different historical periods are intimately related to meanings in other spheres of social life; namely, the meanings associated with practices considered to be gender or sexually dissident. These other meanings are usually condensed into either terms that express stigma, such as *joto* (faggot), *homosexual*, or *nahuilon*, or terms that express self-affirmation, such as *gay*.

A variety of meanings coalesces to form both the possibilities and the modalities for the construction of emotional and corporeal bonds between men. That is to say, these meanings work to form conceptual frames for thinking about and understanding the possibilities of affection between men, to express affection in public, or simply to think of and understand male identity and intimacy in a broader sense.

During my fieldwork in different small towns in the Sonoran sierra, I was able to see photos similar to the one in question here. They usually depicted men wearing cowboy's clothes, holding hands, and usually included personal dedications about the meaning of their friendships. The phenomenon seems to have been more common in the economically developed centers that were in close proximity to the small sierra towns, such as Nacozari, Sonora, and Douglas, Arizona.

Men used to travel to these regional economic hubs to sell agricultural or meat products and to purchase goods such as fabric, tools, and other domestic utensils. The journey to these places was usually long and exhausting, and in many instances quite dangerous. Men preferred to make the journey in the company of another man or a group of men—usually partners, "buddies," close friends with whom they shared labor, adventures, fun, and confessions. Feelings of affection and emotional connection between men were thus cemented by the sharing of daily life and the trust (*confianza*) generated by shared toil. In addition, a sense of equity in attending to "manly" things–as they both were men—underscored the affective elements developed through such relationships.

These affective bonds among men stood in sharp contrast to the productive and reproductive roles and connections that men were expected to have with their wives. In the context of marriage obligations and of a highly segregated and dichotomized gender social ideology, these distinctions were especially noticeable. What is particularly interesting about the type of photographs that were taken in this context is that in such representations the notion of masculinity—indexed through the men's clothes, pose, and "look" as defined by the social conventions of manhood—does not appear in contradiction to the corporeal and affective proximity also apparent in the image. I would argue that the significance of the image lies precisely in the reversal it advances of the same elements: here, masculinity enables the bond between the men, forms it, feeds it, and sustains it. Masculinity thus appears as the possibility of affection in and of itself; the thing that makes possible the bonding represented. This semiotic "reversal," whereby masculinity and expressions of male intimacy converge instead of negating each other, is all the more significant because it is out of step with the politics of signification about masculinity prevalent in contemporary Mexican and Sonoran societies. In both places today, the effects of such a politics of meaning is to exclude "manliness," on the one hand, and the act of two men trying to represent their friendship through holding hands and having a picture taken on the other hand.[6]

Paying close attention to Don José Pedro's testimony, we notice that the friendship he describes with Chico, expressed graphically through the photograph, is articulated by him in relation to a playful arrangement of various experiences and signifiers. For instance, he is talking about two friends, specifically two male friends, but not just men defined in a biological sense; instead, these are men who stand for the socially sanctioned ways of being manly. In other words, they are *hombres-hombres* (manly men). Manliness or even manhood is constructed in Don José Pedro's discourse through the following: the men's work ethic, their responsibility as providers for their families, the clothes they wear (even their hats give off signals of virile self-assurance), their fulfillment of certain social values such as *no rajarse* (not giving up, or not cracking under pressure), and their responsibility to be honorable or serious and to command respect.

In this case, therefore, friendship appears as a by-product of the men's induction into male socialization. As Don José Pedro remarks, they shared rituals of manhood: going down to the river (i.e., to an isolated area) with more experienced men to learn about sex, something that "girls don't do." The terms Don José Pedro uses to designate his childhood antics turn on military metaphors: a *cuadrilla* (band) and a *tropa* (troop) refer in both cases to groups of men engaged in a mission or a common task. Friendships between men are thus nurtured and enabled by the bodily proximity derived from working together in the fields or in work-related errands or through what is simply called *andanzas* (hanging out, or partying). In the social context, all these activities are presumed masculine (not things that women do). A man's first heterosexual experience, characterized by Don José Pedro as *conocimiento de una mujer* (to "know" a woman, or "to be" with a woman), is expressed through the semantic expression *vaquetonada* (an act of a tough guy, a real man). But that expression is also used semantically to connote distinctive and unequivocal acts of masculinity in other social realms and usages. Hence, the bonds of male friendship are solidified through the exchange of these kinds of nonambiguous male behaviors shared by men through stories and experiences.

The terms *vaquetón* and *vaquetonada*—still popular sierra expressions well known in Hermosillo—are also interesting for another reason. In everyday speech, these words carry a significant ludic connotation as they refer to playful modes of behavior related to sex, but not exclusively. The same words can also refer to subtle transgressions of *deber* (moral and social obligations) without falling into disgrace for obvious deviancy. A *vaquetonada* is a mischievous act (*travesura*), a transgression that breaks the rigidity of Catholic morality in its extreme forms. But as the word is used in male contexts, this last meaning is extended to include "worldly" experiences that men must have and partake of (to "know" the world) and that women, secluded in their domestic realms, do not have access to.[7] *Vaquetonadas* are thus male socialization rituals that contrast males' ability to play with the social rules—to disobey—against the mother's moral teachings and women's modesty in general. The mischievous acts construed in the local speech community as *vaquetonadas* are expressions of masculinity that reinforce men's right to autonomy: in their bodies, their decisions, and their sexuality (Núñez 2013a).

Another interesting term used by Don José Pedro is that of *nahuilon* (sissy or effeminate). The term has Opata origins, referring to the *nahuas*, or a woman's skirt. A man described as a *nahuilon* is someone who acts like a woman, as if he were literally wearing a skirt. In other words, the term is a semantic expression of male gender transgression in which masculinity and clothing are linked together. To break the code of masculinity is also to break the code of proper clothing. Clothing configures the body publicly. The term *nahuilon* does not refer to erotic conduct, although that meaning can appear occasionally as well. The term points primarily to gender conduct. It does not function to designate someone with a different "identity"—as is the case discussed by Foucault of the homosexual in the 19th century, condemned to have a "different" life. As José Pedro indicates, the man found in women's clothing behind the bushes was married, had children, was hardworking, and did not have to choose a whole different life-style. His actions could be seen as a "relapse," a sin, or, as his own brother tells him, a crazy thing to do, but they do not necessarily make him a man of another "species."

At one point during our conversation, José Pedro seems confused by the proper pronunciation of the word *homosexual*. He asks me about men who are "hombresensual." But his apparent semantic confusion reveals a broader social difference at stake. The *nahuilon* is stigmatized because of his transgression of the expected social conduct of a man. The "hombresensual," on the other hand, can be constructed in today's social context as a man distinguished by his erotic difference, for being a "sensual man." Rather than being a simple slip of the tongue, I believe the difference between the two seemingly related terms points out the very different ways in which gender and sexual differences between men can be understood (or misunderstood) in Mexico today.

Don José Pedro's use of the term *vaquetonada* to refer to himself and certain ludic and heterosexual behaviors in his youth as well as to refer to sexual relations between men also strikes me as interesting. "Men have always engaged in *vaquetonadas* [mischievous behavior]," remarks Don José Pedro, when I ask whether in his time there were men who had sex with other men. In this manner, forms of illicit sexuality—transgressive modes of sexual pleasure obtained outside the boundaries of marriage and for nonreproductive purposes—are codified in Don José Pedro's testimony with a word that allows room for a certain playful indulgence, even though it is still a word that marks a difference from the norm. One does not turn into a *nahuilon* by having sex with another man. Such an act, although it is not the prescribed behavior, is comprehensible within the frame of "things that men do"; it is, in other words, a *vaquetonada*.

However, the *nahuilon* and the men who have sex with a *nahuilon* (an effeminate man or a man who acts like a woman) and the contemporary homosexual or "hombresensual" [*sic*] are not the only expressions of male sexuality at play in the social discourse. What about those things that happen between men who are close friends, pals, buddies (*camaradas*)? Don José Pedro speaks vaguely about a couple of possible scenarios. First, he tells me about young men who pair up with other young men and go down to the river to talk about sex openly and to do *vagancias* (things to pass time, kid's sex tricks) when the boys' bodies "begin to change." Other informants in the same region, younger than Don José Pedro, have also reported such pairings between adolescents for the purpose of exploring sexual practices. In the small towns in which I conducted fieldwork, on more than one occasion I heard men talk among themselves—or "ourselves" to be exact—(in confidence or *en confianza*) about group masturbation sessions, mutual masturbation experiences, or having sex with farm animals during their adolescent years.[8]

Second, we learn from José Pedro that his friendship with Chico included moments of close corporeal contact: they traveled together on the same horse and slept together at improvised spaces along the way. There's only one instance during our conversation when a single word and a joking context seem to hint—but no more than that—of a closer physical contact between the two men. Don José Pedro uses the verb *conocer* (to know something or to meet someone) in his discourse in two ways: to express the experience of having a first-time sexual encounter with a woman, which can be read literally as "gaining knowledge" about being with a woman, and to revindicate, jokingly, the primacy of the friendship between the two men over the marriage bond of José Pedro with his wife. Chico said pointedly: "yo lo conocí primero" ("I met him first," or "I knew him first"). Relaying the story to me, Don José Pedro added: "y era verdad" ("and he was right," or "he was telling the truth").

Whatever the true nature of their relationship may or may not have been, it is exceedingly clear that the affective relationship between Don José Pedro and Chico represented for them a unique personal and social experience. It is also clear that from and through their friendship the two men derived important insights about their self-image, their ways of understanding each other, their personal sense of happiness, their overall life dynamics, and the formation and affirmation of their individual masculinities. It is important to keep in mind that the affective bonds described up to this point are always constructed within the dynamics of gender politics. These politics, which in turn construct the masculine and the feminine as two distinct realms of social life, make it difficult for men and women to develop similarly strong bonds of friendship and trust with each other. The conjugal relationship thus represented for many men of Don José Pedro's generation a different type of affective relationship, one primarily based on the exchange of work roles (and value) and sexual rights: what is socially sanctioned as the *relacion de pareja*, or "married/couple life" (Núñez 2004a). It is no wonder then that in a social order segregated according to gender roles, affective relationships will also follow the same route. Homosociality[9] among men and women, respectively, becomes the main mechanism for establishing social bonds. The affective bond between José Pedro and Chico takes place therefore within the patriarchal context that establishes these sexual distinctions.[10]

I feel it is important to remark, however, that homo-affection and homoeroticism, as human relationships, are neither dependent on nor merely a function of homosociality and gender segregation. There is simply no evidence to support such a claim. Societies that have experienced significant changes with regard to the desegregation of gendered social spaces, where more equitable and accessible relationships of friendship and camaraderie among men and women have been made possible, have certainly not showed evidence of reductions in homoerotic interests. What I think can be asserted, instead, is that different social configurations will result in different modes of expressing and experiencing homoerotic feelings. The anthropological contribution to our understanding of the meaning of men's physical contacts with one another, as these contacts are produced within the parameters of the social regulation of the body and according to specific gender politics, has been up to now rather negligent. In Mexico, in spite of an upsurge in interest in masculinities and homosexuality in recent years, the field of ethnographic knowledge in these areas remains sparse. Much of the recent literature on homosexuality in Mexico has placed an emphasis on sexual roles as opposed to the broader spectrum of homoerotic relations and homo-affective bonds between men. The result has been a considerable gap in knowledge about these practices.

Bodies: Proximities, Distances, and Contacts

My experiences researching the field of men's corporeal and affective relations in Mexico's northern region have been complex and contradictory. In general, there is some truth to the generalized perception that men tend to have difficulties expressing physical affection for one another in public. Men's bodies are repeatedly subjected to surveillance when it comes to their public expressions. The way a man talks, his way of addressing other men, the way he walks, the way he expresses his emotions, the way he engages in conversations, and the way he dances, are all subject to scrutiny. Men feel the effects of such a state of constant vigilance regarding social norms of manliness in quite specific, everyday terms. One man I interviewed told me that when he saw there were many people in the plaza, he never walked across it; he preferred to walk around the perimeter instead. A friend of mine told me about the extreme case of a cowboy (*vaquero*) that said that just thinking that he would have to walk down the aisle of a church for a wedding, he would rather never marry. In fact, when the man finally got married, he refused a church ceremony.

The body can be a great source of personal stress for some men, especially when it becomes the object of attention of others in myriad everyday performances. In my field interviews, several young men told me that walking through a group of men makes them nervous, that they are afraid they will trip or that their legs will give out. On the other hand, men who carry themselves confidently, whose stride is firm and determined, who are perceived as being "in control" of their bodies, tend to be highly admired.

Legs wrapped in blue denim, feet snuggled into workboots or cowboy boots, arms covered by long sleeves, heads protected by hats or baseball caps—these body parts contained in specific garments and accessories stage a form of closure. The physical or corporeal closure symbolizes a communicative closure—men are thus rendered inaccessible, "impenetrable." The act of walking manifests subjectivities associated to manliness: the movement of the shoulders should be tempered, the hips must not swing, the arms must not fling out of control, the neck must be kept straight, and the facial expression must suggest concentration. If two men suddenly meet face-to-face on a trail or pathway, a greeting is expected, but it must be as brief as possible: barely a couple of words ("quihubo," or "what's happening"), a laconic exclamation ("hey," or "yep"), or a quick whistle. Public greetings between these men rarely include kisses or embraces. A handshake is usually considered the only necessary and appropriate greeting, and only among men who share other social bonds (of a personal or professional nature). Everyday acquaintances are greeted with only a passing "good morning," "what's up?" (*que hubo?*), or "how is it going?" (*que paso?*). Meeting strangers requires an added sense of formality: men usually get up if they are seated, and the custom of older men is to lift their hats slightly with the left hand while extending the right hand for a handshake.

Men's social greetings contrast significantly with those of women. Women's clothing also exposes more of the body, such as legs, feet, shoulders, arms, or even hair. Most distinct of all, however, are the ways women usually greet each other. It is not uncommon to see public expressions of happiness, surprise, fear, pleasure, sadness, or even crying when women meet in public. Women are also comfortable expressing public gestures or actions that signify tenderness to one another. These marked distinctions in the areas of emotional and affective expressions are precisely what feminists have referred to as "the social division of emotions." The responsibility for carrying on emotionally charged domestic tasks has also fallen primarily on women. That is, women organize the family gatherings, offer support at funerals, take primary charge of caring for the sick, bear the responsibility of cultivating emotional bonds with the children, oversee the children's education and their appointments with the doctors, and, of course, take the lead in their spiritual education and participation.

I have observed that in certain contexts where men are more relaxed and open to social interactions—where their guard is down, so to speak—it is possible to identify other modes of bodily proximity and contact not usually found in the course of everyday life. Sometimes the contrast between the two realms and the behaviors displayed can be quite surprising. One of these sites of openness are parties (or *el baile*—any social gathering where dancing is allowed). Parties to celebrate a community event, a wedding, or a girl's fifteenth birthday are the classic sites for the expression of happiness, affection, and sexuality. Even if from the outside those occasions and the dances that take place in them seem contrived or ritualized, compared to less rigid social settings in which dancing can be more free and sensual, these traditional gatherings are fertile sites for a wide diversity of bodily expressions by men and between men. In such gatherings, men sometimes can be seen retreating together to a spot nearby to urinate or throwing their arms around each other in good spirits while holding a conversation.

Of course, these behaviors are sometimes greatly aided by the consumption of alcohol. In fact, it may be hard to say with precision whether parties encourage alcohol consumption or it is the other way around. One thing seems clear, however: alcohol plays a role in helping configurate the range of possibilities for more open bodily expressions of affection among men. At many communal or family parties, it is common to see young and adult men form their own separate gatherings somewhat distanced from the main event. These gatherings to the side are occasions for more drinking, rough talk, and dancing. There it is common for a man to start dancing all by himself to the tune of a song he likes, to be followed by other men dancing alone, and sometimes for two men to dance together as a couple. This scene has become so familiar that sometimes children can be seen imitating the same behaviors.

Certainly, as these observations illustrate, many forms of physical contact between men seem to contradict the otherwise strict surveillance of men's bodies and masculine identities the majority of the time. In today's social context, it is highly unlikely that two friends from the Sonoran sierra would pose for a photograph holding hands. The closest that two young men would come to that action today would be to throw their arms around each other's shoulders. Today, the gesture of holding another man's hand to express affection in a portrait carries connotations of romance and homosexuality. In the short span of two generations, something has changed in the social structure about our understanding of male intimacy. And yet, it is still possible to glean spaces and possibilities for the public expression of male affection. Unfortunately, the lens we use to see these social dynamics between males in Mexico today has been colored by a persistent bias in favor of so-called dominant "Mexican gender ideologies," which render much of what we see as "odd" from the outset. In many instances, such reductionistic viewpoints have been abetted by an anthropological glance to begin with.

The public presentation of men's bodies proceeds according to a binary pattern of closure–openness, which is in turn symbolized and reproduced as masculine–feminine respectively. Along the same lines, it seems to me, among themselves men reproduce this binary by marking two distinct times and spaces: either "everyday life/party life" or what has been called in the anthropological literature "ordinary/extraordinary" experiences. Hence, even though manliness or maleness (*lo masculino*) depends to a great extent on the presentation of a closed body in its gestural and clothing patterns as discussed earlier, the arrival of party time signals a time and space where transgression of the quotidian ordinary is allowed, within limits. The party as such does not exist or function outside the norms; quite the opposite, the norms themselves configure the possibilities for exploring gender and corporeal expressions contained and repressed within the norms all along. I do not want to argue here, however, for the uniqueness or "licensed" singularity of the party as an isolated instance, perhaps on an annual basis. In fact, what happens in real life is that the social milieu of the extraordinary, the festive, is continually absorbed and reproduced within the parameters of ordinary life. In this sense, informal evening gatherings, the drinking sprees of weekends, birthday parties, vigils for patron saints, and a wide range of other social occasions, instigate the possibilities for party time within the flow of everyday life.

In many communities, to be sure, alcohol provides the incentive for creating these distinctive festive times–spaces that stand in contrast to the quotidian. In northern Mexico, the convergence of alcohol consumption with the creation of a set-aside festive moment, without any particular special occasion to call for celebration but simply for the pleasure of gathering and drinking, is denominated a *pisteada*. Traditionally, *pisteadas* have always been exclusively male events. In recent years, however, as a result of the dramatic increase in women joining the manufacturing labor force and the parallel shifts in relationships between young men and women as coworkers, some women have started to participate in *pisteadas* as well, even at the risk of "soiling" their reputations (Núñez 1998). The body and alcohol conspire within the homosocial spaces of the *pisteada* and the fiesta to authorize and justify the exploration of other means of bodily affection and expression. These explorations entail in the first place new modes of presentation of the embodied self and from there extend to affection, eroticism, and reach as far as the expression of pain, suffering, anger, and even violence. Through the intervention of alcohol (as catalytic agent of the emotions), the presentation of the "everyday" body as a closed, controlled, disciplined body is upset. A man who alters these prescribed patterns because he drank too much usually finds a certain degree of tolerance and social leniency for his behavior. The leniency, however, is not absolute. Even then, a man must uphold his honor and dignity for the sake of himself and his family.

The binaries closed–open and masculine–feminine are rearranged through the consumption of alcohol in these festive moments to activate yet a third binary set: that of inside–outside. The man who "has a few drinks in him" at these festive gatherings occasionally breaks out into song or tears or confessions, and in doing so (when he opens himself up, or in Spanish *al abrirse* or *rajarse*) he exposes an interior life that is unusual in the prescribed closeness of his everyday life. In this sense, *pistear* becomes a verb, an action that encompasses all of these possibilities at once or at any given moment. This kind of association and mis-association between the binaries described above seems to structure some of the ideas expressed in the following monologue by Raul, an inebriated forty-five-year-old man, who throws his arms around me at an alley behind a cantina:

> Don't pay me any attention, OK? I am drunk. But do you want to know why I am drinking? Because I am a man. Because men . . . you are a man and I know you will understand me . . . because men, we know about things that women don't know anything about. You understand . . . right? Let me explain . . . do you know why a man starts to drink? A man starts to drink when he loses that thing from his childhood, that innocence, you understand? When he has feelings and things inside of him that now he must keep to himself, when he carries pain, when he has committed a sin or two . . . yes, my boy [*mijo*]? Do you agree? I know you understand me because you went to school. I did not go to school, but I know what I'm saying. Shake my hand, come on. I am going to tell you something: a man only knows what he carries inside; no one else really knows him. When you carry something deep inside yourself, it is almost as if you carry another silent man inside.

If there is something to be learned from this drunken monologue, from this maneuvering between conscious and unconscious speech, it is perhaps the central role played by the inside–outside binary in figuring this man's understanding of his actions. Raul, however, is not an isolated case. I would argue that his words ring true for many men. Raul's explanations are part of the subjective dynamics by which many men justify their drinking and their particular assessments of what it means to be a man. Such explanations express a vision of gender identity in relation to the loss of innocence, sin, and secrecy. When Raul describes his emotional/personal self as another man inside oneself, he activates fundamental assumptions about the ideological aspirations of masculinity and the kind of work it requires to keep the space of those emotions locked up in everyday life.

"With a few drinks in him," so to speak, Raul throws his arms around me, confessing his deepest feelings and motivations; he aches as he describes his inner struggles and treats me as an accomplice who certainly understands him because I, too, am a man. At one point he addressed me with tenderness, calling me "my boy" (*mijo*), even though we only know each other from passing. A few days later, now sober, Raul walks past me in the street. He barely says hello; his previously open self is now sheathed back into a stern and locked-down body.

Ventura: The Ambiguity and Difficulty of Love Between Two Men

I met Ventura quickly after my arrival in the town of Los Corazones, through an accidental encounter at a government office. Later on, he saw me at the Plaza and approached me. Ventura is forty-two years old, is married, and has four children. He has had many occupations, but is mainly experienced in mining. Tall and slender, his normally light complexion tanned by exposure to the sun, Ventura always has a smile on his face when he speaks. The smile has become a symbol of his public image; in this town, he is well known for his ability to make people laugh. One afternoon later that autumn, he invited to me to come hang out with him to talk while he worked as a night guard at a warehouse along the highway. Thus, we began a series of very fruitful conversations. In fact, Ventura became one of my key informants.

Ventura is not originally from Los Corazones. He came here from Dátil, a small mining community in the high sierra, fairly isolated and generally less impacted by modern communications and life-styles. Ventura came to Los Corazones after a series of circumstances having to do with his romance with a young woman he had known since he was a teenager. Nevertheless, it is here that he also developed a deep friendship with a young man of his own age. Over the course of our conversations, Ventura revealed to me in great detail the story of this unique friendship that, as he said, he had "never been able to talk about with anyone." I sensed that he was especially thankful to be able to talk about it with me at last.

Ventura begins: "I met Rodrigo at the local bar. Listen to this: I met him just a short time after arriving in town. I was working at the time in the mines up there in the sierra . . . you know where they are located more or less, no? I had gotten paid that day. I walked over to the bar looking my best—shaven and wearing clean clothes, very 'pretty' [he says smiling]—and since I was a young man then, well, even prettier. So I went to the bar, asked for a beer, and hung out quietly for a while. Soon after, the man that took care of the bar put some money in the jukebox and began to play music. I got really melancholic, thinking about my family that I had not seen in a while. I also got depressed thinking about my failure with the girl that I told you about and one thing led to another, and before I knew it tears rolled down my face, from sadness and nostalgia."

He continues: "In the bar there was only another young man and I, well, and maybe a few others on the other side. The thing is that unexpectedly that young man [*chavalo*] sent me a beer and then he came over and we started talking. He asked me if I was from around here, if I was sad, and that's how we became friends. Then he asked me to come over and have dinner with him at his house. From there the friendship sort of took off. Later on, after we'd been friends for a while, he told me that he paid attention to me that day in the bar because he had seen me cry, that when he saw the tears roll down my face he was surprised because, well you know, around here most men boast of being so tough and macho [*se las dan de muy machos*], and here I was, acting differently, and for that reason he noticed me. Deep down inside, he said, he and I were the same kind of men. Check it out, that's what he said to me. What do you think? [Ventura asks with a smile.] We became the best of friends and since I did not have family here and I was renting a room from this one lady, he said that I should come live in his house. And I did. I lived there for a long time."

Then Ventura says: "Soon we started hanging out, going together to the community dances and that kind of thing. And, let me tell you, I taught him how to dance, because he did not know how. He was a shy young man, overall. So, I began to give him dance lessons when we were alone in the house. Later on he hooked up with a girlfriend, and so did I. Sometimes the four of us would go out together."

"Listen, Ventura," I interject. "Did the two of you ever have sexual relations?"

He says: "No, you will see; I will tell you the whole story, OK? I believe that he liked me that way, because I could see that he would get jealous if I hung out with other friends. He asked me once if I had already learned how to kiss and I said, yes, that I had. Then he asked me what it felt like. I told him that I didn't know how to describe it; it was just something you felt. Then another time when we were at the ranch by ourselves . . . I was laying down resting and he was next to me and he said, 'Kiss me, so that I can know what it feels like; I want to learn how to kiss.' I laughed and said to him, 'Oh, you are so naïve, no, no way; how am I going to teach you such a thing?' And he answered me, 'So what? There's nothing wrong with it. I want to find out what it is like.'"

"And did you ever kiss?" I ask.

"I did not want to. Well, not exactly; the truth is that I wanted to do it, because he was quite a handsome stud [*estaba bien chulo el cabron*], but I was embarrassed," says Ventura, smiling. "But for a long time we slept together holding each other, especially when we were out working in the countryside. Hey, what do you say to that?"

"Do you still see him?"

Ventura says: "No, not anymore. He went to the other side [the United States] to work and he stayed there, in Tucson. He hasn't come back, he hasn't . . . he left the woman he had here and hooked up with another woman over there. Ah . . . there was this one time when he came back . . . oh, for God's sake, yes . . . I was working right there in the Plaza, trimming some trees way up high in the branches, and he saw me and you should have seen what an uproar he made. I hadn't seen him in so long that I almost didn't recognize him. He was always excitable, like that . . . when I came down from the tree he embraced me and kissed me repeatedly . . . [he laughs] . . . how about that? Then when he left, all the men around me, there in the Plaza, started teasing me because they saw how distressed and sad I became."

"Have you had another friend like him since he left?" I ask.

Ventura speaks in a deeper tone of voice and his whole body language changes. He seems to be overcome with emotion.

"Well, with Chalo, like I had mentioned earlier. But I am going to tell you something here, only between you and me: I think I truly am in love with Chalo. If a day goes by and I don't see him, I feel sad and I come up with any excuse to find him and see him. He does the same, he looks for me in the same way. Did you notice that I even have his photo displayed in my house? He gave me a photo of himself."

"Oh, yeah? And where is it? Where do you display it?"

Ventura says: "Right there in the living room . . . seriously, you didn't notice? There he is, standing tall and proud, my pal [*compa*]. I bought a frame for it."

"And your wife, what did she say about it?"

"Nothing . . . well, she said: 'Ay, how come you have his picture there, as if he were pretty or something.' She laughs when she says that. I responded to her: 'Come on, I don't keep his photo there because he is pretty, but because he is my friend and he gave me that photo.' The truth is that I really do find him pretty but I don't tell her that, of course [he laughs]. But there's nothing to it, I have photographs of other friends displayed in the house. But Chalo and I, well, we are different. I have told him straight out that I love him and that I want to kiss him and feel his body . . . all of that."

"And. . . ?"

"Yes, we have kissed, a few times when we both were drinking . . . but not the real thing, not a real kiss, just pecks on the mouth, playing around, that's all."

"Playing around?"

Ventura answers: "Yes, more or less. See, let me tell you: the thing is that Chalo told me about his father, who by the way was a very macho kind of man. I mean so much so that he even died as a result of a rumble with some guy. Well, Chalo told me that when he and his siblings were kids his father had a custom of kissing them lightly on the lips . . . like birds do, beak to beak . . . barely touching. He has good memories of his father, but one of his brothers doesn't. As it turns out, the old man liked to drink and he had a temper. And Chalo's brother . . . well, he is effeminate. Someone told the father once that they had seen the boy, barely fourteen years old at the time, have sex with an older man . . . a man from the area. The father got drunk and hit the boy really bad, he also threatened to hang him, if you can believe it. That's the reason why Chalo's brother does not care too much for the old man."

Ventura continues: "I also think that's the main reason why we only kiss lightly. I think he feels guilty, because he comes forward and then he retreats, and then he comes back. He has told me it is not easy for him. But when we go to sleep, I embrace him and he cuddles up in my arms, and I give him sweet caresses, as if he were a little boy [*un chamaquito*]. There was this one time when I had to travel to the countryside to watch over some farm equipment and he went with me. Over there, we acted like two people in love . . . at nightfall, we walked along the river holding hands. But something sexual? No, he does not want that and I don't insist, you know? In that manner, we carry on. Nobody in town knows the truth. I mean, people know that we are very close; they always see us together, but that's it. But he and I are not the type to be making a big fuss about things. And besides, you can tell, I act manly, and so does he. We are not going to be carrying on like that guy, what's his name, the one who acts like a faggot [*joto*] . . . all he needs are a few drinks and he makes a fool of himself acting out like a woman. That's why I say that people see us and they know about our closeness, but I don't think they have any idea, I mean . . . they can't possibly imagine the truth . . . that is, that we are in love with each other."

Ventura smiles as he speaks and his eyes shine with the peculiar glint of someone who is deeply moved.

Ventura never uses the word *homosexual* to refer to himself. It is not a word that he considers to be applicable to him, for after all, he acts manly and is married, as he frequently makes it a point to remind me. He would not use this word to refer to his friend, either. Their relationship is safely sheltered within the social space of friendship. Conforming to the conventional parameters of manliness and camaraderie between men, they take advantage of whatever concessions for intimacy they are able to find.

In the two friendships with other men that he describes, falling in love has always been a real possibility for one or both parties. In both cases, the expression of romantic love has been channeled through the institution of friendship. Yet, invariably, such expressions of affection stumbled repeatedly over the ghost of sexual prohibitions, over the threatening proximity of homophobia and its sequels: shame, guilt, silence, and the difficulties in manifesting one's feelings. For Ventura and for most of the men in town, at least as he describes them, a *joto* (faggot) is someone who violates the canon of manliness: he is effeminate, or when he drinks he behaves "likes a woman," making a public spectacle of himself with his behavior or letting others know about his preferences, as in the case with Chalo's brother. More than an elaborate discourse on homosexuality as a "repressed" social experience that demands to be released or does not dare to free itself from social prejudice, what we find here instead is a particular way of articulating desire, gender identities, and affective relationships.

In this context, it is worth asking the following questions: (1) What are the social coordinates that mark and define manhood and manliness (*hombría*) in Mexico? (2) What social coordinates, in turn, mark and define homosexuality? (3) Are the boundaries and limits of these two notions established once and for all? and (4) How are the borders between these two notions defined, and what room is there left for enacting different possibilities, actions, and connotations?

The experiences documented in these ethnographic interviews suggest the need to investigate something other than specific objects of speech reified at certain historical moments: homosexuality, heterosexuality, gay identity, and so on. These testimonies issue a call instead to examine expressive possibilities for affection and eroticism as a field of social relations that has been subjected to various and divergent regulations throughout different historical moments. This field of expressive possibilities is manifested in different modes, forms, and meanings at various times. As such, it also results in different consequences for the subjects who embark in its various practices and demarcates in general different possibilities around how power and pleasure are experienced. To renounce this kind of analysis that I advocate in pursuit of general ahistoric discourses about homosexuality, masculinity, patriarchy, and so forth, represents a renunciation as well of the richness and complexity of the human experience in general and of the manifold strands through which freedom and power intersect.

Not until recently, with the expansion of the field of men's studies and queer theory, has it been possible to explore theoretically the topic of male intimacy in the way in which the ethnographic subjects in this study seem to understand, live, and negotiate this experience. By putting into question the constructed nature of the meanings attributed to masculinity and the possibilities for male expressions of affection that such constructions police, queer studies and recent inroads in the emerging field of men's studies have opened a door for the kind of experiences illuminated in this book. Only by understanding the intricacies of a social system intent on mastering the power/knowledge to define the subjectivities and bodies of men are we able, in turn, to understand how the possibilities for being a man and loving other men—affectionately and sexually—are regulated and hence denied.

Sharing the Bed: Experiences of Male Intimacy

During the three years I spent doing fieldwork in rural Sonora, I received multiple invitations from male informants and collaborators to share their bed.[11] The first time it happened was only two days after I took temporary residence in Los Corazones. In the process of getting to know the town and the people who lived there, I attended a wedding that was taking place in a public park, which did not require a previous invitation. While I stood on the side observing the wedding party, I began conversing with a man in his early thirties who asked for my help to move a group of chairs.

The man was an employee of the father of the bride. He was dark-skinned, of medium built, with thick eyebrows and a thick mustache, and single. When we finished the chore, he asked me my name and thus we began an extensive conversation. After an hour or so, aided by the buzzing sensation of uninterrupted beer servings offered by the brothers and cousins of the bride to all present, we both felt relaxed and comfortable in each other's presence. The man expressed happiness over our impromptu friend-ship. He told me: "Man, you are good to hang around with; it is easy to have a conversation with you!" He then asked whether I had any relatives in town or any friends. When I said I didn't, he immediately tried to be helpful and asked me in a concerned tone: "Where are you staying?" Be-fore I could answer he said: "If you want to come and stay at my house, it is a pleasure for me to offer it to you; I live with my mother, that's it. My brothers and sisters are all married and live in Hermosillo. You can stay there with me; I have a big room and a big bed, big enough for the two of us. We are poor, but we can manage."

I answered politely: "No, don't worry about being poor. I am a simple person. I would feel comfortable there, I am sure." I then proceeded to inform him that I had already paid for a room in the town's guest house. He replied: "As you prefer, but if you ever need a place to stay, you are more than welcome to do so." His tone was kind, sincere, firm, and atten-tive. It was clear that his offer had no sexual hidden agenda; it was an act of hospitality from one man to another borne out of empathy, *confianza*, and friendship.

Throughout the duration of my fieldwork, I eventually had the experi-ence of sharing the same bed with male friends I had made along the way. Rubén was one of those men. He was twenty-three years old, of white complexion, good-looking, and masculine. I met him through one of the inevitable rides in my truck that I either offered or was asked to help others with between Hermosillo and so many of the small sierra towns where I was working. He was a university student and traveled every weekend be-tween his small town, La Mesa, and the state capital. After approximately one year of knowing each other, we attended a dance with his girlfriend and some friends and stayed up almost all night. Considering that I was in no condition to drive home, Ruben asked me for the keys to my truck and drove me to his house, where he lived with his parents and three siblings. When we arrived, he showed me the bed we would have to share and or-dered me to bed. He helped take my boots off and folded my shirt over a chair. "Feel at home," he whispered. He filled a pitcher with water and put it on the night table next to the bed in case I became thirsty during the night and pointed out the bathroom down the hallway. Then he stretched alongside me in bed and pulled the covers over both of us. At dawn I woke up and noticed that his body was lying close to mine and that his arm rested on my shoulder. I also noticed that his sister and his nieces slept in a room directly across from where we were and that only a thin curtain separated the two rooms. I fell asleep again. Later that morning, Rubén woke me up with a cup of coffee in bed and invited me to come to the kitchen to eat breakfast with him and his older brother. During breakfast we talked, commented on the news, and laughed about the events of the night before.

I found out that in many of the small rural towns in Sonora, sharing a bed among male friends is considered an act of friendship and affection. Most of the time, the occasion to share the bed comes about through special circumstances such as being in transit between towns, having to travel somewhere for work reasons, or having to spend the night when it gets too late and one has had one too many drinks. As such, this act is performed in plain view of other members of the family or friends. There is no shroud of secrecy imposed on the invitation to share a bed, and it is rarely something that invites scrutiny from the social group. In the same manner, when a man sleeps with another man in such contexts this act is not inscribed in the framework of a homosexual experience. Most of the time, it doesn't even raise suspicion along those lines. The sexual and gender norms of these communities allow for the possibility of an affective and corporeal intimacy between men that questions dominant conceptions about what counts or not as sexual as well as general definitions of what is normal, what is manliness or homosexuality, or even queer.

I contrast these experiences in the Sonoran sierra with the discovery I made when I lived in Tucson, Arizona, and went to the movies one evening with a heterosexual male friend. As we sat down to see the movie, he left an empty seat between us. Later on I was told that leaving an empty space between seats in a theater is a common practice among young heterosexual men in the United States due to the fear of giving the impression that one has a homosexual interest in the other man.

The gestures of intimacy I have described are not only found among men. In fact, they are far more common among women who often find occasion as friends to spend the night in each other's house and to sleep in the same bed. Sharing one's bed with another person of the same sex is an act that signals for both genders a desire to express corporeal and affective intimacy considered appropriate within a friendship. It is an act that is usually framed along with other acts of solidarity, such as keeping one another company (especially among women), helping someone with a large home project, helping a friend fix his car, or giving someone a ride to attend to some kind of errand. Family members usually become witnesses and participants of these types of exchanges among friends. For instance, when a man visits another man in his house—when a friend drops by or comes along after sharing a chore—it is common that the brothers, the father, or the mother of the one whose house it is will invite the friend for coffee, to eat, or simply engage him in conversation. Sometimes a friend becomes a "best" friend precisely on account of the extended family activities in which he participates over time. The expression "so and so's friend" becomes a code for those types of friendship that share in these more intimate spaces. Eventually, becoming someone's compadre is a means to institutionalize and add religious meaning to these types of unique liaisons between close friends. It is quite common to hear friends start calling each other by the word *compa* (short for compadre) quite some time before an actual act of baptism of a child takes place.

As time went by, Rubén and I developed a very close friendship. He came to my own house in Hermosillo and on several occasions shared my own bed. I was able to share with Rubén many questions that came up during fieldwork about gender expectations, behaviors, and relationships among men. He always offered interesting perspectives that allowed me a closer look into the sexual behavior and values of young men his age, because of not only his own experiences but also those of his friends. He also shared quite a bit of information with me about the sexual and affective dimensions of his relationship with his girlfriend. One day he asked me directly whether I "was able to distinguish when a man is good-looking or not." I answered affirmatively and told him very honestly that I considered myself capable of loving a man or a woman in the same way, as in effect I had had the opportunity to do in my life. He listened politely to my answer and never brought it up again.

In spite of Rubén's apparent acceptance of the possibility of bisexuality or homoerotic desires among men, not once did he ever bring up the subject of sexual orientation or any statement related to the notion of homosexuality. However, the few times that he used the word—*homosexual* it was always to criticize and correct other derogatory terms such as fairy[12] (*joto*) or *fresco* (fresh or cool) that some men imputed to other men when they refused to drink more or accept a dare.[13] He always rejected these kinds of situations as being *machista*. Conforming to a strongly held value in many of these small communities about being a "true man" by respecting the privacy of people's lives, I never heard him call anyone *joto* or even homosexual. To talk too much or spread gossip about someone else's private affairs is not considered a manly characteristic in this region. Only on one occasion did I hear Rubén use the words *pansy* (*maricon*) and *loca*, but it was in reference to a joke that made fun of someone's hyper-effeminate gestures. I found that comment from Rubén particularly interesting because it revealed an implicit and hidden homophobia in someone who by any other account had given all indications of being comfortable with male affection and intimacy. It is possible that Rubén perceived enough evidence of the heterosexual side of my life or felt comfortable enough with my own expressions of manliness that he accepted the possibilities of male intimacy as something that simply belongs "among men" or among good friends (*buenos amigos*).

After a couple of years of friendship with Rubén, mostly around weekend get-togethers, one day he made a startling confession and proposition. While drinking beers one afternoon, he told me that he "loved me very much" (*me quería mucho*) and that he thought "we would always be friends no matter what happens" and I could "always count" on him for anything I needed. He told me that he often talked to his girlfriend (by now fiancée) about me and the kinds of things we talked about and that she also thought I was a very nice person.

Then he added: "Guillermo, my fiancé and I were talking . . . and I was thinking that maybe when we get married, if you haven't married yet, that you could come to live with us. She told me she liked the idea; what do you think?" I smiled and made a couple of humorous remarks, primarily to aid in helping me get over the surprise at this new proposed configuration of our friendship. It was clear that the bond of intimacy that Rubén allowed himself to live with me called into question the dominant conceptions about male subjectivity and the contemporary identities and relationships around homosexuals and heterosexuals that I had encountered in the literature coming from Europe and North America as well as in certain dominant urban, modern, middle-class discourses in Mexico. Rubén constructed an affective intimacy with me that was deeply steeped in a discourse of love and corporeal proximity. Yet, he did so from the subject position of a man (a young man from the countryside with some access to higher education and limited urban experiences) and not from that of a homosexual.

Rubén's subject position and his understanding of the range of meanings of a friendship were akin to Whitman's notions of "adhesive love" (Whitman 1973) or to the stories of male intimacy and affection among men in the United States in the mid-1800s described by Jonathan Katz in his book *Love Stories: Sex Between Men Before Homosexuality* (2001). At the same time, I was keenly aware that Rubén's subjectivity and identity position in this regard could not be understood as an expression of a unique and liberating dominant local model of masculinity. Quite to the contrary, Rubén repeatedly affirmed a critical attitude to what he termed *machista* modes of thinking among many men and women in the region. In other words, the subject and identity position claimed by Rubén involved a very deliberate act on his part of resubjectification toward the dominant modes of male subjectivity in his community. At the same time, within the framework of certain select possibilities in his community, the friendship that I had cultivated with him around critical questions of intimacy pertaining to this research project had also assisted his ability to perform this action. Rubén's marked discrepancy with his social context, however, cannot be understood as a difference articulated around sexual orientation but more so as an enhanced capacity for affective intimacy within a set horizon of cultural negotiations and debates about the meaning of being a man.

The ethnographic experiences of corporeal and affective closeness that I have been relating so far, as well as my own difficulties in making sense of them, confront me face-to-face with two main threads running through this book: the culturally constructed nature of the meanings often attributed to physical contact and emotional intimacy between men; and therefore the socially constructed character of men's possibility for affective and erotic intimacy, and the inadequate character of dominant sexual categories (such as fairy, trade, gay, or homosexual) to account for these intimate relations. Several instances of physical contact and emotional bonding that for me would have immediately represented erotic interests and would have pointed to a gay identity, turned out to be ordinary masculine behavior for many of my informants. Along the same lines, everyday bodily performances, gestures, and postures that for me suggested excessively rigid expressions borne out of the local modes of machismo, were considered by many of the men that I interacted with as normal modalities of being a man (*de ser hombre*). In several other instances, I was left to ponder actions and behaviors that from my point of view seemed rather ambiguous.

The meanings attributed to affective and corporeal intimacy among men are always constructed in relation to certain meanings in other areas of social discourse: namely, meanings about what counts as manliness and conversely what does not count as such (and is thus considered feminine, effeminate, less masculine, less manly, *joto*, or the proper conduct of women). The semiotics of gender are thus implicated in the social regulation of what it means to be a man, and these regulations are in turn mobilized to establish a horizon of possibilities for exchanging intimacy with other men. Some of these intimacies certainly transgress somehow, to a greater or lesser degree, the dominant conceptions of being a man in those communities.

However, are the semiotics of masculinity and manliness always transparent, fixed, homogeneous, and inflexible? The testimonies of the men that I met and my own experiences in the field seem to suggest quite the opposite. They point, instead, to negotiation, flexibility, heterogeneity, and dispute with regard to the meaning of "being a man," even in traditional communities in the northern sierra of Mexico where one would assume the opposite to be the case.

At the same time, I recognize that the cultural significance of the practices of masculinity and intimacy that I discuss here were apprehended through a research process and experience that implicated my own performances of manhood in relation to that of my research subjects. Or, better yet, I should refer to the dialogic nature of what has been learned in terms of my own knowledge and trajectory in grasping the politics of masculinity and intimacy in contrast to the processes undertaken by my informants toward the same end. Yet, in what may seem at first glance a paradox or perhaps a disclaimer, this contrast between myself and my research collaborators makes all too obvious a point that I argue in the next chapter: the meanings of masculinity in Mexico are not always the same for all men, in all places, and at all times.

CHAPTER TWO

Disputes over the Meaning of "Being a Man" in Mexico

Applications of Queer Theory

Masculinity as Challenge

Field Note, January 27, 1999

While I sit on a bench in the Town Square in La Mesa, around the time when people retire to take their siesta and the streets look deserted, I see three boys approximately six or seven years old playing around and climbing a large olive tree nearby. One of the boys climbs to the highest branch. Looking down, he says to his friend below: "Let's see if you are really a man. I dare you to climb as high as I did." The boy below responds: "I'll show you," and rapidly ascends the trunk until he reaches the same branch where the first boy sits. Intrigued, I focus my attention on their conversation. The second climber now begins to taunt the third boy who has stayed behind, close to the ground.

"Don't be a *bizcocho* [sissy]. Climb up, nothing bad will happen to you! [The Spanish word *bizcocho* has been translated as "sissy," but a literal translation would be something like "don't be a sponge cake."]

The third boy, who is also the youngest of the three, responds in a fearful voice: "No, I will fall."

"Come on, climb up; nothing is going to happen, try again," says the second climber.

"Leave him alone, he is very *culón* [sissy]," adds the first boy from the tallest branch. [The expression used by the boy in Spanish is *es bien culón*; a literal translation would be "he has a big ass," but in this context the connotative meaning is the same as sissy.]

The second boy now turns his attention to the first climber and issues another challenge:

"Let's see who is more man—I dare you to jump from here all the way over there," he says, pointing toward the end of the long branch on which they are sitting.

"I'll do it," says the first boy and jumps in a hurry.

The boy who issued the challenge retorts:

"Well, I can do it, too . . . look, look," and he jumps daringly only to land next to where I am seated, his knees badly scraped.

"It's OK to rub yourself," says the boy on top sarcastically.

"That didn't hurt me," responds the second boy confidently and quickly gets up and dusts himself off.

The boys continue to carry on a little while longer and finally move away to play some other game.

I am surprised to hear these boys, at such a young age, compete to prove who is "more man" than the other. Socialization into gender identities, as many studies have already confirmed, begins literally from the moment of birth (Badinter 1995; Chodorow 1978). Yet, other studies have indicated that this process of gender socialization is not universal, but rather that in some people groups gender differences are established through specific rituals performed around the age of puberty (Herdt 1981). Certainly, most of the ethnographic studies about masculinities have focused on such rituals of masculinization. In general, however, there is agreement in the literature about the deployment at some point in a boy's life of experiences that transform his subjective understanding of himself as "male"—a process that is a matter of the construction of the boy/man as subject as well as of establishing the social and personal dispositions of what Bourdieu calls "habitus." In fact, the behavior of the boys in the field observation above reveals a point that Bourdieu theorizes in his book *La Domination Masculine*: that the construction of masculinity also involves the formation of an *illusio*. That is, the social struggle to obtain the symbolic prize of "manliness" often involves the desire to place a "bet" or dare others to give you the opportunity to "prove it" (Bourdieu 1998).

Taking into account these dynamics, something becomes exceedingly clear: manhood and/or manliness is neither a given, a fact, a fait accompli, a substance, nor an intrinsic quality. Manliness appears to be, instead, a social "good" that is in short supply—the object of everyday disputes that must be adjudicated through competitions, games, and burdens of proof. Manliness is the result of certain specific actions and ways of signification and of the capacities of subjects to enact those actions and meanings corporeally and subjectively. The meanings of what may or not constitute manliness are also objects of dispute: "Let's see if you are really a man." It is a meaning process experienced through attributes of quantity and quality: "Let's see who is more man." In these instances of competition, meaning is relational; in other words, meaning is defined by what it opposes, in this case the feminine ("he is very sissy").

On the other hand, the use of the adverb *very* in the boy's description of the youngest boy as "very sissy" seems to suggest the possibility that what is opposed to manliness is also a matter of degrees and quality. In Spanish the use of the adjective *bien* before the word *culón* produces the same semantic effect. But in either case, both masculinity and its opposite are apprehended in terms of bodily images: in Spanish *bizcocho* (a sponge cake in the shape of a ring) and *culón* (a big ass) are both connotative references to sissiness. In both cases, the words are used to reference fear or the inability to overcome fear, or being excessively cautious (timid). In both cases the reference is to qualities at odds with virility. Being a man is thus configured as a matter of courage, self-control, a daring attitude, and finally, suppression of pain. The deployment of these meanings is mediated through sarcasm, mockery, scorn, and disqualification, as well as by a conception of the male body as closed and impenetrable. In other words, a real man does not have the openings of a *bizcocho* (a ring) or of a big ass. On the contrary, a *culón* has an open and exposed body. The boys' game makes clear important insights of queer theorists like Judith Butler who refers to the performative character of identity construction, a quotidian performance in a social context where complex technologies of power are in place, from ostracism, or mockery to physical or psychological violence as we will show later (Butler 1990).[1]

Another small detail in the boys' exchange catches my attention: the youngest boy was not able to resist or revert the meaning attributed to his behavior. Recent studies about masculinities and gender socialization have emphasized the importance of agency as a reminder of the complexity of these processes. I do not discount the importance of agency in approaching the construction of masculine identities, but I am also compelled to note the pervasive character of the "exigencies" (Welzer-Lang 1994) or requirements—the compulsory calls to conform that seem so integral a part of the gender socialization of boys. These demands are even more difficult to resist when one's own peers issue them, when children function as agents of order and conformity among themselves.

According to Bourdieu (1990, 1998), once subjects enter a socially configured field (in this case the field of gender and sexuality[2]) and common interests are recognized between the subject and the social context, a mechanism of shared functionality sets in motion the reproduction of distinctions. In this case, the distinction refers to manhood and its privileges. But this line of argument begs the question: do subjects ever have the option to resist, differ, and contest? In the case of the boys playing in the tree, the answer to that question comes almost too easily. And that easiness in itself makes me wonder what may be at stake in the candid, almost commonsensical way in which two boys issue a call to a third boy to step up and represent his manliness. Is this process between children always so effective?

A few days after my observation of the children playing in the tree, I had the following experience.

Field Note, February 2, 1999

While I sit writing field notes in the small living room of the adobe house where I am staying, I hear two girls and a small boy playing house in the courtyard. The boy plays the role of a small child, and the two girls play the role of mother and *comadre* (mother's friend and godmother of her child). At one point they stage a scene in which the young boy is severely scolded by the girl playing his mother. Upon seeing this, the *comadre* intervenes and says to the mother: "Comadre, it's not a good thing to scold your child so harshly; please count to ten before you do it." And then, addressing the small boy, she says: "Remember that children like us have a right not to be mistreated or abused." I am surprised and amused to hear such a clear reproduction in the play of these children of the messages from governmental campaigns to prevent domestic violence.

The existence of a social discourse against domestic violence and the rights of children contrasts with the usually violent exchanges that characterize children's play in the first place. It occurs to me that maybe the experience and process of childhood is not as ideologically homogeneous as it has been made out to be. Maybe there are possibilities of resistance to the traditional values and child-rearing practices passed on through socialization. These possibilities are not abundant, but they are present nonetheless. At same time, it is important to outline the gender identity of children involved in both cases. Boys emphasize gender distinction and proof of masculinity, while girls reproduce a discourse of respect, nonviolence, and human rights. This seems to suggest the resilience of dominant discourse of manhood, but also the complexities of interpelation of governmental discourses against violence.

To Be a "Man" or to Be "Macho": Disputes over Meaning

I saw Rogelio for the first time when he was pushing a stroller and walking with his wife in the neighborhood. Both he and his wife are twenty-three years old. They caught my attention because during the time that I lived in that town I had never seen a man pushing a stroller. Many young couples used to take walks in the late afternoon, but either they were alone or the woman was always in charge of the baby. After seeing Rogelio that afternoon, I always recognized his face whenever I ran into him in other locations around town. The few other times that I saw Rogelio, he was always in what could be generally described as "unusual" situations for men in that area: grocery shopping with his wife, wearing shorts, or practicing karate moves on a baseball court with a foreign guy.

Over time, we became friends. Rogelio told me he was pleased to find someone with whom to share what he called his criticisms of the machismo prevalent in the town. I, in turn, was pleased to find such an excellent informant—a native of the town and well versed, as he put it, in the "ways of thinking" of people in the area. One afternoon, as we sat in the living room of the guest house where I lived, I brought up the subject of his differences with respect to the behaviors of other local men.

"Listen, is it common for men around here to walk their babies on a stroller the way you do?"

"No, not at all," he smiles. "Don't we wish, Guillermo. Haven't you noticed that people around here are very *machista* and they would feel embarrassed to be seen strolling a baby?"

"Yeah? And why is that?"

"Because, as I am telling you, they are *machistas*. It's the Mexican machismo; you know how that works," he says, expecting the meaning of his words to be self-evident.

"And what kind of things could happen if a man was seen strolling his baby?" I ask.

"Well, nothing," he seems impatient with my questions. "What could possibly happen? Nothing has happened to me yet."

"You think they are afraid that people would say something to them, insult them?" I ask.

Rogelio answers: "Yes, that's right . . . they are afraid to be called *mandilones* [submissive to their wives, to be commanded; in Spanish *mandar*]. OK, let me explain it to you. There are people in this town, men mostly, not the women so much, although there are women who think in the same way—well, there are men who like to make fun of other men; if they see you, for example, playing with your child, they say: 'Oh, look at that guy, what a sucker [*mamon*], making a fool of himself.' Or, if you go out carrying the baby on a stroller, all the same they talk about you; they say, 'Look at that guy; his wife orders him around,' and things of that sort. I know what to expect from guys like that. Since they always make fun of other men, then they restrain from doing things that they know will cause others to make fun of them. There are men that even restrain from hugging their children for fear of being ridiculed."

"No way!" I say, pretending to be surprised.

"Yes. Haven't you noticed? Yes, they are ashamed. They horse around with the boys and pretend to play rough with the kids, in order for them to look tough themselves," [he tells me with a smile]. "They act in the same way with regard to other things ... not so much the older folks, they change as they get older, but the guys more or less my age, they are full of themselves and pretend to be real tough; they are always boasting that they can beat the crap out of anyone, that they gave so and so a good beating, that they can hold their drinks ... things like that ... I guess they like imagining that they are the tough guy on some old Western movie, or the hero of a *corrido* [he laughs]. I find it all very funny. I laugh to myself, but sometimes it also makes me mad."

"You don't act that way. Why not?" I ask.

Rogelio continues: "I don't want to be like that. Well, to be fair, not everybody acts in the same way. It's mostly the guys who come from the 'ranchos,' have less education, and are a bit more boorish. But me, ever since I was a little boy I said I did not want to be that way. I am different, and even if they make fun of me, I said to myself, it is they who are wrong, not me. Once, when I was about fifteen, some guys wanted me to smoke cigarettes with them. They kept saying: 'Come on, smoke, be a man,' and I said to them: 'And what does being a man has to do with smoking? I am a man, and I don't want to smoke.' The same guys later on insisted that I drink beer with them. I refused and they began to insult me: 'Sissy [*bizcocho, culón*], he must be a faggot [*joto*].' They grabbed me and poured the beer over my head. I got really sad. When they let me go, I went back to my house and I felt real sad about what had happened and I even shed some tears about it, but I didn't tell anyone.

"Let me tell you, there was a time when I felt depressed because I was different. I used to wonder if there was something wrong with me, because I was ... how can I say it? Uhm ... so sensitive. I used to pray to God that I could be tough like other men. I wanted not to give a damn about anything. And I used to think: maybe they are right; maybe I am a faggot [*joto*]. I used to have these fantasies that I was a bully, that I would throw punches at anyone who crossed me. But at the same time, I used to think: no, I am fine the way I am; they are the ones who are wrong. One day some boys around my same age instigated a fight and they said: 'Come on, are you a man, or what?' And that day I finally had it in me to tell them: 'Yes, I am a man, but fighting has nothing to do with being a man; you guys are just caught up in some idea about machismo. Why would I get into a fight with someone over nothing?'"

"But that made you different from other men in town. Why do you think you are this way?" I ask.

Rogelio says: "Uhm, who knows! I don't know, I was always more sensitive, so to speak. I remember that I had this teacher, and he was a priest also . . . he was really nice, and he used to talk to us in a different way, and I noticed that he acted differently from other men that I knew, because he was more affectionate and he always used to tell us: 'Never be ashamed to express your feelings.' In a way I am different, but I am not the only one who feels this way. There are people who change over time, who do not agree with those ideas about making fun of other men. It's only a matter of ignoring those types of comments. You can't live your life to please other people. That's exactly what I told one of those tough guys once. I said: 'Come to think of it, I am more man than you are, because I have the courage to take a walk with my wife, to wear whatever clothes I feel like wearing, of kissing my brother when I run into him somewhere. You, on the other hand, are always thinking what people would say about you, even if you feel like acting the same way I do. You are not you,' I said to him. 'You are afraid. I, on the other hand, am more man than you, even though you are a *machista*. For you being a man is always acting tough and mean, but deep inside you wish you could be like me, but you do not dare.' And, guess what? He stood still and very quiet."

"He just stayed quiet, nothing else?" I ask.

"He looked at me and not knowing what to say, he said: 'don't be such a pussy . . . I was only joking with you, man.'"

Rogelio surprises me once again. He is a sui-generis kind of man, not only because of his uncommon public behaviors but also because of his discursive clarity. He has the ability to articulate an alternative discourse about the meaning of being a man and to resist the pressures around him to conform to a fixed set of ideas. Ironically, Rogelio comes from a neighborhood with a reputation of being a place where people are "mean," "vulgar," and "bully."

My conversation with Rogelio reaffirms my realization that the meanings of masculinity are disputed, even in small traditional towns like the ones in the sierra. He is living proof of the fact that some men are capable of articulating an alternative discourse that resists the demands and restrictions imposed on behalf of a particular version of manliness or manhood. We also see, again, how terms of insult such as *bizcocho, culón, mandilon,* or *joto* (sissy, softy, submissive, or fairy) are mobilized as threats against the fulfillment of certain idealized forms of masculine behavior. It is interesting to note that in this usage, *joto* (fairy) is not a term that describes a man's sexuality, but his gender identity. Specifically, Rogelio is called a fairy because he is sensitive, is a pacifist, refuses to smoke and drink beer, enjoys doing things with his wife, expresses his affection, and insists on his own aesthetic choices—namely, he likes wearing brightly colored shirts.

Rogelio, on his part, mobilizes in his discourse the term *machismo* as a powerful argumentation intended to subtract validity from the actions of so-called masculinity. As Mathew Gutmann (1996) points out in his book about meanings of manhood in Mexico City, the term *macho* has lost currency, and very few men use it nowadays when talking about themselves. Being macho is no longer considered a desirable quality. The term has become associated with notions of underdevelopment, premodernity, and ignorance. In other words, macho is now recognized as an inappropriate way of being a man. Behaviors associated with being macho, such as violence toward women or failing to share in the care and upbringing of children, have also lost social legitimacy. In general, there is now greater diversity in Mexico about the behaviors that count as manly and a social dispute over the meanings of masculinity.

The expression "Mexican machismo" used by Rogelio is represented discursively as an image clipped from a film, or as the fantasy character in a *corrido* (popular song). In both cases the emphasis is placed on the masking function of the concept ("deep inside you are afraid"). At the same time, Rogelio invokes the same tropes associated with mythical conceptions of Mexican machismo to affirm other ways of being manly ("I am more man than you are"), almost suggesting that his is a more authentic version of manhood and hence lending legitimacy to his unconventional behaviors.

Diversity and Disputes over "Being a Man" in Mexico: A Poststructuralist Analysis

Departing from the work of Samuel Ramos in the 1930s, the general intellectual conceptualization of the Mexican man has been dominated by an essentialist perspective that refuses to examine not only the diversity of manhood manifested in Mexico but also Mexico itself as a nation-state. The Mexican man that became the object of analysis for most of the twentieth century was thus represented as disorderly, hypersexual, and aggressive womanizer who drank excessively, and someone incapable of expressing his true feelings (as Octavio Paz [1959] so eloquently describes him in his seminal work, *The Labyrinth of Solitude*). For Paz and his followers, the peculiar phenomenon denominated the Mexican man operates as a kind of protest enacted by men to hide what is otherwise an alleged inferiority complex. This sense of inferiority can be attributed in turn to processes of conquest and colonization, the rape of the archetypal Indian Mother, and the abandonment or distance from the Hispanic Father. In this light, the complexity of sociocultural formations in Mexico is reduced to a pseudo-psychological plot fitting for a soap opera.

I want to argue here for a fundamentally different conception of this ideology. Taking into account a variety of ethnographic materials about men's lives that has been produced in Mexico and elsewhere in the last few decades, I begin by stating the obvious: Mexico is not a single homogeneous cultural entity. As such, Mexicans are not all the same, not even all Mexican men. There is no such thing as a uniform, stable, predictable, and fixed Mexican man. That kind of man has never existed. The only possible way of invoking something close to a Mexican man is to refer to him as an object of discourse, the product of a series of rhetorical maneuvers linked to a very specific political goal—namely, the construction of the nation (Anderson 1983). The substantialization of the nation into a human figure is a political and rhetorical strategy mobilized to accomplish projects of state formation (Alonso 1995). In post-Revolutionary Mexico, this nationalist substantialization has acquired clear connotations of male identification (Muñiz 2002; O'Malley 1986).

Setting aside the rhetoric of a national male prototype, we are left therefore with a vast diversity of experiences that configure men in Mexico. Mexican men are diverse in terms of class, ethnicity, life-styles, sexual practices, age, skin color, notwithstanding the complex processes of subjectification elaborated by the Church, the state, and the capitalist economy. This diversity that now seems so obvious, however, was not always identifiable under the weight of conventional mythical constructions of the nation and its subjects. Since the 1960s, a persistent popular struggle for democratization in tandem with several ideological crises in the nationalist ideology has helped open up theoretical and political spaces to acknowledge this diversity.

It is not enough, however, to limit the argument of being a man in Mexico to an affirmation of the diversity of experiences of manhood between and among men. We also need to examine critically the notion of being a man in the first place. We need to recognize that the difference established in the first instance is a gender difference. In other words, we need to recognize that in Mexico there are many ways of conceptualizing that which we uniformly call being a man, as well as many ways to understand masculinity, and hence different ways of organizing gendered social distinctions, even among biological males.

The theoretical argument that I am advancing proposes that instead of referring to the Mexican man or simply to man as a conceptual category, we need to make the categories themselves the objects of study. The term *man* seen from this perspective, as Bourdieu (1990) points out, is part of a struggle over modes of representation that encompass more than a singular experience but that have to do with the power to represent reality in the first place and the power to achieve legitimate and adequate representation. The concepts man, masculinity, virility, manliness, and so on are mobilized as part of politics of signification that debates the very meanings of these terms and their uses to represent actions, ways of feeling and being, objects, and relationships.

The extent to which these terms are in dispute, however, is tightly connected to the ways in which the same terms participate in the organization of social distinctions (Bourdieu 1988). Ostensibly, these are terms that (1) differentiate people from one another and (2) assign status of distinction to some to the detriment of others (Bourdieu 1998). In patriarchal societies, notions of masculinity and manliness are privileged markers of distinction that assign values and symbolic powers to some at the expense of others, and that translate into forms of "capital" in other social fields (Bourdieu 1998).

These theoretical considerations throw into a whole different light how we conceive of our object of study, properly speaking. In contrast to essentialist tendencies prevalent in the emerging field of men's studies that purport to study the practices and subjectivities of men as a natural group defined by common biological characteristics, in this book the objects of study are not simply men who do manly things or a distinct group of men with different and idiosyncratic interpretations of their masculinities. I would hope that in place of these seemingly positivist conceptualizations, this book can focus attention on men as a group of people who have been socialized according to divergent and contradictory semiotics of gender that coexist in contemporary Mexican society. The codes that establish the divergent meanings of manliness and masculinity" are disputed in every-day life and account collectively for the determined male character of specific forms of subjectivities. Put simply: notions of who and/or what are men or masculine are not transparent and cannot be applied unambiguously in all cases. The processes by which subjects are designated as men are part of political dynamics of signification that ultimately define the gender identities by which people are differentiated. In this scenario, of course, a certain presumption of masculinity is attributed through processes of socialization to those subjects who bear male genitals.

Manhood and the "Male" Body: A Problematic Relationship

Fragment of a Conversation with Jose

I met Jose at a bar in Hermosillo that is known as *de ambiente*; that is, a place where a certain homoerotic audience and permissiveness predominate, even though it is not formally designated as a gay bar in the conventional sense of the word. Men from all walks of life—from blue-collar workers to government employees to hairdressers to white-collar professionals, and intellectuals—converge at this location to play dominoes, talk, or in some cases for flirting. Women are not denied entrance to this bar, but for the most part it is a male-dominated environment. Some women come to the bar in the company of gay friends. It is common to find a great variety of gender representations in this place—some men carry the hyper-virile look of blue-collar workers and cowboys, whereas others appear to be what I would call androgynously gay. On Friday nights, one can also see a few transvestites in attendance.

I have seen Jose come into the bar several times. He would usually come alone, dressed in a cowboy outfit but without a hat, and sit at the bar to order a drink. He usually stayed there the whole time he was at the bar, staring at the TV monitors that showed movies or sporting events. In another part of the same location, a TV has been installed that shows heterosexual soft-porn movies. We never talked, but on more than one occasion I have observed him leaving the bar discreetly in the company of another man, usually a man identified as gay.

Sometime later, I ran into Jose at a party in one of the small towns where I was conducting fieldwork. Each of us were equally surprised to find the other there. We exchanged greetings and started a conversation. I had a feeling that our conversation was facilitated by a sense of complicity about having spotted each other previously in the same bar in Hermosillo. I learned at that moment that Los Corazones was Jose's hometown and that he had moved with all his family to Hermosillo four years earlier to work at a *maquila* (assembly plant). He said he only came back to town for special occasions or when he was on vacation. He asked me what I was doing in town, and I explained to him the nature of my research project. Satisfied with my explanation, he then made it a point to tell me that "nobody in town knew what was going on" referring to his affective and erotic attraction to men. I quickly let him know that I would keep the matter confidential.

Later on that day he asked me whether I was headed back to Hermosillo and whether I could give him a ride. On the way back, indicating that he thought I was someone who could understand him because "I knew more than he did" about life and such matters, he shared his life story with me. I could tell that his compliment was genuine. Over the course of our conversation that day, he shared with me what he said were things that he "had never talked about with anyone": his adolescent escapades as well as his fantasies and crutches, topics that provoked a certain degree of embarrassment in him.

My conversation with Jose was one of the most unusual exchanges I had had with anyone during fieldwork. In my view, it revealed just exactly how complex can be the intersection between predominant ideas about being a man and the practices and conceptualizations about eroticism among men. By the way, it is worth mentioning that Jose's demeanor and behaviors were conventionally masculine, as evidenced by his gestures, attitudes, and style of clothing. In other words, by the standards of the town of Los Corazones, at first sight he does not project any sign of sexual dissidence or gender playfulness.

At one point during the conversation, Jose saw fit to go into details about some aspects of his sexual life: "Listen, I don't know what you think, but look . . . I want to be frank with you . . . even though I am twenty-two years old, I have just barely started to have sexual relations of this kind . . . well, the thing is, you see, I am the one who gets penetrated and . . . well, I don't like it too much, I am not sure. . . ."

"Do you feel guilty?" I ask.

"Well, yes, sometimes . . . but it is not so much that . . . maybe with time it will pass . . . more than anything I am afraid."

"About AIDS?"

Jose answers: "No, not that . . . well, yes, that too, but . . . well I don't just do it with anyone, a prostitute fag . . . no, I do it with a guy who is pretty quiet and reserved, like me. I met him this one time when I took my girlfriend to a 'Norteño' dance at the Stadium, and we got along just great, it was really happening, so we agreed to meet at another time to drink some beers . . . and from then on, we continued seeing each other, and we get it on, that's for sure . . . and he is the one that I have allowed to penetrate me."

"So, what are you afraid of?" I ask.

"Oh, geez, let me see . . . it's not really fear, how can I put it? I don't want to continue doing it because I think that if I am always being penetrated maybe over time, who knows, it's almost as if my body would turn more feminine, my hips would grow wider, and I would get breasts. What do you think?"

Utterly surprised by his confession about what sounds to me almost like a superstition, I ask: "And why do you think that such a thing could happen? Who told you that?"

"No, no one . . . I have noticed those changes in other people . . . haven't you noticed how the faggots [*jotos*] have large breasts and large hips; they almost look like a woman?"

I explain to Jose that those men he has seen around town that have the features he describes, that look like a woman, in most cases have had silicone breast implants and surgery to modify their bodies. Trying to provoke further reflection on his part on this confusing subject, I ask him: "Have you ever met men, masculine men, like you, for example, who have sex with other men?"

He pauses and thinks and then says: "Yes, that's true, isn't it? Because I remember that I met this guy who plays in a baseball team, a professional team, mind you, and you see the guy and you could never imagine that he also likes to get it on with other guys [*el cotorreo machin*]. I know that guy likes to be penetrated and I hardly doubt that he is new to this . . . and I tell you, you see him and he is all man. Yes, you are right."

In Mexico's nonindigenous rural communities, a man is immediately identified in commonsense terms by having a penis and testicles; in other words, with being identified as having a male body in the biological sense. This commonsense association between maleness as a biological marker and manhood can be interpreted as a symptom of the hegemony of a patriarchal system that declares things normal in their most obvious ways while working to conceal the contradictions among the key markers of such a system: in short, by rendering seemingly natural the trilogy male–masculine–heterosexual as if one term inevitably and logically followed the other and so forth. These contradictions are particularly evident when we focus our attention on the term *man* and the politics of representation that invest that word/category with meaning, as is most notable in the case of subjects such as effeminate men who always appear peripheral to the center of the sex/gender system.

The term *man* is therefore inflected with the following contradictions: having a male body is not enough to achieve manhood; men who are effeminate are still men; behaving like a man has nothing to do with having a "male body. A number of particular ideologemes have been activated in order to achieve the ordering belied by the following contradictions: (1) men who are effeminate partly belong to a third sex (even though they appear to have the attributes of a male body, that body is not in fact really all male). (2) Effeminate men and other biological males who engage in practices considered not masculine are mentally and socially deviant. Insofar as these beliefs become operational, it is not hard to see how the perception of a normalizing correlation between male body, manhood, and masculine behavior justifies and abets homophobia.

The concept of man in Mexico is therefore more complex than it seems. The same can be said for the concept *joto* or homosexual, as I have argued elsewhere. So-called homosexuals are not necessarily those who have sexual relations with persons of their own sex (a topic that I will explore in more detail later). As far as the concept of man is concerned, my previous research on male identities and subjectivities revealed that although male genitalia is required for identifying those who are not men (i.e., females), the presence of genitals alone is not enough to define who is or is not a man. What happens instead is that the male body is subjected to a set of prescribed cultural readings that specify ways of presenting and acting with (in) the body. As a result of these compulsory dynamics, the body is endowed, so to speak, with male qualities and the equivalent socially assigned value of manliness.

This process that I describe above becomes all too apparent when we consider the concept of man in relation to transsexuals, transvestites, or *jotos*. The category of hermaphrodites or intersexuals, which would cast serious questions about the normalizing trilogy described above, does not even figure in the discourse of manhood (Fausto-Sterling 1992, 1993). There is a euphemism used in some parts of Mexico to refer to *jotos* that captures some of the normative weight of the category man as well as some of the ambivalence with which *jotos* are regarded socially. The made-up word *machomenos* has a double meaning: it means literally *menos macho* (less male), but it also calls into play phonetically the expression *mas o menos* (more or less), which in this instance means *mas o menos macho* (male . . . more or less). Intended to be a clever expression, the word *machomenos* condenses the ambiguity that permeates the concept of man and the allegedly natural relationship between manhood and the biologically marked male body. Jose's confession and his story in general underscore the social relevance and prevalence of these ambiguities.

Far from being the natural and safe site (residence) of masculinity or femininity—ground zero for the construction of gender identity—the body is burdened and crisscrossed by multiple demands and preconceptions that entail ideas about desire, erotic practices, and the ultimate expected configuration of one or another gender identity (masculine or feminine). Gender, therefore, enunciates the possible understandings of sex and body (Butler 1993). Of course, it would not be sensible to assume that all the young men in Jose's town who more or less share his characteristics think alike about these matters. In general, we can say that in Mexican society the possession of a male body is associated to manhood and manliness. However, the mechanics of this association are not clear or homogeneous.

"A Man" and "a Real Man": Internal Distinctions in a Cultural Fiction

In semantic and political terms, there is another area of contention about being a man in Mexico that deserves elaboration. I am referring to the similarities and differences among various cultural communities within the same country regarding the gender designations of a wide array of everyday actions, objects, relations, and presentations of the self. Such similarities and differences, particularly with regard to the meanings of masculine behaviors, underscore the construction of distinctions and hierarchies among Mexican men when it comes to determining their manliness and/or manhood. These distinctions are manifested in the use of expressions such as "he is a real man," "show that you are man," "I am more man than you," and so forth (*un verdadero hombre, qué tan hombre eres, menos hombre*). The stories and commentaries by the men introduced up to this point in this book—José Pedro, Rogelio, Ventura, and the children—demonstrate the currency of these conceptualizations.

Mexican men experience and express the semiotics of masculinity differently. By the same token, people in Mexico differ about how they understand, even in the broadest terms, what are masculine or feminine behaviors. Rather than assume that we know in advance how social conventions resonate with people's emotional links to gender categories, we should study the exact ways in which these processes unfold. For example, in Tzotzil communities men hold hands when they walk together. For them, such an act is a sign of manhood that expresses the values and meanings that define their masculine sense of self. In contrast, in nonindigenous communities in Mexico, holding hands between men is predominantly considered an effeminate behavior (because women, for the most part, are allowed the freedom to hold hands in public as an expression of friendship).

Another example of a divergent interpretation of gender designation can be found in a small community in the Sonoran sierra. In this community, wearing shorts can be interpreted in a variety of gendered ways. In fact, the very ambiguity and multivocality of this action testifies to the ongoing struggles over the meanings of masculinity. Although wearing shorts to play soccer (also a new interest in this community) or to hang out around the home is becoming increasingly popular among young men, it is also quite common to hear comments among men and some youth against the practice for fear of not looking masculine or being identified as *jotos*. This connotation is so prevalent that many of the male high school students resist wearing shorts during gym classes or playing any sport where shorts are part of the required costume.

In stark contrast, in the city of Hermosillo, barely 150 kilometers from this sierra community, wearing shorts in itself is not a relevant gender marker, but the style, color, and design of the shorts worn are. If the shorts are too short, or have buttons instead of zippers, or are made of soft, colored fabrics, then they are not considered masculine. This diversity of interpretations about the meanings of masculine or feminine markers of identity is not exclusive to distinctions between rural and urban communities or among ethnic groups. These variations in gender signification can be found even within the most close-knit communities.

This diversity in values and judgments testifies to the saliency of social struggles over the meanings of masculinity, or of the right kind of masculinity, to be exact. Rather than assert with certainty that one set of values is predominant, the practices under review so far demonstrate that the meanings of masculinity intertwine in a complex way with many other elements and that such meanings are disputed often. Hence, when it comes to the wielding of these meanings in scholarly investigations, contextual factors must be taken into account and afforded analytical preponderance.[3]

In the rural communities in which I conducted fieldwork, men act out values related to their masculinities depending on the cultural repertoires available to them as well as their personal histories (which is another way of saying that configurations of desire also vary from one man to another). Given these variables, men become adept at manipulating the multivocality of the available signs in order to negotiate a range of actions and identifications. For instance, in the community described above, a man who holds a baby and takes him for a stroll around the neighborhood can be seen as someone who lacks independence or autonomy vis-à-vis his wife and his familial duties; in other words, he is described as a *mandilon* (someone who gets bossed around). However, these same actions—and the identity indexed through them—can be seen as expressions of manly responsibility, paternal care, and family affection in another context; in other words, characteristics that configure the values of a real man.

A brief excerpt from my fieldnotes reinforces this point.

Field Note, June 12, 1998

This morning, as usual, I walked over to the food stand on the corner where Pedro works. Placing myself at the stand every morning has proven to be a good decision for my ethnographic interests. This is a site where men gather regularly during the course of their daily activities. Some stop by quickly while running errands; others rest here a bit after getting off work or come to pass time after finishing their early-morning agricultural chores. Most of them, like me, come by for a bite. Pedro . . . is a twenty-four-year-old man who displays an unusual charisma—whether due to his good looks, his masculine demeanor full of anecdotes, challenges, and dares, or on account of his courtesy and charm toward the children and grown-ups that approach his counter. In general, the clientele around here, as well as this researcher, finds him quite seductive. This morning upon my arrival, four other men were hanging out in addition to Pedro; they included Pedro's older brother, Victor, two blond guys from the adjacent neighborhood, and my friend Ventura. Victor was telling the rest of us about the funeral of an older man who had just passed away and of how the deceased man's sons were "carrying on a big crying show" (*tenian una llorona*).

Pedro interrupts the story and says: "That's not even the custom anymore . . . why cry and carry on like that? He is dead, so bury him and that's it."

The men present listen quietly. Then one of them says softly: "Yeah, that's right . . . that's the way it is, no?"

Surprised and eager to provoke further conversation on this topic, I say: "Let me see. How is that about crying being out of fashion?"

"What?" asks Pedro, apparently disconcerted by my intervention.

"Well, sometimes I cry, and I didn't even know it was something that can fall out of fashion."

I go on paying attention to the food on my plate, not wanting Pedro to become defensive. In a casual and detached yet self-assured manner, I add: "Man, I cry all the time . . . in fact the other day I was watching a TV program, one of those where they present a mother reunited with a son she has not seen for twenty years, and I broke down crying . . . made a mess of myself over it."

I immediately take a bite of my food, reinforcing the comfort and naturalness of my conversation and letting my comment linger.

I lift my head from the plate, look around me, and notice that Pedro has stopped chopping onions and that he is now staring at me, disoriented and serious, without uttering a word. Everyone else is silent, also.

Suddenly, Pedro's brother, Victor, a thirty-seven-year-old man who drives a truck and earns a living selling and buying cattle, erupts and says, obviously moved: "Ah, yes! Was that in the show of that blond lady who comes on in the mornings? Maybe two weeks ago? Yes, I also saw that program. No, man . . . when I saw that story I was choking with emotion, I almost cried."

"That's the one, yes," I respond with no added emotion in my voice.

Pedro asks, again apparently surprised and disconcerted, but in a soft tone of voice: "What program are you talking about?"

One of the young men present adds: "Man! The same happens to me . . . for example when the war, remember, the war in Iraq . . . things appeared on TV that made me want to cry."

I notice that all it took was for one of us to validate feelings of sadness for the rest to feel free to share their own tearful moments. I was curious, however, about how the men interpreted my initial emotional confession, especially Pedro who seemed so disconcerted.

Later than afternoon I saw Ventura and asked him about the men's perceptions of me in the morning. He told me: "Man, that was great that you said that . . . you fucked with their minds."

"How so?" I asked.

"Yeah, bottom line is that by saying what you said the other men see you as being more of a man, if you will . . . the real deal . . . because you are so manly that you are not even afraid to say that you cry, and you say it with such conviction and naturalness, and they see that you are not afraid of being criticized . . . you know what I mean? No, man . . . Pedro was in awe of you. . . . I saw it in his face; deep inside he admired what you did."

As an expression of emotion, crying can be read through different lenses: on the one hand, it can be seen as an expression of weakness or softness. On the other hand, to expose one's feelings before other men by saying "I felt like crying" or "I cry sometimes for this or that reason" can be considered a gesture that affirms manliness because the person in question demonstrates the courage (valor) to express it. Courage, assertiveness, and determination to face one's fears connote masculinity. These actions, therefore, must always be read within the framework of the gender politics that regulate manhood. Paradoxically, the commonsense notion that crying represents a gesture that diminishes masculinity was disputed by me and other men present, resulting in the end in the legitimization of an action that signified increased manliness. Against Pedro's masculine anti-crying performance, I constructed another more efficacious performance that put into evidence the inherently contradictory meaning of cultural actions (Herzfeld 1985).

Masculinity as Unfinished and Anxious Performance

I reflect on the discomfort expressed by Pedro as noted in the above anecdote. Pedro is well known for his ongoing urgings to virile competitions, as he usually takes part in all kinds of contests: from sports, to verbal exchanges where comparison and masculinity are present, so his apparent "loss" in this situation put him in an odd position within the group. I ask myself: if the meanings of masculinity are in fact more unstable, heterogeneous, and subject to negotiations than they at first glance appear, what are the repercussions (emotional, psychological, social) of such instability, heterogeneity in the personal projects of manhood as Herzfeld (1985) conceptualizes the personal quest for masculinity.

Butler (1990) and other poststructuralist authors describe the "performative" character of gender identities in everyday rituals. These routines of body comportment are described as instances of "complex technologies of power." In the poststructuralist argument, identity is not conceived of as an essence or an ontological truth about the self, but as an artifice, a fabrication, a social and historical construction within a given set of discursive coordinates. Apprehended semiotically, identity must be understood as a construction that straddles symbolic frontiers of the self (the "I"), which are subjected to constant surveillance and performance. Male identity, therefore, references those symbolic frontiers of the self that are elaborated through practices, relationships, objects, attributes, and bodily and subjective dispositions that connote manhood.

Male identity is, so to speak, a project under construction, a practice of being constantly reenacted in conformity with given sets of observances, performances, and behaviors. The meanings of the symbols that constitute these frontiers of identity are never stable—not only because of the intrinsic qualities of the difference as observed by Derrida (1976)—but also more important because of the social struggles involved in the constant efforts to fix the meanings of masculinity in a more general sense. Given these characteristics of male identity, I ask myself: how are the flux and ambiguities of these meanings experienced by subjects who are simultaneously under tremendous social pressure to demonstrate or prove the "right" kind of manhood and manliness?

Those of us who are born males (biologically) are expected from the moment of birth to act socially masculine. We are expected to express our manhood and, to lesser or greater degrees, make efforts to comply with these expectations. Our compliance is manifested (or put into evidence) through specific actions, relationships, and behaviors that express the values and meanings considered masculine in our specific social contexts. A great part of what has been described as socialization, therefore, involves becoming familiar with the semiotics and politics of gender that spell out our intentions to be appropriately recognized as one or the other gender. The majority of the rituals and routines implicated in this process make the body and bodily subjectivities a locus of these enactments. It is through the putting on stage, socially speaking, of these rituals that we constitute ourselves as male and as virile. When the social exigencies or demands to be masculine coincide with our internalized expectations of ourselves, those of us born males feel our manhood, our masculinities, and our gender identities fixed and secure, at least for a few brief and seemingly "magical" moments. However, the process of feeling one's own manhood and of constructing masculinity is never homogeneous. The values attached to the meanings and to the subjects who perform these meanings are open to interpretation and hence are disputed first and foremost among males themselves.

From the psychoanalytic perspective, other authors refer to the "anxious" characteristic (therefore unstable, fragmented) of the masculine psyche and relate this situation to masculine violence (Badinter 1995; Jefferson 1994; McBride 1995). The semiotic, anthropological perspective allows us to understand this phenomenon at a much deeper, more complex level. In as much as meanings of masculinity in different cultural communities are always disputed, people socialized as men do not all live their manhood as natural, homogenous, and stable forever, but as an anxious process of "making oneself a man" (*hacerse hombre*) through daily decisions and actions always in dispute, negotiation, and imposition. This is why it is preferable to refer to masculine identity as an "ideological project of manhood," as mentioned by Herzfeld (1985), and not as something achieved and stable.

As has been noted in the present study, subjects (especially males) dispute among themselves the level of masculinity or the authenticity of the "manhood that their actions and identities proclaim. Hence, it is not enough to simply refer to someone as a man—authentic manliness must be demonstrated. A number of idiomatic expressions in Mexico index and reinforce notions of authentic manliness on an ongoing basis: one example is the phrase "he is a manly man, no fucking around with that" (*un hombre-hombre, no chingaderas*). This need to reiterate manliness points out the fragility of male identity and manhood as a social/ideological project. At the core of this anxiety, we find among men a culturally induced fear of moving toward femininity and its fundamental implication: becoming an object of oppression. Masculinity is not simply relational vis-à-vis femininity, it is also reactive against femininity, as several authors have previously noted (Badinter 1995; Kimmel and Messner 1995).

Styles of Manhood

Field Note, November 15, 1997

Sergio and I approach the municipality of Chiltepin, a subdivision of Los Corazones where he lives with his wife. Sergio is a man who has "opened up to me," as he put it, and lately we have been spending a lot of time together. He has asked me to drive him in my car to Chiltepin to run an errand. After we cross the river and begin entering town, Sergio tells me: "Put on this baseball cap," referring to a cap that sits on the dashboard of my truck. I look at him puzzled. Sergio is thirty-three years old, married, and the father of three girls. He works construction and when work is slow or he can't get hired working the temporary crops of chiltepin (a piquant wild chili pepper of this region), he goes to Hermosillo or to the border towns to find some way of earning money. He is slender, dark-skinned by the sun, and always wears blue jeans and cowboy boots. He does not wear a Western hat because he says he is not tall enough and hats do not look good on him, but he often wears a baseball cap. I do not question him and promptly put on the cap as he tells me, even though I am not clear what is going on.

After he finishes his errand and gets back in the car, Sergio explains: "The thing is that in this town people are very nosy and closed-minded, always criticizing other people; haven't you noticed? I know them well. Here it is expected that a man always covers his head with a hat or a cap when he is in public. If he doesn't, they will consider it odd, since only women go out with their heads exposed like that; do you understand?"

Of course, I understand what he is saying, but that does not make it any less surprising. I ask: "Is that so?" Sergio replies: "Hard to believe as it may be, the other day I was wearing shorts just to relax at home and an old lady from the neighborhood said to me, 'What is that you are wearing? Don't tell me that now men wear skirts as well.' Later the same day, she saw me washing my underwear in the backyard, the kind that is now in fashion, bikini type and in all colors, and, man, laughing at me she asked why I wore women's panties [he laughs]. I did not respond. On another occasion I did, I tried to explain to her . . . but that's how people are around here; they either don't understand or pretend that they don't."

Field Note, March 4, 1998

Today I overheard a conversation between my neighbor Martha and a lady who came by to visit. They were criticizing a man recently widowed.

"Oh, you can see him already wearing short-sleeve shirts and no hat, as if he were a young man or single," says Martha's visitor ironically.

I understood their criticism to be a commentary on how the man in question deviated from the modesty expected of adult men in this town. I have noticed that even when the heat is most intense, adult married men are expected to cover their heads in public with a hat and to wear long-sleeve shirts. That is the compulsory clothing code in this town.

The diversity of stylistic forms or poetics of male identity and the importance of these signs to represent authentic manhood or appropriate masculinity must always be taken into account when talking about men. So-called Mexican men are not exempted from the same dynamics. Habits, ideas, and bodily manners such as a man's stride, his way of holding a cigarette, his choice of clothes, the way he talks or dances—these are all important signs that other men read to evaluate a man's manhood and hence establish social distinctions and relations of power with one another. Of course, these stylish elements condense other social and personal dimensions: class, ethnicity, religious affiliation, political ideology, nationality, sexual orientation, level of education, morality, and so on. These multiple factors combine with the visible signs described above to render an assessment of the level of manhood of a given man in question.

In the displays of everyday life of the sierra communities in northern Mexico, it is possible to encounter a wide range of stylistic proposals for the appropriate presentation of male subjects. In addition to the forms so-called "traditional," the exposure of many men in the region to radio and television, magazines, travel to other regions for school or work, as well as the presence in these localities of foreigners (mostly men engaged in business transactions but some social scientists as well), has increased the range of possibilities for the presentation of the self in everyday life. Clothing and accessories play a central role in marking these differences. It is also true that the process of economic and social modernization in these communities has impacted the stylistic diversity now found in there. For instance, it is not uncommon for older men—grandparents and fathers—to argue with their younger sons or grandsons about wearing baseball caps instead of Western hats, tennis shoes instead of work or cowboy boots, or about piercing their ears, wearing chains or bracelets, wearing their hair longer or stylishly, shaving their mustache, or wearing a goatee. Through jokes and bantering, young men themselves dispute the legitimacy of certain choices in clothing, accessories, or styles in general. Peer group approval can be so important that many men think twice before buying or wearing an article of clothing or accessory that may invite comment or ridicule from other men.

Each of the elements of a so-called style plays an important role in the composition of that modality insofar as these elements represent an aesthetic and ideological proposal and positioning. Stylistic posturing becomes an important part of how subjects negotiate their roles within a community in relation to notions of significant social and local consequence. Some examples are giving off the appearance of being modern, foreign, or urban; pretensions about belonging to a given social class; simulating youth or being younger than one's real age; being associated with a marginalized group (such as *cheros*); being labeled as less than masculine or possibly even effeminate; having the "look" of a drug dealer or of a federal agent (*placoso*); or being perceived as a member of a religious sect (e.g., Mormons). Each one of these identifications is related to a greater or lesser degree to holistic gendered evaluations about a person.

Cultural ideals of masculinity come to us embedded in aesthetic and ethics choices (see Luciano 2001; Mort 1996). It is therefore productive to study the specific manifestations of these practices to better understand the parameters of the imaginary that defines individual and collective manhood. The recognition that in a multicultural state such as Mexico there are a variety of modalities, forms, and styles of masculinity becomes a necessary step toward a critique of the generalizing notion of Mexican men. Examples of these differences abound. For instance, in a small river-bed community in Sonora that I visited, wearing *huaraches* (leather sandals) is a sign of poverty, "Indianness," and a practice associated with southern Mexico. A Sonoran man wishing to portray a manly image would never wear huaraches. Instead, it is expected that he would wear cowboy-style boots. Boots, in turn, connote a variety of masculine styles depending on their color and form. Although it is well known that indigenous men wear huaraches, in Sonora this style of footwear is considered a sign of weakness—this, of course, is due greatly in part to the fact that it is precisely Indians who customarily wear them. The implied message is that an Indian man is "less of a man" than non-Indian Mexicans and hence less virile and less powerful. On the other hand and for no apparent reason, in the neighboring state of Sinaloa it is a common practice among men associated with the drug trade (*narcotraficantes*) to wear braided huaraches. Along with pickup trucks, guns, and jewelry, huaraches connote in this case a kind of raw masculinity—one that is also crude, aggressive, and less refined. In recent years, working-class youth in Hermosillo began emulating these markers of fashion, including the wear of huaraches, to construct a more deliberately powerful masculine identity evocative of the drug lords. The narco or drug dealer is mythologized by young men as a masculine image that privileges adventure, risk, economic power, dominion, revenge, immediate gratification, and emotional distance. It does not come as a surprise, therefore, that the narco image, as an aesthetic proposal for expressing masculinity, has come to be intrinsically connected with the narco trade as an economic option for many young men.

Sometimes, stylistic choices can be appropriated by subjects to express masculinity or manhood independent of sexual preference. In other words, as the following fieldnote reveals, the politics of gender operate in contradictory and playful modes to render new and often implausible modes of masculine expression.

Field Note, April 25, 1999

Very few men in Los Corazones are openly known as homosexuals, *jotos*, or gays. There are considerably more men who have had homoerotic relations without assuming or being designated with those labels, as are my friends/informants Ventura and Jose. But Miguel is one of those few. He has been identified as a homosexual mostly on account a series of public scandals that he was involved in several years ago when he drank excessively and before he embraced sobriety. Although most people in town recall the events and speak about it behind his back, it is considered impolite to confront or embarrass Miguel to his face about what happened.

For this reason, I was very surprised this morning when I witnessed a young man banter Miguel publicly about his sexual conduct as Miguel walked past us. The young man in question is a seventeen-year-old who, Ventura told me, is the lover of an older man "who gives some gifts in return." As Miguel walked by with a pocket knife hanging from his belt, the young man—perhaps wanting to show off or to get back at him for some personal reason or simply for being socially inappropriate—said in an ironic voice: "Ahh, fag [*loca*] . . . a pocket knife and the whole nine yards [*con navaja y toda la cosa*]."

And Miguel, serious and stern, obviously angered but ready to confront what would be considered by any standard a *falta de respeto* (a lack of respect literally, but culturally, a violation of social etiquette as well), responded, "Yes, and boots and chaps and hat, and rope and horse as well, and you should see how good I can lasso an animal; and when it comes to working hard, I am first in line. I don't crack [*no me rajo*], rising earlier than anyone to put in a hard day of work. What do you think about that?"

The young man did not say a word. Instead, he lowered his head, embarrassed and aware of his insolence. I am not sure whether my presence there, as a witness, had any impact on how the situation went down.

Miguel always wears cowboy-style clothes, and he indeed has a reputation as a hard worker. He is not effeminate in his mannerisms, yet stories abound about how faggish he would act (*se ajotaba de a tiro*) back then when he used to get drunk.

Against the young man's ironic remark, based of course on his prior knowledge of Miguel's homosexuality and the apparent dissonance of Miguel's display of a pocket knife—a sign of virility—Miguel responded by affirming his masculinity. He reminds the young man that he always wears cowboy clothes and accessories, making clear the significant power of those articles to reference masculinity. But in addition, Miguel stresses his quality as a hard worker. In other words, the kind of attribute that Don José Pedro once described as key to being considered a "true man." Miguel's tone of voice and the directness of his answer are enough to quiet the young man.

It seems to me that Miguel, in his irrefutable affirmation of masculine "belonging," may have also been pursuing a parallel objective—perhaps the right to be respected for who he truly is, a modicum of social legitimacy. Masculinity works here as an index to the moral dimension of a person: responsibility, discipline, seriousness, respectability, and courage are some of the qualities that it activates. It is common to hear in Mexico the phrase *no me rajo* ("I don't break under pressure," or literally, "I don't crack open") to express this moral imperative. Miguel's response to the sarcastic young man manifested the power in action of this corporeal metaphor. Instead of "taking it," or accepting the young man's appellation of him as a fag (*loca*) and breaking under that word with shame, Miguel "does not crack" (*no se raja*). He puts to work this conventional cultural notion of impenetrable masculinity on his own behalf as a mode of empowerment. By doing so, he demonstrates, once again, the complex politics of meaning that constructs men's gender and sexual possibilities in Mexico.

CHAPTER THREE

Acá Entre Nos *(Just Between Us)*

Cultural Notions About *Rajarse*, the Body, and the Negotiation of Male Intimacy

Introduction

When I began this research project I, often wondered what difficulties I might encounter trying to obtain personal information from the people I interviewed. I questioned my ability to get answers about issues that for most people are shrouded in privacy. Even though I entered the field with previous experience in the research of homoerotic practices, I felt that I was dealing with a different field of social relations. After all, my previous research had led me to interview informants in places that were clearly identified as "flirting" spaces (*espacios de ligue*), or the *ambiente*.[1] Many of the men I encountered in those locations had already invested considerable time on self-reflection about the subject of their sexual practices or identities.[2] Now my topic was broader and therefore more elusive. What kind of questions does one ask of ordinary men to elicit knowledge about their sense of manhood? Uncertain about how to proceed, I worried and anguished about my research project. An excerpt from my field notes reveals some of this internal struggle.

Field Note, September 12, 1997

How exactly should I go about producing knowledge about men and their possibilities for affective and/or sexual relations with other men? This is not the kind of information that I can presume to find on the surface of everyday life activities, consciously accessible to an ethnographer in a simple conversation. I know this from my own experience as a man, but it also has been well documented in the literature on masculinities and intimacy. Nonetheless, the very fact that such a literature exists is evidence that it is possible to obtain that information, although, to be sure, none of the authors that I have read explain exactly how they managed to get men to open up to them. In fact, the same literature makes repeated references to concepts such as "emotional illiteracy," silence, hermetic postures, naturalization, and repression, to name some of the difficulties of getting men to talk about their feelings of intimacy. (I may have gotten myself into trouble by picking this subject.)

From personal experience I know how difficult it can be to assume and stay focused on constructing a different kind of masculine identity—one that, as they say, is not *machista*. I have found it particularly difficult, sometimes even painful, to confront the limitations, anxieties, and troubles that the dominant politics of gender and sexuality involved in the process of masculinization prescribed for me. I was greatly helped along the way by the literature produced by the profeminist men's movement, as in the case of the British group Achilles Heel and several others. Discovering the writings and manifestos of these groups certainly supported my own individual quest to transform my masculinity and, more broadly, aided my mental health.

It is clear to me that in studying these topics I study myself, so to speak, or at least find a sense of meaning that connects my professional life with my personal life. How do I go from that realization, however, to actually producing knowledge so that others can understand aspects of these intimate processes? I began to explore aspects of my own subjectivity and to discuss my feelings openly when I was around twenty or twenty-two years old and joined my first self-help group. The group gave me the confidence I needed. Yet how does that relate to my task as a researcher today? Ethnographic work is not meant to be therapeutic. Maybe what matters most is being able to develop the trust necessary (between researcher and informant) to open up. I am not sure, though, how trust is accomplished in the cultural contexts in which I am doing fieldwork and around the topics that I am investigating.

A few days after writing these reflections in my journal, I entered the following field note.

Field Note, September 18, 1997

This afternoon I traveled to El Amanecer, a small town close to Los Corazones, where I took residence after two months of travel in the high sierra and the Moctezuma River area. The main highway cuts across this settlement of approximately one thousand people dotted with old adobe residences that have large windows covered by ornamental iron grills from floor to ceiling. In spite of the highway, the town is very quiet. A small assembly plant located there employs around twenty-five people; the objects it produces carry labels in French, Japanese, and English. The main economic activity, however, is the cattle business. People from this area have a reputation for being very clean and quiet.

I noticed that the town's cantina seems to be highly patronized by the locals. This is somewhat surprising because in this area men generally go down in pairs to the river or to the town outskirts or drive around in their trucks when they want to have a few beers. The cantina has a very modern feel and look. It has a large TV screen, which I am told is continually tuned in to a large sports cable network from the United States. But come to think of it, this is not really surprising. In contrast to similar small rural towns in other parts of Mexico, towns in the Sonoran sierra have a lot more access to advanced technology.

I must confess that, although I am used to entering cantinas in many different towns and hanging out comfortably, in this instance I felt a bit apprehensive. When I went into the cantina only a few people were there—in total around eleven, I would say—who were all gathered in a small side room. As I came in, they all turned around at the same time to look at me. I took a seat at the bar. The bartender, a robust middle-aged man sporting a thick moustache, approached me. The whole place became silent as I told the bartender what I wanted. Once I had spoken and everyone had heard me, I turned around and some of the men across the room greeted me with a slight head nod, returning quickly to their heated discussions about the local baseball teams. Nobody was paying attention to the TV at the moment. The men seated at the closest tables all had their backs to the TV. All the men present wore blue jeans, work or cowboy boots, and either cowboy hats or baseball caps. They ranged in age from approximately twenty-one to fifty. At one of the tables I noticed two men talking in very close corporeal proximity. As they talked and gestured, they touched each other's shoulder.

In general, the atmosphere of this place was very relaxed, but as is common in Mexican cantinas, the emotional dispositions of those present functioned in direct proportion to how much alcohol they had consumed. These two fellows I was observing looked particularly "sensitive" at that point. When the jukebox began playing a song by the popular ranchero singer Vicente Fernandez, one of the two men squalled what could be called "a typical Mexican *grito*," and two other men across the room responded likewise with *gritos* of their own. Suddenly, the place was filled with a new emotional intensity. As the song played, several men got up to the jukebox and selected the same again and again. The song rendition by Vicente Fernández is accomplished with deep, heartfelt emotion. An excerpt (song lyrics written by composer, Martin Urieta Solano) goes like this:

Acá entre nos	Between you and me, let me say this . . .
quiero que sepas la verdad	I want to tell you the whole truth
no te he dejado de adorar	I have never stopped loving you
y allá en mi triste soledad	and in my loneliest and saddest moments
me han dado ganas de gritar	sometimes I have felt like yelling
salir corriendo y preguntar	take off running and ask around
que es lo que ha sido de tu vida	whatever became of you
Acá entre nos	Between you and me, let me confess
siempre te voy a recordar	I'm always going to remember you
y hoy que a mi lado ya no estás	and today when you are no longer by my side
no queda más que confesar	all that is left for me to do is to confess
que ya no puedo soportar	that I can't take it anymore
que estoy llorando sin llorar	that I am crying even when I shed no tears
porque respiro por la herida	that this wound is my last breath of life

I believe this song is relevant to understanding something about the subjective dynamics of masculinity as well as the possibilities for men "opening up" their emotions. The song makes me think about Octavio Paz's (1959) misguided and incorrect statements about the phenomenon of *rajarse* in Mexico (cracking oneself open or breaking down). Men indeed experience openings, fractures, and wounds. The core logic of masculinity does not rest on the absence of openings and fractures but on the pretense of absence as well as in the regulation of the discovery and visibility of such openings. The expression "between you and me" (*acá entre nos*) summons a call to enter a space of trust where those emotional wounds can be displayed, where a man can show a vulnerability that goes against the everyday performances of masculinity in which he feels he has to pretend to be different.

Certainly, being a man does not mean that one does not "crack open" (*que no se raje*) or, more literally gendered, that one does not "have a crack" (*no tenga rajada*). What is predominant is the social regulation of the processes for expressing those cracks among men themselves. Learning about those regulations is part of the socialization of becoming a man. From personal experience I can attest to the difficulties one faces in understanding those regulations and the awkward negotiations one has to engage in to express sensibility, affectivity, pain, love, and desire, especially when these emotions are not circumscribed to an exclusive heterosexual context. In the process of understanding and learning these regulations, the socialization into masculinity becomes a form of "pedagogical violence," which in most instances results in plain and concrete acts of homophobic violence. I believe that the phrase *acá entre nos* holds clues to help construct a methodology for researching men from the perspective of gender and to help launch a systematic reflection about what it means to engage in the study of men, masculinity, and politics of intimacy.[3]

The Politics of *Rajarse* and of "Being a Man"

A possible English translation of the Spanish, or in this case Mexican, word *rajarse* would be to "break down." But the word in Spanish has more of the emotive force, which is implied in saying in English to "crack open." *Rajarse* is a very powerful concept in Mexican society that enjoys wide circulation among the working class. Among men, phrases that make reference to the implicit or explicit action of breaking down abound. For instance, expressions such as *el que se raje es puto* (a man who breaks down is a faggot), simply *pinche rajón* (damn sissy), *no seas bizcocho* (don't spread it open), and *piche culón* (damn chicken) can be overheard among boys at an early age as part of male socialization rituals. In fact, it is not uncommon to hear *no rajarse* (not breaking down) as one of the desirable characteristics a man should have, at least if he is a manly man (*hombre-hombre*), as Don José Pedro once told me. The concept seems to issue a call for men to submit themselves to an emotional and bodily "lockdown," lest they risk losing their manhood.

At first glance, the construction of male intimacy and the value placed on not breaking down would seem impossible to reconcile. Yet, the song by Vicente Fernández suggests the opposite—a mediation made possible by a symbolic space created "between you and me" through which one is able to "breathe," to expose one's "wounds." The expression "between you and me" (*acá entre nos*) suggests a kind of social bracketing wherein it becomes possible to transgress the dominant codes that include, among several things, the prescription of bodily and emotional closure. What relationship does such a license to open up have with the dominant definitions of being a man? To what extent are these codes related to the construction of other identities such as homosexual? And, to what extent are these codes related to the social possibilities of male intimacy? The use of the verb *rajarse* in these instances demonstrates how inadequate it can be to think of language in strictly referential terms that point to transparent meanings outside of very specific contexts (Silverstein 1977). *Rajarse* as used in these various instances is introduced in speech as a metaphor, and the various meanings that the word acquires are related to its use in context. As a metaphor, the word does more than simply denote a known fact; indeed, it leaves open a myriad of interpretations. As Dell Hymes has perceptively observed, in this case, too, language is not simply an unmotivated mechanism, but a modality of social action (Hymes 1964).

Rajarse is thus a metaphor placed in the confluent space between language, gender (particularly masculinity), power, and social relations that makes possible or inhibits access to intimacy. As a concept, it structures the possibilities and modalities of expression and therefore of social action (Bauman 1987; Sherzel 1987). Specifically, the fear that one's actions could be interpreted as instances of "breaking down" conditions, in turn, the practices one chooses to engage in in the first place. To understand better the nature of these social and symbolic connections, it is advisable to study those speech acts in which certain words and expressions occur and at the same time function to socialize individuals in the proper use of those words (Ochs 1990). In other words, it is imperative to pay attention to the linguistic (social) practices in and through which certain words make their entry into a cultural milieu (Hymes 1964; Sherzel 1987; Silverstein 1977). The linguistic practices in which the word *rajarse* plays a prominent role can be read therefore as moments of intervention in a social struggle over meanings. This struggle is at the level of representations—over the power to be able to represent reality as one of the fundamental dimensions of social struggles more broadly defined (Bourdieu 1990; Duranti 1990; Sherzel 1987). In this case we are referring to those representation related to the moral construction of identities, gender identities, and social relations (Irvine 1992; Duranti 1992).

The ranges of situations in which the verb *rajarse* (or its variants as adjectives or adverbs) can appear as part of a communicative act are plentiful. The following is an attempt to classify some of the most common instances of the word *rajarse* in Mexico today.

The first meaning is associated with a situation in which an individual "abandons" or "desists" in pursuing a task or project in which he or she has been previously involved, particularly if that task or project involves a certain degree of commitment and honor. It is illustrated in the following field note.

Field Note, November 8, 1999

I ran into "El Prieto" this afternoon.[4] He was standing in the corner of my house looking out to the empty streets. El Prieto is a recently married young man, approximately twenty-eight years old. People call him Prieto because of his dark complexion. He told me he has been out of town for a few days, *chambeando* (working). I assume he meant he was working in Hermosillo, which is where most of the people from the town go when employment opportunities are scarce and they don't own land or cattle or are employed in assembly plants or the public sector. Those with less education go to work in the vineyards nearby Hermosillo, such as Estación Pesqueira. Those who have a trade—bricklayers or carpenters—work construction. Still others work temporary jobs in government-sponsored road and infrastructural improvement projects or go to the United States looking for work.

I ask El Prieto whether he has been working in the United States, and he laughs: "No, man . . . I wish. I would have fared better. I was deep inside those evil hills, up in the sierra, as far as you can think of, picking chiltepin [a local wild chili pepper].

"But why so far away?" I ask.

"Well, there's no more chiltepin down here, and my compadre is so damn stubborn so up we go, son of a bitch. I fell. I scraped myself. I am all screwed up," he says smiling, as if making fun of his misfortune.

"Do you usually go to pick chiltepin?"

"No, well . . . kind of, I have done it before, but it is shitty work, and then this time I went up with this big hangover and nothing to help me get over it; we had been drinking for two days straight, not my compadre and I, but with another buddy of mine, and I had forgotten that I had made the commitment to my compadre to go with him. A long time ago I had said I would go along with him for the chiltepin harvest. My compadre even said to me, 'You better not break down, compadre' [*no se me vaya a rajar*], and I said to him, 'Come on, what do you mean? Of course I'll be up to it.' And what you know that the day came and it caught me all messed up [laughs]. I felt so sick but what could I do? No way I was going to hide from my compadre. I know how he gets; he would have become all depressed about it and besides, he had already bought all the supplies we needed and he had arranged for transportation. So, there you have it, we faced shit together," says El Prieto still smiling.

"Man, I tell you, up there in the sierra, I couldn't find my way around, and I felt all fucked up. I even considered the idea of returning, but whenever I thought about that I said to myself, no, I am already here and there's no way that I am going to break down and let my compadre down" [*no me le puedo rajar a mi compadre*].

I reflect about El Prieto's story and this matter of commitment and the value of a promise. I am also aware of the value that men in this region place on their labor. As far as I can see, not breaking down (*no rajarse*) is a concept that plays an important role in stimulating following through with one's actions, no matter how difficult these might be.

In the situation in the next field note, *rajarse* means not fulfilling a commitment one has made, or giving one's word and then backing out.

Field Note, May 7, 1998

While I am at the town's electrical workshop—a business establishment owned by Fernando, a rather prosperous forty-year-old man—I listen to the jokes exchanged between the workers and their boss. The jokes, puns, and verbal games can get rather heavy and vulgar, but the code of honor is simply to withstand it all—or, as the men say, "take it, faggot" (*aguantate puto*), or "don't take it too seriously, it's a joke, learn how to carry on" (*no lo tomes en serio, es una broma y aprende a llevarte así*). Somehow my presence only serves to stimulate even harsher and more direct taunting, as if the men were putting on a performance just for me. At the same time I can tell that there is a spirit of loyalty and camaraderie among these men.

While I am talking with one of the workers, Fernando approaches him and says: "What do you think, Lucio?"

"About what?"

"It broke down" (*se me rajo*).

Lucio says, "It broke down? Psss. . . [laughs] I told you . . . but you are such an ass. I told you it was no good."

Another worker hears the conversation and yells from across the room: "You said that it broke down?" [laughs]. Yes, we told you that asshole is all talk, a pretender. And now what? You see that happened to you for being a bad friend; remember you said you were never going to take us for a ride [laughs]."

"What happened?" I ask.

Fernando explains that a man had come by to offer him a very nice car, and that he had agreed to buy the car from the man for a set price, right on the spot, because he wanted the car to take his family for a trip to Tucson. "We had come to an understanding," he says. He adds that he had already gone to the bank to get the money when the man sent word that he had changed his mind and could not sell him the car for the price they had agreed on.

Fernando says, "What makes me so mad is that the man broke down at the last minute, that his word was no good" (*que el bato se haya rajado a ultima hora, que no tenga palabra*).

A third meaning of *rajarse*, illustrated in the next field note, has to do with revealing a secret or divulging information confidentially. Sharing this kind of private information denotes a special social bond, especially if the person revealing information stands to suffer any kind of social or emotional damage for being so forthcoming. The possibilities of this kind of information circulating as secondhand information or as gossip or rumor are in the specific context of *rajarse* constrained by the implicit assumption of responsibility and personal loyalty when one is a participant in such a valued exchange (Hill and Irvine 1992).

Field Note, June 26, 2000

From the looks of it, it appears that Cabezon (Big Head) was sent to jail a few days after the rumble at the wedding last Saturday. Of course, this is not the first time that something like this has happened. It wouldn't even be considered news if it were not for the fact that this time they admonished him that if it happens again he will be turned over to the district authorities and charged with more serious crimes. Maybe this imminent threat will produce some positive results at last.

Generally, in these small rural towns people try not to get into trouble with the authorities. With the exception of adolescents who get into scuffles at parties, most people deal with their conflicts with others by either simply stopping to address those who grieve them (*dejándose de hablar*) or filing a complaint at the local police station. Police officers sometimes act as mediators and in many instances are able to persuade both parties to settle their differences. In extreme cases when a man feels that he is being singled out, mocked, and constantly harassed by another man, he has three options: he can fight him, he can threaten to file a complaint with the local police, or if he gets no results, he can complain to higher authorities. In many instances, the threat of a lawsuit is quite effective. Fights or major physical confrontations are not as common as one might think. Because the fines imposed on those found guilty of engaging in public fighting can be very high, the law in fact serves as a deterrent to street violence.

Cabezon is a young man who works as a ranch hand. He is tall and thin, but well built. He has a reputation for being serious, standoffish, and introverted when he is sober. But when he drinks he gets belligerent, he can say some nasty things to people, and so he has a reputation for becoming hypersensitive to comments others make, even his closest friends. For all these reasons, Cabezon is one of the town's most peculiar characters. He has a reputation for being boorish, acting like a burro (donkey), a man whose true manhood is lacking as demonstrated by his inability to control himself, to reason, and to treat others decently.

On this occasion, a group of men gather outside my house; the incident of last Saturday is being discussed and Cabezon happens to be present.

He complains: "The problem is that Martin is a lazy ass [*culón*]; he went and broke down with the police commander [*se fue a rajar con el comandante*]—why did he have to do that? The issue was between him and me. Why can't he just face things like a man?"

One of the neighbors answers his questions: "No, Cabezon, things do not work that way; get on with it, man . . . [*no es así el rollo, agarra la onda*]. The man had lost his patience with you. Besides, he had already told you what to expect if you insisted. You were wrong, no matter what reasons you may have had; you should not pick a fight with him. In fact, check this out; it was you who broke down first [*el que se rajó primero*], because you promised the police commander not to pick any more fights with him."

Cabezon gets very quiet and stays that way for a long time.

I think this incident is interesting because of the way in which the term *rajarse* is used in reference to notions of masculinity. The concept is used as a term that questions the behavior of an individual. In this instance, Cabezon affirms the assumption that within the homosocial contract, conflicts between two men should be faced off as men and that to involve the police is to act cowardly. He also alludes to the violation of a pact of silence between men—"nobody had to know"—therefore, talking about the conflict with others, confessing what should have been private is also understood as a form of *rajarse*. On the other hand, the neighbor reminds Cabezon, not fulfilling a promise one has made is also *rajarse*.

In the following field note, *rajarse* is used in relation to an individual making an effort not to open emotionally, a man who tries to control his emotions or affections.

Field Note, February 11, 1998

Recently, Ventura told me that he has been distant from his friend Chalo, because he found Chalo having a good old time with his friend Miguel one evening while the two rode around in Miguel's car. "What the fuck does he have to do hanging out with that asshole?" Ventura tells me. Besides, he tells me he was also upset because when he saw him, Chalo was almost drunk, when Chalo had promised him that he would stop drinking from the beginning of the year until Easter.

(Many men around here make those kinds of promises and most of them abide by them. I think it is a way of getting their economic and physical priorities in order, but most of all, a symbolic way of getting themselves under control. During the time leading to Easter many men change their behavior: they become more serious, responsible, and disciplined.)

In any case, it is obvious that Ventura is mad at his friend, but he is also very sad. I would say he is almost depressed. He brought beer so that I can keep him company while he talks about his sadness. Ventura tells me that he is pleased to at least have someone like me to talk things over with, because before he met me sometimes he felt he would go crazy because he could not share "his feelings, the things that really hurt him" about his friendship with Chalo.

Ventura promises that he will not go looking for Chalo anymore until he asks for forgiveness. I doubt that he can keep that promise. He tells me that when he sees Chalo around town he pretends to lack interest in him, to show Chalo that he is not so easily taken by him. I laugh tenderly when I hear the story, so typical of love affairs, and I am also amused by Ventura's contradiction: he claims he does not want to see Chalo, but then he looks for him and when he sees him he pretends that he doesn't care.

I tell Ventura: "I don't believe you; you'd better not make any promises because sooner than you think you'll be looking for him again." Ventura replies: "I'd rather tie one of my balls off [*me amarro un güevo*], but I swear I won't break down [*no me rajo*] . . . mark my words, this time is for real. No way, no way am I going to accept his behavior; it's pretty shitty what my compadre did, don't you think? There, showing up like an asshole with that prick [*ahí anda el güey exhibiéndose con ese cabrón*]. It's not that I have anything against that guy Miguel, but come on!"

Ventura's expression about *amarrarse un güevo* catches my attention. It's not the first time I have heard it, but it makes me think of how testicles function metaphorically as the "residency" of virility. *Amarrarse un güevo* (tying or cutting one ball off) is to endure a great deal of pain in a body part visibly identified with maleness. He says he prefers to do that than to break down (*rajarse*); that is, confess his needs, his heartache, desperation, sadness, and longing for Chalo. Through this expression, Ventura seeks to regain self-control and hence emotional closure—the capacity to control his own emotional boundaries.

The events that describe the various instances of *rajarse* can be classified as instances that (1) imply a threat, (2) describe an act, or (3) affirm a purpose or ability. The concept of *rajarse* entails a semantic codification of a set of social values implicated in the regulation of social relationships. These values—discretion, trustworthiness, truthfulness, reserve, control— are used to represent, produce, and evaluate ethical and aesthetic behaviors; and they play a central role in the configuration of the moral identities of various subjects. Adhering to those values makes an individual a person of honor and integrity (social values that have specific gender connotations; Alonso 1995). Going against those values, and therefore departing from the behaviors that they prescribe, leads subjects in certain situations to experience a type of communicative event in which *rajarse* becomes a real possibility. Of course, how and when and what moral effects the concept of *rajarse* is capable of accomplishing are always subject to negotiation—a negotiation over assumed identities and gender positions indexed by the term *rajarse* itself.[5] This in turn becomes a negotiation over systems of meaning and social distinctions (Bauman 1987; Bourdieu 1988).

Masculinity and the Indexicality of *Rajarse*

As an idea and as a linguistic element, the concept of *rajarse* indexes indirectly, through references, to affective values that I am calling here "moral identities." In turn, these moral identities index gender identities, especially as these are manifested in a social ideal type for what counts as masculine. The transaction that links these different fields of signification together can thus be expressed as:

Rajarse→ moral identities (coward or valiant, etc.)→ manhood

To understand how this chain of signification and social regulation functions in everyday life, it is necessary to move beyond a simplistic correlation between *rajarse* and the set of assumptions and behaviors that have been popularized as the practices of Mexican men. In his famous essay on Mexican masks, Octavio Paz designates *rajarse* as a masculine verb, related to the dialectic of openness and closure. According to Paz, Mexicans understand one who breaks down *(que se raja)* as a coward and the act of confessing or opening up to a friend as an abdication of manliness. A social record imbued with "threats" and a generalized hostile social environment are presented as the causes for this necessary urge toward "closure" among Mexican men. In this central element of the "Mexican character," Paz finds an explanation for many cultural practices and preferences otherwise difficult to understand. For instance, the Mexican bent toward romanticism and the licensed "openness" (aperture) that takes place during fiestas are examples of times and moments in which Mexicans *se rajan* (crack open), expose themselves to the world, cry out, and laugh loudly. Women, according to Paz, cannot break down because they are already cracked open—a condition of their very own sex (Paz 1959).

If Paz's reflections fall short in attempting to account for the relationship between Mexicans and the act of *rajarse*, perhaps one possible explanation can be found in his lack of attention to social practices, including the linguistic use of the term *rajarse* in everyday life. Specifically, this refers to the fluidity and negotiated nature of the term and its meanings, as studies in the field called the "ethnography of speaking" have amply demonstrated (Hymes 1964, 1971). Despite Paz's assertion, in Mexico women can also break down. Women apply the verb *rajarse* to their own actions and those they are socially expected not to do, as well. Although it might be true that the term is less common among women and that women generally are not subjected to the same pressures imputed to the act of *no rajarse* as men are, a woman can say to herself, "I am not breaking down" *(no me voy a rajar)*, or she can be called *rajona* (quitter, crybaby) by another woman or man. Paz seems to forget that the dyads open–close and inside–outside are subject to negotiation by the simple fact that they are cultural constructions. Whatever is considered closed or open in relation to emotions or linguistic expressions depends on the cultural construction of boundaries in the first place—on constructions of inside and outside, the I and the other, and of social bonds expressed through metaphors of space (Fuss 1991). Contrary to Paz's assertion, a Mexican man can break down without being considered a coward. In fact, by doing so he might even be considered a good friend or an exemplary *comadre* or compadre.

In the same manner, not all Mexicans wait until Independence Day to cry, shoot their guns, and expose themselves to the world. Paz's conceptualization of holiday (fiesta) is so radically different from everyday life that it makes it almost impossible to apprehend the expressions of laughter, tears, and confessions that form part of daily living for so many Mexicanos. In fact, it is quite possible to encounter festive behaviors in nonfestive spaces, such as on the bus or in a school classroom. The right time for festive behavior is also determined according to negotiations. For instance, people negotiate the act of *rajarse* (as does Vicente Fernandez in the song when he calls out a space "between you and I" to open up emotionally) in relation to spaces and discourses that may be at hand at some moments and not others. The ranchero ballad (or bolero) is one example of a discourse that enables the creation of the space required to transform certain elements of a person's subjectivity.

An ethnographic outlook oriented toward actual practices can help us understand the use of the expression *rajarse* in a variety of forms and contexts: when it takes the form of an accusation between men and women; as a mode of explaining the huge success of the romantic ballad genre (bolero ranchero); instances of gossip and reported speech; the importance of friendship bonds and the role of complicity between men (the culture of homosociality); and the excessive amounts of confessions, flirting, and love connections that take place between men in Mexican cantinas. Does this ample circulation of the concept imply that *rajarse* is not especially related to practices of masculinity? No, not at all. What it implies is the need for further study, in the same way in which it becomes necessary to investigate further why and how women acquire the designation of breaking down and what such an act (of *rajarse*) represents in terms of women's subjectivities and the power relationships in which they operate.

Homophobia, Misogyny, and Masculinity in *Rajarse*

The type of communicative events in which *rajarse* usually appears provides many clues to a deeper understanding of the concept. It is common to find the term *rajarse* in the company of other words and phrases that usually have sexual connotations. For example, expressions such as *pinche culón* (related to the expression "asshole" in English but with a more emphatic gender mark), *puto rajón*, (something like "bitchy crybaby," although the word *faggot* is present), or the phrase *el que se raje es puto* (he who quits or breaks down is a faggot) are often used in tandem with expressions that feminize men such as *pareces vieja* (you act womanly), *pinche comadre* (fucking sissy), or *lavandera* (a literal reference to a woman who washes clothes turned pejorative in as she is considered to like gossip).

To abandon a task, reveal a secret, or go back on one's word—all these actions are associated with feminine qualities and are hence considered denigrating to males. Similarly, there is a range of colloquial expressions that are used to mock or ridicule someone who is not able to keep a secret or control his or her emotions. These expressions are enunciated as sexual idioms that reference lack of control (control of the body and of desires).[6] Some of the most common expressions are *se te calentó la garnacha* (one possible translation could be "your skirt got on fire") and *le faltaron guevos* ("you don't have the balls to do it"). These expressions imply that *rajarse* entails a deficiency in a person's sexual powers (or sexual desire) or in the transparency of their gender identities. Thus, men who break down can be assigned the stigma of being a *vieja* (old female), *maricon* (faggot), *poco hombre* (not man enough), or *hombrecito a guevo* (little man).

In turn, the act of not breaking down (*no rajarse*), even when a person wants to do it, can be expressed through phrases such as the one used by Ventura—*me amarro un güevo*, or "I'd rather cut one of my balls off." In Hermosillo and other sierra communities, I have also heard expressions that convey sexual images to describe someone who has courage, someone who is firm in his or her convictions, or someone who keeps his or her promises. Some of the most common ones follow: *tiene güevos así*, or "he has balls this big" (indicating with a hand gesture the alleged size of the testicles); *los tiene de dos yemas*, or "his balls are double-yoked" (referring also to the size of the testicles); *ese bato es lechudo*, or literally "he has a lot of milk [semen] in him;" and *es un tira-leche*, which can be translated as "he can sure squirt a lot of milk" (again in reference to the amount of semen). As is evident from these examples, the act of *rajarse* always points to a semantic field crisscrossed by gender and sexual references and as such to a set of discourses that construct and imagine masculine and feminine subjectivities. In fact, in the logic of these semantic expressions, these gendered subjectivities are seen as the products of sexed bodies or, put another way, as psychic economies resident in corporeal entities.

An interesting question derives from this scheme: how, then, are men and women whose gender and sexual identities are manifestly dissident subject to the semantic dynamics of *rajarse*? Och's concept of indirect indexicality[7] can help shed light on this apparent dissonance. As a practice, *rajarse* alludes to social values that must be honored because they in fact constitute the substance of social relationships. Values such as courage, trustworthiness, truthfulness, sincerity, self-control, resistance, endurance, and discreetness are held in high esteem. Observing or preserving these values indexes moral identities and meanings. In turn, those moral identities index social conceptions about egos underwritten by clear gendered subtexts. Women can break down (*rajarse*) insofar as they too are expected to uphold the values that hold society together. What is sexually conditioned is not whether women and other morally "deficient" persons such as *jotos* are expected to fulfill the said values, but the range of social expectations that exist for fulfilling those prescribed roles and positions. For example, in the case of men who are not manifestly perceived as *jotos* (fags or queers), the expectation is that they will adhere more closely than *jotos* to the prescribed social values that define male gender and identity. Gender differences, therefore, entail different levels of social expectations about the fulfillment of social values and hence the moral capacities of gendered subjects. Ultimately, these differences are reflected in systematic sexist conceptualizations in society (Irvine 1992).

Nonetheless, this sexist system has its own ambiguities and counterarguments. Women, for instance, are considered more trustworthy and in many communities are often chosen for public positions that have to do with the handling of money. Men are considered to be more prone to dishonesty and corruption. Similarly, a woman who does not break down (*que no se raja*) is highly valued and respected, for this quality usually indicates her inner strength and a special commitment. On the other hand, a man who does not break down could be said to be simply acting according to what is expected of a man. In other words, the action of *rajarse* or *no rajarse* proves a man's value as a masculine subject. Some of the phrases in common usage reveal this assumption. For instance, if a man or woman identified as a *joto* or morally deficient breaks down, or fails to uphold his or her commitment, it is common to hear people say: "What did you expect?" or "You couldn't expect more [from a fag or a woman or a sissy]."

Paradoxically, these social expectations applied to those who have been publicly identified as homosexual or *joto*, or to those men who are suspected of being one, often result in an increased self-imposed expectation to "prove people wrong" and hence excel in adhering to social norms of respect, responsibility, discretion, and seriousness; in other words, an increased adherence to the values that define being a man. The added pressure of these expectations is sometimes more noticeable in men whom "everyone knows about" or that "have been rumored to be" or that "it is not hard to imagine" what their "true" preferences might be. An interesting case in point is that of Irving, a twenty-year-old man from La Mesa who, as do many other young men of sierra communities, lives and goes to school in Hermosillo.

I met Irving at his part-time job in Hermosillo where he works as a clerk in a department store. Noticing his name, I asked him whether he was from La Mesa, and in that way we established a conversation that eventually led to friendship. I ran into him a few times at various places around town, mostly on weekends and usually accompanied by various family members. As it is the custom in Mexico, I was always greeted politely and acknowledged as a friend of Irving's by his siblings and his mother. Although Irving is not clearly effeminate, he also is not someone who wears the usual cowboy outfits typical of the region. He is thin, fair-skinned, with delicate or elegant facial features, and generally introspective and quiet. According to his own words, it is not hard for someone "to imagine" that he might be "gay."[8]

Speaking of his ambiguous look, Irving says: "Let me tell you, I have never had any troubles in this town. No one has ever said anything offensive to me, anything that may have bothered me, because the fact is I have never given anyone any reason to speak badly about me, never. People respect me. They greet me politely; I greet them back. I don't know if they talk behind my back; that's their business. If they do, in the end, the ones who look bad is them, because people around here know that I am someone who gives respect and gets respect. I have never been embroiled in any scandal, first of all because I don't care for them, and that's what people like about me."

"Do you think you have to live up to higher expectations?" I ask.

"Yes, a whole lot higher. That's so good that you say that . . . because it is the truth, I believe it is. People pay a lot more attention to my behavior, that's why I feel I have to be more serious and dedicated to my projects, more discreet, more respectful of others, be more careful about what I say, not get involved in gossip, all of that. I do that not to mean that I am not gay, but because I think people put more attention to people like me. Most people they don't have those worries, but I am always so much more aware. I am not sure if you have noticed, but look . . . those of us who are 'like this,' or that people imagine or kind of put together that we are this way, or maybe simply that they know . . . because people know these things, even if they can't prove it . . . well, we are a lot more considerate, careful, and respectful. We work harder, we help people more than usual, we excel at what we do; even the fact that we pursue more education, I believe it is all related. There are those men who are the same as I am, I mean they like sex with men, but they are more . . . uhm . . . hombres . . . they think of themselves differently . . . tougher, or they are married, things are different for them because for people once you are married, even if they have suspicions, they no longer judge you the same. Sometimes they don't even pay attention, or maybe they can no longer 'imagine' that a man may be like that."[9]

A three-prong exercise structures the dynamic that I have been describing: the failure to adhere to predetermined social values, demonstrated by specific practices, indexes moral identities, which in turn index the failure to uphold a social idea or expectation about masculinity (Herzfeld 1985). This chain of signification is possible insofar as moral identities are sexed identities and vice versa. Concepts such as honor and integrity—when applied to the idea of maintaining a secret, keeping one's word, persisting when one has committed to do something, or controlling one's emotions—are central elements of the social definition of the male self and the power status of men. The same dynamics and values are present in women's sense of self, but they do not play the same central function that they do in men's lives. As researcher Ana Alonso has noted, following Peristiany's insights (1968) on Mediterranean-derived cultures, in Mexico women's sense of honor and integrity is more a function of their sexual practices and is codified instead as chastity and modesty.

The Politics of Control and Excess: *Rajarse*, Body, and Sex

As already noted, *rajarse* indexes a sexed conception of subjectivity. Male subjectivity may be apprehended through an economy of desire that is dependent on the body for its expression. In other words, the male body is the locus of practices that define the male subject. These practices are often characterized through metaphors of fluidity and solid matter: toughness, resilience, resistance, impermeability, closure, and so forth. *Rajarse* (or a literal crack down) connotes not only a fissure in the body,[10] but also a fissure in a metaphoric body: the masculine self. The male ego, constructed metaphorically as a body, is thus expected to be solid, coherent, unitary, hard, disciplined, closed, and hence independent, autonomous, self-sufficient, and not vulnerable.

Certainly, *rajarse* also points toward a symbolic ordering of cultural forms arranged according to gender. A number of dualities construct such a symbolic system; masculine–feminine is the most obvious binary but also closed–open, hard–soft, hot–cold, solid–liquid, clear–viscous, straight–crooked, right–left, among many others. The hierarchy of this symbolic ordering can be discerned in the terms that are usually employed to describe a man who is effeminate or less manly (*menos hombre*): *rajon* (big-mouth, open), *bizcocho* (sponge cake), *blandengue* (softy), *fresco* (fresh), *se le hace agua la canoa* (literally, "his canoe is filled up with water," meaning that one's abilities are suspect), *ni agua ni limonada* (literally, "neither water nor lemonade"; similar to the English idiom "swings both ways"), *raro* (odd or queer), *torcido* (crooked), and *corre para tercera* (literally, "he runs to third base"—in baseball the third base is always on the left side—similar to the English idiom "he scores for the opposite team"). In the sierra communities I also found the localized duality *puntiagudo–chato* (literally, "pointy–flat" but could also be "sharp–dull"), manifested in the expression to refer to a highly virile man who is not afraid to fight if he has to—*picudo* (literally, "sharp-edged").

The symbolic system that expresses masculinity is even manifested in the use of certain phonemes.[11] A man in the sierra once told me about an effeminate child of his times whom other children called simply by the letter *i* because, according to this informant, children have the feeling that "the letter *i* is neither *o* [the masculine suffix in Spanish] nor *a* [the feminine suffix]." The man also explained that the letter *i* "is kind of weak." Another informant, this time in the city, told me about a nickname for another effeminate boy at elementary school using simply the pronoun *lo*—because it is "neutral," neither *el* (masculine) or *la* (feminine). The preferred symbols to represent manliness in many of these communities are *lo cerrado* (references to things that are closed or locked down) and *lo duro* (things that are hard-surfaced).

Many social practices associated with the presentation of the body in public, such as dress styles or gesturing, tend to reproduce the ideal masculine ego as described above. Some examples are the practice of wearing hats or baseball caps as a way to always have the male head covered; wearing long-sleeve shirts, tight-fitted blue jeans, or never exposing the feet by wearing huaraches or sandals; and the use of certain accessories, such as polarized sunglasses, or in the car, as an extension of the body, the use of polarized windows. All these artifacts and practices mark the presentation of the male body as closed and consequently suggest that male subjectivity is something in the same order—a projection of emotional enclosure.

The social presentation of women's bodies does not seem to pivot around the same kind of expectation. For instance, women's legs are visible through shorts and skirts; women wear their hair long and loose; they wear sandals often and short-sleeve or sleeveless blouses. Of course, this hasn't always been the case for women. Scarcely two generations ago, women were also subject to the same social expectation of bodily closure through the use of hairstyles that gathered their hair in buns or braids or the use of long skirts or dark-colored stockings. But generally, we can say that changes in dress style have corresponded with a larger structuring binary conceptualization of bodies and subjectivities wherein maleness is associated with seriousness and hermetic behaviors, whereas female characteristics are stereotyped as always being more communicative and open.

Nonetheless, I venture to say that in both instances (male and female) we can find that the social conceptualization of subjectivities as described above, insofar as they represent a psychic economy of desire, are always subject to "eruptions," disorders, disciplinary acts, or *calentamientos* (hot-headed moments). The social and cultural norm is to consider these instances of disruption not characteristic (*propios*) of being a man, but significantly more tolerable as far as women are concerned. This differential conceptualization of gender subjectivities rests upon a sexist understanding of power and ability expressed through body metaphors such as *guevos* (balls), *panocha* (pussy), *culo* (asshole), and so on. This sexist construction of language and gender differences imputes to women's bodies, as well as to the bodies of *jotos* and men who are *poco hombres* (not manly enough), an alleged irrationality, madness, or lack of control. In other words, it is the female sex who make women hysterical and hence who make men who are identified as homosexuals as *locas* (mad ones, or mad females, literally).

This notion perhaps also explains the culturally held belief about men's high tolerance for pain and the social expectation that real men do not whine or complaint. A man who expresses openly and frequently discomfort or physical pain becomes the object of ridicule by his peers. The assumption is that a real man takes it (the pain) or he must *aguantarse* (hold it in), or else he must minimize how badly it actually feels. David, a thirty-eight-year-old man whom I met during fieldwork, told me that when he was a child and worked with his father in the fields, he would sometimes get thorns in his hands. His father always commented that "there was no time to waste" in complaining about thorns, that those kinds of minor things were dealt with "on Sundays" when men took time aside to "clip their nails, pull out thorns from their skin, and that type of thing." Other than Sundays, the rest of the days of the week were "work days" or "days of discipline."

The various instances in which men break these social norms and engage instead in acts of *rajarse* support the existence of a social discourse around the question of desire that is manifested through speech acts such as intimate and affective confessions, or through pledges of silence and discretion. The inability to hold it all inside can be characterized then as excesses of desire (*excesos deseantes*) or, in colloquial speech, a loss of control, that correlates with the subjectivities (and hence, bodies) of women or of those men identified with feminine attributes (*jotos*, or men who suffer of deficient manhood). The colloquial term used in Mexico *cruda moral* (literally, a moral hangover) to refer to shame, guilt, or regret among men who talked too much or became too emotional when they were drinking or were under the influence of alcohol is a visible, and pathetic, sign of the social control effected by these ideologies and cultural attitudes. Simultaneously, they point to the intrinsic anxious nature of "normal" masculinity (Jefferson 1994; McBride 1995) to keep the masculine system of domination.

The study of this vernacular modality called *rajarse* enables us to access the discourse that organizes the social surveillance of men's expressive possibilities as "desiring expressions." It allows us also to look at the power technologies that provide the meaning of the excessive and the need of control of men subjectivity, as part of the organization of an economy of desire with gender connotations.[12] In this sense, we are capable of seeing and understanding how the social dynamics of power (in this case, patriarchy) function as practices of regulation of intimacy as well.

I noticed the interesting use of the word *sujeto* (subject) as a term of admiration among adults in sierra communities and among Serranos living in Hermosillo to refer to a man who has self-control. Don Manuel, for instance, referred to a ranch hand whom he recognized as a responsible and skillful worker as *es muy sujeto* (he is very much a subject). On other occasions, I have heard the same expression used to refer to someone who is reliable, responsible, and levelheaded, as in the phrase: *con ese hombre no hay problema, puedes tratar sin recelo, es muy sujeto* (you can trust that man; you won't have any problems with him; you can deal with him without reservations; he is very much a subject). In these usages, to be a subject is in fact to have the capacity to subject one's basest impulses down or under control; in other words, to have self-control, to monitor one's own behavior, and hence to be reliable or predictable.

This self-control must be first and foremost exercised over one's body and hence one's emotions and social relations. In this vernacular reference, we can see or evoke Foucault's concept of the subject as a condensation of a parallel process of subjectification/subjection, manifested in this instance with a clear masculine connotation.[13] We can see how this subjectification both is part of a gender identity process in which the very subject is implicated, and is a process that gets recognition and therefore, in some way, pleasure. But, if the process of subjection does exist, is there any room for "resubjectification," as Foucault put it at the ends of his days?[14] Is it not any stylistic practice that speaks of a process of self-invention? I think that the expression *acá entre nos* should be seen as indexing such stylistic intervention in the process of resisting masculine subjection, at least in its most orthodox form. It also indexes the existence of a social space in which men can become intimate.

Acá Entre Nos and the Negotiation of Intimacy

If, as I and others have argued, it is true that so many practices among men in Mexico are conditioned by the notion of *rajarse* and the fears derived from the enactment of such an act in particular communicative events or moments, how are we to account for possibilities of intimacy among men and the ability of Mexican men to establish intimate relationships? According to Paz, Mexican men cannot confide in a friend without feeling simultaneously that they have "given in" or surrendered some part of their masculinity (1959).

Men's emotional confessions to one another are a phenomenon linked to the broader conceptualization of the male self and to an ideal (and rational) masculinity that is expressed through linguistic and nonlinguistic means. To "open up emotionally," much like *rajarse*, is the manifestation of a speech economy, or rather of an economy of silence that is part and parcel of a psychological economy of desire with high social stakes. Silence is frequently recognized as one of the methods employed by men to assert their power over a situation or a person (Gal 1991; Sattel 1983). But silence also functions to reaffirm a certain poetics of masculinity among men. Through silence and lack of expression, men often signal the limits to which they are willing to go in a conversation while simultaneously affirming their positions of power in their relationships. In the same way, men often dismiss and devalue the expressive behaviors of others (mostly of women) as signs of weakness and in the process assign themselves the leading role in determining what communicative strategies are or are not valuable. Silence functions as a performative practice that activates the codes of normative masculinity and enables men to distance themselves emotionally.[15] This is not to say that talking always guarantees emotional connection and communication. Seidler (1989) has already mentioned how men tend to use modern rationality in bureaucratic, economic, or scientific speech to create identity and power relations (or legitimize social institutions) with the effect of marginalizing or oppressing less educated people and alienating themselves from their own emotions, pains, and affections.

Male intimacy in Mexico, therefore, can be said to be conditioned by the politics that regulate the act of *rajarse* (breaking down) but perhaps not in the absolutist and one-dimensional way described by Paz. The fear of *rajarse* does not control with absolute certainty the openness or closure of the self. But insofar as that fear is an indicator of an idealized notion of masculinity, it is also an element that must be continually negotiated, disputed, and resisted by male subjects within their emotional lives; a negotiation and resistance that speak of a way of resubjectification.

The construction of intimacy in everyday life involves a certain organization of social links through communicative acts, primarily acts related to speech (Giddens 1992). *Acá entre nos* is one of those phrases that once it has been uttered functions to construct a sociolinguistic context that prescribes specific gender identities and social bonds. When a man tells another man (or possibly even when he tells a woman) the phrase *acá entre nos*, the phrase instantly creates a socioemotional space that allows for a range of expressive possibilities almost always entailing intimacy: closeness, openness, and affection. The phrase *acá entre nos* (between you and me) addresses the listener as an accomplice in an act of affective connectivity. The phrase is a linguistic resource that bets against the odds of *rajarse* by forming a sideways alliance with the listener. It is a way of appealing to the listener's need for intimacy to construct a new socioemotive context wherein it becomes possible to expose emotions and hence to deepen social bonds. For men, this new context holds great potential for the transformation of normative gender practices. Thus, *acá entre nos* tends to appear as a moment of "rupture" (of the normative self that is called upon to remain closed). In such a moment, men dare explore other possibilities of being, thus transgressing the alleged naturalness, universality, and even the desirability of the prescribed social ideal of masculinity.

Acá Entre Nos: Intimate Confessions and the Production of Knowledge

Field Note, October 14, 1998

I am not sure how to start writing about what I am feeling at the moment. I am deeply moved, touched, surprised, and at the same time excited about what I think is confirmation of a methodological intuition I have felt for a long time. All of this was brought about by running into Pedro today. Pedro is an interesting person because he seems to embody through his everyday actions the values that define the ideal of masculinity in this community, albeit with a certain degree of ambiguity. He is handsome, and the confidence he derives from his good looks helps him establish rapport with people. His line of work exposes him to many different people, and on account of his charisma he is usually surrounded by men all day long. In these informal gatherings, the men comment on everyday situations, hold discussions, and take positions on a variety of issues. Always careful to uphold his virile image, Pedro usually injects comments that reflect his competitive nature, drive, courage, and his self-control and work ethic. Pedro has a fine sense of humor to add to his charisma; he is usually attentive and courteous with women and children, sometimes displaying gestures of tenderness toward them that I have rarely seen manifested among men in this region.

Through interviews with other men in Pedro's community, I learned that many of them perceive Pedro as highly compelling and intriguing. At the same time, I was able to elucidate at least two aspects of Pedro's persona that do not speak well (*no hablan del todo bien*) about his standing in the community. These are his social linkages with men who "move drugs" (small-town drug dealers) and his getting a woman of the community pregnant, whom he has yet to marry. If the first issue caused several men to distance themselves from Pedro, the second issue provoked a strong reaction among many of the women who used to like him. A woman named Alicia told him: "Beware of the fact that men also suffer social embarrassment, they also get burned on account of a pregnancy, because if a man does not stand up to his responsibility, then he loses a whole lot of credibility . . . you can be sure." Given all this complexity, Pedro became a difficult subject for me to understand and grasp through my investigation. In fact, aside from my observation of his behavior and commentaries in social settings, I had seriously doubted that I would be able to engage him in one-to-one open conversation as I had the opportunity to do with other men such as Ventura, Rogelio, Chalo, Juan, and Irving. I also erased from my mind the possibility that I would ever have with Pedro the kind of affective friendship that I had developed with men like Joaquin (who took me on that interesting trip down to the river).

This afternoon, however, I was gladly shaken out of all these assumptions. As I was making my way down from my house toward the main street, I passed as usual in front of Pedro's house. As I passed, Pedro was in the front porch organizing boxes related to his business. I said hello and he reciprocated the greeting in his usual laconic style. I had not advanced more than fifty yards when I noticed a car pulling close along the sidewalk where I was walking. It was Pedro calling to me from his pickup truck. He asked whether I wanted a ride. The circumstances were somewhat awkward, because the center of town was merely two hundred yards away and it would have been perfectly fine for me to keep walking. I accepted the ride nonetheless, realizing that it was an opportunity to connect with Pedro that might not come up again. I also thought of the fact of how impolite it would be to reject the offer from such a central character in this community, and that given what I had observed about Pedro's competitive nature, I might even offend or embarrass him.

When I jumped inside the truck, I noticed that Pedro was carrying a sixpack of beer in the front seat. Pedro had already opened one can and offered me another. For many of the same reasons mentioned above, I accepted the beer. In addition, it is a strong cultural value in this region never to reject a drink offered socially, unless one has a highly compelling excuse such as taking medication of having taken a temporary religious vote of abstinence. To reject a beer because one is on a diet is considered one of the most faggish things (*joteria*) one can possibly say. In any case, I have long been aware of the fact that beers are usually an excuse to engage in moments of masculine intimacy. Some people would go as far as saying: "other than for drinking, what other reason would a man have to get together with other men?"[16] Alcohol, as I have noted many times, plays a critical role in helping men drop their inhibitions and hence in achieving emotional closeness.

I noticed that Pedro was restless, almost nervous. As expected, we reached the main plaza quickly, but jumping out without finishing my beer would have been yet another sign of disrespect, so I sat in the truck a bit longer. Pedro then told me that we could continue talking on the outskirts of town, at a place by the side of the road that local men like to frequent to drink and hang out together. I agreed that it was a good idea. When we got there, Pedro turned off the truck and asked me what I thought about the people in this town. I answered with positive but vague statements. Then a sudden silence enveloped us, made all the more awkward by the fact that we were sitting close to each other in the truck. Pedro stared at me, with a strange combination of intensity and sensibility.

Looking straight into my eyes, and placing his hand gently on my shoulder, Pedro said: "Here between us [*aca entre nos*] . . . and I say this because I know that you are someone that can be trusted, because I have seen how you are, what you talk about. In the same way in which you observe people here for your study, I have also observed you . . . and I wanted to tell you, how can I say, Guillermo, well . . . that I am like you."

I became very disconcerted. His tone of voice was deep, sincere, as if he was finally making a confession that he had long considered. I felt an emotional connection emerging between us that I was not sure how to assimilate or treat.

Pedro said: "I am like you. But you know what? Around here it is very difficult to show that side that one has inside."

I was not sure what he was referring to. Was he talking about my precise–imprecise bisexuality, or my comfort with sexual diversity, whatever one wants to call it? Was this confession a platform to express attraction? I found myself unable at that moment to sort out all these competing interpretations. After all, here was the man who embodies the ideal of masculinity in town, and he was talking to me in this personal manner. And, more important, what was the meaning of his words? A bit awkwardly, I began to talk. I only remember that I asked: "Are you concerned that people would make fun of you?" In spite of how trite my question seems now in retrospect, Pedro did not seem to be moved from his intention to express whatever he had in mind.

He said: "I feel that there is a way of being buried inside me, a way of feeling things that is very different from what people generally know about me. I am the kind of person who is moved by sunsets, who enjoys the singing of the birds in the trees, even feeling a light breeze brush my face. And I have often wondered, do other people feel the same way I do? For example, I get deeply upset when I see animals being mistreated. I mean, I get upset! I even feel like crying. But do you know what? Around here, you can't express those feelings. Even if that is how you feel, even if everyone else feels the same way as you do, you can't express it because people would make fun of you. Around here you have to be *cabrón* —manly, do you understand? A man must learn how to hold all of those feelings down."

"I understand," I said.

Pedro continued: "I like you, Guillermo; I feel that I can talk to you about how I really feel inside. I have always wished to meet someone like you, because it is not always easy for me living here. Around here you have to always demonstrate that you are macho—that you are tough, that you almost have no feelings. You have to comply with that way of being, even if deep inside you feel differently. But being a man who, how should I say, who is tender and affectionate . . . no, that is not possible. Look, I am going to tell you something I have never told anyone: the fact is that I am very angry at my father. I feel resentment toward him; it is a wound that although not visible, I have inside me. My father never showed us any affection; never a hug, or a kiss, or saying 'I love you.' I really would have liked to have received a kiss from my father; up to this day I do not know what a kiss from a father feels like. He believed he met his obligations as a father because he worked and provided for the household . . . but he came short, because that's not all that a father must be. It is not all that a child needs. That's why I feel resentment. When my mother got sick, yes, it is true that he worked hard, but I never felt that he was really there for us, because that situation was very difficult for all of us and it was almost as if he was not feeling anything about it. That affected me a lot. Even today I still carry that with me and when I think about it, I get mad at him."

I noticed that Pedro's eyes became watery as he spoke.

He continued: "But don't believe for a minute that my family was alone in having this kind of experience. I see that the same thing happens in other families, in many cases, it is actually much worse. At least in my family we had brothers and sisters that supported each other. You know what I mean? We held each other up."

I responded: "I too have noticed many of the things that you talk about. I have also heard many men of your age talk about having the same difficulties with their fathers. And I am going to tell you something that might surprise you: in the same way as you feel, many men have also told me that they wish they could talk about these feelings in the open without risking being ridiculed."

"No kidding?" Pedro responded.

"Not at all," I said.

"*Orale*," he said. He looked at me and smiled as if I had revealed something new to him.

"Have I bothered you with my things?" Pedro asked and then answered himself. "No, I know that I haven't. I know that you are different and that's why I approached you to talk about these things. The good thing is that this won't be the only nor the last time we get together and talk . . . do you agree?"

"Of course, I do . . . of course," I replied.

"Listen . . . do you want to go watch a boxing match on closed circuit . . . they usually charge a cover charge, but don't worry, I'll cover us. It is in Daniel's house, do you want to go?"

"Sure, let's go."

We begin driving toward Daniel's house. Pedro opened another beer and offered it to me with a complicit smile. When we arrived at our location, Pedro made his entrance in his usual self-assured and manly manner. For a moment, he looked at me with complicity.

That experience with Pedro impacted me profoundly. I have not stopped thinking about it ever since it happened. I think that Pedro's confession moved me so much because through it I was able to get in touch with an unconscious desire on my part as a researcher that had to do with the need to validate my own intuition about male intimacy. Here was this man who holds around him the quintessential aura of male virility, confessing to me his deep feelings about a dimension of his emotional life that he suppresses and denies publicly. As he calls it, a "wound" that he cannot show on account of the censorship produced by the politics of gender.

I am compelled to make a confession of my own: now that I am writing about this, I feel that the most personal dimension of this research project has been precisely the "discovery" that my own sensibility is not that different from what other men experience. Or rather, that other men are not so different from me, except that in my case I was able to break the barriers of that emotional censorship and made a commitment to transform the politics of gender that regulated my emotions. I realized that it was somehow the presentation of myself in everyday contexts that gave Pedro the confidence to provoke an encounter wherein the subjectivities of one another could be exposed as we each feel them. Ironically, I was observing Pedro to know the other in his normative expression of manhood, and that "other" was observing me in order to assess whether I was the right person to reveal what the construction of such an image of manliness has entailed. Pedro constructed his own knowledge of me to, in turn, expose himself and thus find complicity and echo—in other words, to establish intersubjectivity.

After this event, I noticed how in small ways, Pedro's behavior changed after his confession. This effect is not surprising: it has been well documented how the research process changes both the investigator and the research subjects. As a matter of fact, my presence in Pedro's community brought about changes in many other unexpected and small ways. I noticed that several men other than Pedro also observed me. Many others speculated about me, asked questions, and sought out my company. The process of gathering knowledge about these men entailed an interrogation of the prevailing gender politics that attempted to keep silent, or at least make seem natural and universal, what it means to be a man.

The gesture initiated by Pedro to make his confession—that "between us" space (*acá entre nos*) that he called out to show me his wound—signaled the invention of a metaphorical space of complicity for the encounter of subjectivities and for a process of resubjectification. In that space, a sui-generis knowledge of men as gendered subjects becomes possible. The between us space marks a path and a methodology for the production of knowledge about men and manhood. At the same time, the between us gesture marks a space of intimacy. Confronting the obstacles and the exigencies of normative manhood and its prescribed closures of the emotional lives of men, the space of intimacy enabled by this social gesture can in turn intervene in facilitating various modes of resistance to the dominant forms and discourses.

CHAPTER FOUR

Male Intimacy and Homophobia

Different Subjectivities, Powers, and Resistances

The Multiple Forms of Subjectivity in Male Intimacy: Fieldwork Experiences

Gonzalo and Mariano

Mariano is a friend of mine—a dentist, divorced father with custody of his two children—who worked for several years in the small town of El Edén. He confessed to me one day that for a long time he had maintained a "very intimate" friendship with Gonzalo, the brother of his friend César, whom I had had the opportunity to interview when I was conducting research on the topic of homophobia. Quite different from César, whom everyone identified as *joto* because of his effeminate manners and to whom many men in town came to ask for sexual favors, Gonzalo looked and acted masculine. He always dressed in cowboy clothes because he worked at a cattle ranch. According to my friend the dentist, on several occasions he and Gonzalo took long walks along the river and had long conversations, all within the framework of their friendship. Nobody suspected them of any other involvement or attributed any erotic content to their relationship. Nonetheless, amid many typically male shared activities such as attending public fiestas, getting drunk together, or helping each other do chores, they also found the space to get away at isolated sites in the countryside and engage in sexual games with each other.

The relationship continued on and off after my friend finished his work as a dentist in the small town, but it stopped abruptly when Gonzalo got married. According to my friend, Gonzalo said: "Now that I am married we have to have respect toward marriage, so we won't continue doing these things." My friend the dentist said he accepted this verdict on account of the "respect" he felt for Gonzalo, even though he would have much preferred to continue the relationship on the same terms. They eventually became compadres when my friend agreed to be the baptism godfather of Gonzalo's first child. At the time of the baptism, they once again experienced a time of close bodily proximity, and Gonzalo gave some indications that he was interested in renewing the erotic liaison. But on that occasion it was the dentist who refused. As he stated: "Now we are compadres and that is a sacred bond established before God, a spiritual union; and even though many people would not have a problem with that, I do. . . . I don't like to mess with spiritual things." He told me that Gonzalo reluctantly accepted the new boundaries and told him with a smile: "If I had known you thought this way I would have not asked you to become my compadre, but it is alright with me, anyway."

Later on, as I was discussing with my friend the dentist the implications, meanings, and identity categories that could be invoked to understand his relationship with Gonzalo, he told me: "Guillermo, I think you get it wrong, it is not like you suggest . . . how can I explain it? For men like Gonzalo it is not a matter of being homosexual. In small towns in the sierra many people don't even know what that word means.[1] I heard a man once say *hombre sensual* [sensual men] when he meant to say 'homosexual.' [I had the same experience with Don José.] Young people know and use the term, but it is not used as you would think. It is more or less a matter of sexual desire (*ganas*), something that emerges out of conviviality; it is not something you talk to other people about, nor even among ourselves do we talk about it. It is mainly a very special friendship that two men keep to themselves and between them. To the world, we are just friends; that's all. The important thing is never to create a scandal, never to broadcast what is happening. For most of the men it is a given—that they will get married, they will have children. Only if you are a *joto*, or effeminate, are things treated differently. You can have as many encounters with men as you'd like [he laughs], but people will talk about you. Furthermore, ever since you are a small boy, things are different for you if you are that way. Your whole life is different; but otherwise, everything remains normal, just as it is for Gonzalo. You see?"

Andrés and Enrique

Andrés and Enrique present a different story. In this instance, they are compadres who have sustained a long-term erotic, and not simply affective, relationship. Enrique comes from a small sierra community, but both men live in the city of Hermosillo. I met Andrés when he approached me at the main plaza one afternoon to ask whether I had ever "been on TV." It was true; a few days before, I had been interviewed by a local channel on the subject of discrimination over sexual orientation. We began a conversation that eventually led to him telling me the story of his relationship with his compadre Enrique.

When we met, Andrés was twenty-eight years old, was married, and had a young daughter. He had completed high school and was employed at a large coffee processing plant; he had held the same job for almost nine years. It was at the plant, during a Christmas holiday party, that he first noticed his coworker Enrique. By means of glances, jokes, and covert hints (*insinuasiones disfrazadas*), Andrés let Enrique know that he was "up to it, that I enjoyed fooling around" (*el cotorreo*). According to Andrés, Enrique signaled back that he was interested. After that moment and their initial sexual encounters, a "very strong friendship grew" between the two men. Enrique was engaged and shortly after he got married. "It was better that way," said Andrés. "His marriage made it easier for all four of us to share times and things." In fact, when Enrique had his first child, this gave him and Andrés the opportunity to "seal" their friendship by becoming compadres and for their wives to share in the social aspects of their relationship. It also gave them the opportunity to continue exploring their erotic connection from time to time under the framework of their friendship.

Andrés told me that not long ago his godson had been very ill, and everyone feared that the boy would die. Andrés made a promise to San Francisco to make a pilgrimage to Magdalena (approximately 180 kilometers away) in return for the favor of good health for his godson. He said: "And yes, San Francisco delivered the miracle; a few days after I came back from Magdalena, the boy began to get better." Such an act of devotion and affection won the heart of Enrique's wife and the rest of the family. Nowadays, says Andrés, Enrique's wife receives him always with great pleasure and is very attentive to him. "When I stay late talking to my compadre or playing dominoes with him, his wife is the one who sets up the bed for the two of us to fall asleep together."

Intrigued, I ask him: "But do you still have sexual relations?"

"Yes, of course," he says. "It is no problem."

I ask: "But do you think that your wife and his wife know about it?"

He replies: "I think that they suspect it; no, I take that back. I am pretty sure that they know. But they make no fuss about it. After all, they know that we are really good friends and that no harm will come of it to anyone."

Ventura and His Companions

I have explored in greater detail in another chapter the story of Ventura. Here I want to make a brief reference to a short anecdote he told me. One day while I was helping Ventura work in the garden of his house by watering and planting, we began the usual conversation, which eventually led to his confessions (always whispered and followed by giggles). The majority of stories revolved around the time when he worked as a ranch hand or as a cook serving large groups of cowboys in Sonora. Ventura is a married man, has several children, and appears very masculine. He is easygoing, friendly, and funny; it is not uncommon to find him surrounded by friends and acquaintances who enjoy his humor and conversation.

Ventura told me that when he worked at the ranches he always managed to find "someone to be with" (*con quien estar*) or to "have relations with" (*con quien tener relaciones*). In one instance he shared a bed with the son of the boss (*el patron*) for more than three months. This was considered a privilege because the rest of the men had to sleep in barracks far away from the main home in the ranch. Ventura was granted this favor because he had known the family for a long time and had proven himself to be an excellent worker. Starting with one occasion in which he initiated genital contact with the young man while they slept, the relationship between them developed to the point that they had sexual contact on almost a daily basis, including oral sex and penetration. According to Ventura, he was always the one penetrated. He insisted on making clear, however, that the young man also shared many other forms of physical affection toward him: caresses, tender gestures, and such things. In other words, he told me: "We became really good friends in spite of our class differences since the young man was refined and I was, well, a common person [he laughs]."

In other ranches he had experiences with cowboys: mutual masturbation primarily. According to him, these types of sexual exchanges are "a lot more common than people think, even though no one talks about it." At one point I dared ask him: "Ventura, with how many men from around here have you had one type or another of sexual encounter?" He stopped shoveling dirt, remained pensive for a few moments, and replied with a mischievous look: "You know that I have never counted? Let's see, do you have a piece of paper with you? Let's count right now."

A very strange and intriguing moment unfolded: Ventura started counting one by one, by full name and enhanced by details of each encounter, each male sexual experience he had had in the area. He found this exercise amusing. The count came to fifty-one encounters, inclusive of both light sexual exchanges such as kisses and rubbing, and heavier sexual activities such as oral sex and penetration. Fifty-one encounters in the thirty years he had lived in this region and in his forty-seven years of life. The majority of the men Ventura had been with still lived in the community and had occasion to maintain social relations with him over time. He told me this group of men included neighbors, friends, and coworkers; in other words, men that he interacts with socially on a regular basis. Similarly, the erotic acts exchanged were not exclusively sexual in nature; they spanned the range of affection, intimacy, camaraderie, and in some instances even "falling in love."

Ventura's experiences also included a range of sexual roles played by the men involved. Ventura himself said he always preferred being the "receiver"—but he applied this principle equally whether the reception was of penetration or of oral sex. In some instances, however, especially in cases of mutual masturbation, Ventura said that both men allowed themselves a freer range of expression through caresses and kisses. Some of Ventura's sexual partners had migrated to Hermosillo, to the border towns, or to the United States; some had married or were already married at the time of the encounter. All of them, Ventura clarified, "were men, real men, not *jotos*." And he added: "I don't like when men act like *jotos*, their little voices breaking, like women . . . no way, if I wanted that I might as well be with a woman."

He turned, looked at me, and asked: "I have been a real *puto* [promiscuous], haven't I?" And he added: "It's just that I like it, why not tell the truth . . . I like the whole fucking scene." He immediately asked that I destroy the piece of paper on which we had made the count. He said such a piece of paper "could fall in the wrong hands." We decided to burn the paper.

I remembered the time when I had first met Ventura and asked him whether he considered himself a homosexual or *joto*. He answered: "No, can't you tell I behave like a man? Besides, I am married." I followed up with another question: "Ventura, are there other men like you around here, who are married, who act masculine but still enjoy having sexual relations with other men?" He answered with a smile, as if enjoying the opportunity to reveal a knowledge he had held to himself for a long time:

"Well, yes, the locksmith, the one who works on the road repair crew, that one you see on his tractor every morning, the other one who works as a clerk at so and so's store. . . ." Then he stopped and said: "Look, we are better off walking down the street and I will point them out to you; in X street this person, in Y street, this one and that one." Utterly surprised I asked him: "How do you know?" His answer: "Because I have had something to do with them or someone that I have been with has had something to do with them and they have told me about it."

I pushed the point and asked again: "Ventura, you tell me you are not *joto* because you are not effeminate and you are married, but do you feel you are different from other men?"

His answer once again surprised me: "Yes, I do. I feel that I am different, because as I said, I really enjoy doing it. For me, it is not just something that happens because of the circumstances, or only at one moment in your life. For me it is different, I really like it. It is true that I have also enjoyed being with women; well, I used to enjoy more long ago, not so much anymore [he laughs]. I even got married. To tell you the truth, there was a time when I suffered a lot, because I did not want to feel this desire; yes, I had a very hard time with it. But, how can I say it? I also realized that I was different because I was never attracted to girly type of men, nor ever got involved in any scandal, nor have I ever felt like I am a woman, nothing like that. I have not even been what you call a 'refined' man, but just the opposite [he laughs]. . . . I have been average, rough. I have always liked men who look like real boys."

He lowered his voice and added: "Yes, I enjoy when a man makes love to me, but the thing I like the most is to feel that love, that friendship and tenderness . . . yes, to feel something really special like that, to kiss and cuddle, all that."

Ventura's narrative is revealing in several ways. First, it makes known the extent to which males in this region have engaged in acts of sexual intimacy with other men and the variety of reasons or motives that lead men to seek this experience. Second, it manifests the different kinds of subjectivities and identities from which men engage in these types of relationships (men, *jotos*, effeminate, masculine, or like Ventura, men who are men but feel that they are different). Third, his story underscores the range of forms of contact and affective dimensions that these sexual encounters entail. Most interesting, however, is the way in which Ventura lives his intimate relations with men from a position of being a man and not a *joto*, yet the form of masculinity that he defines for himself also marks a dissident position in relation to the dominant model of manhood.

Ventura likes other men, but not simply as sexual partners; he also likes to
love them and to be loved by them. This feeling or need has been a source
of pain for him as well as a source of pleasure. He had to learn to accept it
and to integrate that need within a life-style that includes his roles as father
and husband. In other words, Ventura has crafted a subjectivity and an
identity that is simultaneously unorthodox with regard to the dominant
codes of masculinity, yet it does not necessarily involve a homosexual or
gay identity either. He is not "gay," yet he lives with the self-awareness of a
difference between him and other men.

It is important to mention that Ventura's subjectivity is not the only
kind available to men in this region. Certain males in these rural communities live their experiences of intimacy with other men from clearly defined positions of social stigma. In fact, some men have experienced the
stigma of being effeminate, even though they may never have had a homosexual encounter. In every community, one can find characters who have
been singled out and marked as *jotos, puñales, putos, homosexuales,* or
maricones, even though the men in question may never have self-
designated in those ways. Some men, indeed, have accepted such designations; but when asked directly, many of these men prefer to call themselves
homosexual rather than the more aggressive and derogatory terms in common usage.

There are also cases in these communities of men who have been publicly singled out as homosexuals not because they are effeminate but because they have been "indiscreet" with their sexual practices. Some men
who have found themselves in this situation look and act masculine, but
in the majority of cases they are single men. Even though there are married men who participate quite liberally and sometimes relatively openly
in homosexual activities, the fact that they are married—and in addition to
that behave masculine—grants them a more ambiguous position than
what is usually possible within the social categories identified with a homosexual identity. That is, they are able for the most part to maneuver
their subjectivities outside a categorical identity and hence outside the
structuring everyday-life implications associated with a predetermined
sexual orientation as gay or homosexual.

It has been my purpose in documenting the wide range of experiences
of male intimacy to question any attempt—theoretical or otherwise—to
mark only one possible direction for the identity and subjectivity of the
homosexual act between men. My polemics are simple: the emergence of
a gay or homosexual discourse among Mexico's urban and middle classes
to name and classify homoerotic acts and homoerotic relations must not

preclude other forms of experiencing homoerotic experience or of living homoerotic practices from the position of other subjectivities, other identities, and hence other implications in the dynamics of power and resistance constituted around homosexual dissidence. The homoerotic experience is not monolithic. There is no such a thing as one homosexuality with different names—but only different modes of organizing affective, corporeal, and sexual intimacy among persons of the same sex. Each one of those different structures of intimacy has different and diverse implications on the subjectivities, identities, and relationships of power and resistance of the persons involved.

Steeped into a dominant model of gay structuration, it has been difficult to understand and imagine the range of possibilities that power and resistance may take in relation to homosexuality other than the established forms consistent with coming out and adopting a gay life-style. If the term *homosexual* were understood as a complex phenomenon and diverse set of homoerotic practices that transcend the mere designation of a homosexual identity as it has come to be established in Western discourse since the end of the nineteenth century, then we might avoid many of the problems that I have alluded to. If we proceed along the lines that I am suggesting, then it also becomes imperative that certain key terms of the discourse of homosexual identity be revised and attuned to specific cultural contexts. I am thinking particularly of terms such as *homophobia* and *closet*.[2]

What Is Homophobia?: Different Powers, Different Resistances

I want to emphasize some issues that emerge from the data I have collected. First, sexual and affective intimacies among males are diverse in meanings, subjectivities, and social positioning in the sexual/gender system. This would preclude any "stable homosexual experience" that could foreground a homosexual subculture, community, or identity for all those who have taken part in a sexual and/or love intimacy with people of the same biological sex. Second, homophobia is not a stable, unchanging, homogeneous, one-piece structure that runs through gay peoples as a common experience of *injure* (as Eribon calls it) and sustains a common "homosexual subjectivity" in modern Western cultures. Rather it is a historical and cultural phenomenon that should be studied in relation to the sexual/gender regime in which it takes place. Third, masculinity or manhood should be accounted for as a place of resistance to homophobic powers through the various explorations of their contradictory, disputed, and heterogeneous meanings.

Field Note, October 13, 2000

Today I had a touching conversation with Manuel, the young man who lives in "The Other Plain." He is a young twenty-three-year-old man, with a robust and hairy constitution and a copperish complexion. He looks very Mediterranean. This was my first extended conversation with him. I met Manuel through Ventura and Chalo. He is somewhat sensitive, even though he carries himself in a guarded, almost unsociable manner. He is masculine in his demeanor, but when he speaks, a slight hint of restrained femininity can be detected in his gestures and voice. His manner of speech is brief, with a sharp, almost angered tone. Yet, in this tone, Manuel lectures about life, always using profound phrases. Ventura explained one day that Manuel is like this because he is a *cholo*—which Ventura described as "coming from a religious background other than Catholic."

Today as I spoke at length with Manuel, I was able to get inside that secret world of his, "the reserved, put away world" as Manuel called it. As he explained it, this reserved life-style does cause him pain but "thanks to the power of God" he has been able to face it and even talk about it to me.

The conversation occurred when I went to look for Chalo, Manuel's brother. I knocked on the door, and when Manuel came out he told me that Chalo was not home. Neither was their mother. Their father had died several years ago and, according to both Chalo and Manuel, he died from complications due to a severe beating he had endured during a street fight. Yet, other town folk say he died from complications due to alcoholism. As Manuel opened the door, he was very courteous and invited me inside to have a cup of coffee. It was clear to me that he wanted to talk. I gladly accepted. Observing the house's interior and how it was built, Manuel's family clearly had little in relation to the town's standards. It was also obvious that they possessed few things: they had an old metal dish cupboard filled with all kinds of things piled up inside. They had a wooden cupboard that seemed to be newer. Yet some of the same things were kept in the wooden cupboard—plastic cups, medicine bottles, remembrance objects, electricity bills, and the like. They also had a square table covered with a flowered vinyl tablecloth, an old stove, and an older refrigerator that still worked well.

While he prepares the coffee, Manuel asks me whether I prefer to drink my coffee in the back court, a back patio that I can see from where

I am sitting and that contains plants, flowers, and some fruit trees. I also can see an old latrine, a washboard, and a wooden stove where the tortillas are cooked as well as other foods that require a lot of fuel to cook: beans, corn, tamales. Through usage of these wooden stoves, the family saves on gas. I decide to remain in the kitchen in order to have more privacy.

Manuel reaches for a chair and begins confessing that he was curious about meeting me because he had heard "very good things" about me. He adds, "People say that one can converse with you with ease," and that "you are very discreet and that one can talk to you about anything." It was not hard to get to the subject that Manuel wanted to bring up: the experience of feeling he is different and that it is not easy being different in the community "because of the [existing] machismo." When I ask Manuel why he is "different," he replies: "I don't know, I have always been like this, always, since I was a child, maybe because I was the youngest sibling, I don't know. I have always been a bit more tender. When I was very small nobody said anything about it, but then my behavior started to bother my brothers and they started telling me things: that I behaved like a girl, that I should behave well, that I should speak well, that I should walk well, things like that. And I don't know why."

"What specific things did they tell you?" I ask.

Manuel says, "Well, they told me a lot of things. Sometimes they told me I was spoiled, for example, but then they started to tell me that I behaved like a fairy (*joto*). For example, if I fell down or cried, they would say, 'You are a cry baby; you behave like a fairy.' To tell you the truth, it hurt me a lot. At first I didn't understand but later it began to hurt because I felt that I was being pushed aside, that my brothers didn't want to play with me. I don't know, I feel that I then began to withdraw more and I became a child who played by myself a lot." Then Manuel pauses and his eyes are filled with tears, he touches his nose, and he rubs his shirt sleeve against his eye. He then justifies himself by saying: "The truth of the matter is that I have never talked to anyone about this, ever."

"And your dad? How was he with you?" I ask.

"You see, my dad was not well. I understand something that I've learned now that I participate in church. Now I understand that he was not well; he was sick. He was an alcoholic; you know that is a sickness. Yet people here, they don't know about such things. My dad was very violent, a very angry person. He was always grumbling and shouting just about anything. He was very *machista*."

"What do you mean by *machista*?" I ask.

Manuel continues: "Well, that he got drunk, he liked to pick fights, he never hit my mother or anything . . . well, one time, but my mother reached for the hose and began beating him up. He never beat her again. But he did get angry with my mother if she worked, as in washing other people's clothes, because he would say that people would then talk about him, that she was embarrassing him because people would then say that he could not support his family. He would say that others said that he was not a real man, that he was a kept man [*un mantenido*], a goat [*un chivo*] whose wife was washing somebody else's breeches. He said things like that, and I remember one time that he came home drunk and my mom had been washing other people's clothes, and he took the clothes and threw them on the floor. Listen, it is bad that I say this because it is said that children should never judge their parents but, God forgive me, since my dad died we started living better, a calmer life. I don't think that any of my brothers, except Chalo, remember him well, but at home we don't talk about it anymore. It is better this way. I hated him for a long time."

Manuel pauses as if he can't talk because of all the emotions going through him. He then continues: "I am going to tell you something that I have never told anyone. One time, that is why I say that people here in town are mean; well, there are very mean people in this town. One time, a man from here saw me as I was going to the hills to get some wood. I was older then, about thirteen or fourteen, but I was rather withdrawn, as I told you. I seldom went out with other kids. Out there in the hills, an older man from here, from this town, married and everything, saw me in the hills and came close to me, and he began to grab me like this, to caress me, to touch me. I didn't know what to do. He wanted to take my shirt off but I did not want to. I went home. I never talked about this because I told myself, if I talk about this I'm going to get the spanking. I don't know, I was afraid they were going to say it was my fault or something like that. It was going to be worse. But since I was the one who had to fetch wood, I would go by myself and that man, who lives over there, up there, he would follow me and I was very afraid and I couldn't tell anybody. And he would do the same things, he would touch me, grab me, he would tell me to touch him down there and that if I didn't he would tell everybody that I was the one looking for him. I didn't know what to do.

"One time I think someone saw something or someone told my father. I don't know how he heard that 'I did it with men,' because that is what he heard, and he came home like a madman and told me that he 'didn't want fudge packers [*putos*] in the house,' that he didn't want potheads, pilferers, or catamites. And he said that he preferred to see his sons dead than to see them like that, bringing him shame. I remember that I hid, and he pulled me from under the bed and then he grabbed a *cuarta* [a small whip as in those used in herding] and started hitting me everywhere. My mother told him to stop, but he was like a madman and I cried a lot. I was frightened; I was very much afraid and my brothers got scared too."

Manuel says: "My father then grabbed a rope and said he was going to hang me from the roof. He threw the rope over the roof beam and he then made a knot. At that moment, I stopped crying. It was as if I couldn't cry anymore. I thought that I was going to die and then I stopped feeling. I didn't feel anything. I couldn't see anything either, it was as if everything was spinning about me, I was dumbstruck [*atarantado*]. Yet my mother had gone to fetch my older brother, so then my brother and mother were able to stop Dad and they told him, 'Are you crazy?' My brother even told him, 'Why don't you hang yourself? He doesn't hurt anybody and you do. You hurt all of us.' So they grabbed him and pushed him, and my mother kicked him out of the house. My father cried and then he did leave. But within two days he came back and he was even more drunk. He sometimes took to drinking and continued for one or two weeks, drinking without stopping. That time he came while I was asleep and he hugged me and he asked me to forgive him. I remember he was crying but I didn't feel anything by then. [I see tears running down Manuel's cheeks. He is crying but in silence.] I think that I died that time, that I have already died once. It is only through the love of the living Christ that I rose from the dead and now I feel I have forgiven him."[Manuel makes a long pause, and I decide not to interrupt this emotional moment he is experiencing.]

"And how do you feel here, in this town? Do they bother you or say anything to you?" I ask.

"No, they don't have a reason to do so. Now that I am older they don't say anything. I have always respected people. I don't meddle with anybody. Of course, if you meddle with people then they want to meddle with you or they start telling you things. I don't. Moreover, I prefer not even to walk by where people are gathered. When I go to temple I walk through there, through the hills, I cross the little mountain and go down the *cañada*. And I just go that way, without having to cross through the groups of people that gather by the store or at Pedro's business. You know, many good-for-nothing men hang out there."

"Have they said something to you?" I ask.

"Well, they do not shout at me; they are not going to do that. But I know that people are that way. They think things, and maybe they even talk behind your back. I don't know, people here make fun of others and they talk about others. I think there are people here who say things about others simply out of malice. That is why I prefer not to give them something to talk about and I walk through over there," replies Manuel.

"Do you have any friends?"

"Yes, when I was in secondary school and then when I worked at the manufacturing plant. I did make some friends without getting too involved with people. Then I got tired of the plant, although I earned good money and had even been promoted. But I got tired of doing the same things and I started selling. You see, that is what I do. And that is how I met my best friend, the best friend I have had in my life. He understands me. I can speak about anything to him, about how I feel. I have talked about all this, only to him, and now to you. He's not from here; he's from another town. But he is like me, calmer, more serious. Oh, you know him. Do you remember I said hello to you one day in the street while I was riding a bicycle with a young man? Well, that's him." [I observe the enthusiasm Manuel has in talking about his friend.]

"Do you care a lot about him?"(*¿lo quieres mucho?*) I ask.

"Yes, we are like brothers, more than brothers. Sometimes he sleeps over, like when it is getting late. Chalo sleeps in one bed, and he and I sleep together. Sometimes we even hug. [He pauses and I interpret the pause as though he has something else to say. I speculate about the possibility of a sexual relationship, but he continues.] We are very comfortable with each other. We like being with each other and a day doesn't go by without him looking for me or vice versa. He also doesn't speak to anybody; he doesn't meddle with anybody. He is like me. One day I asked him if he thought it was wrong that we loved each other so much, and he said that he didn't. Yet he is planning on getting married someday, and he said I should do the same thing. I always tell him that I don't want to get married, but that I do want to have a child. I love him a lot because it was through him that I learned about the living Christ. His family already practiced this religion, and he was the one who taught me the word of God. The truth of the matter is that I have a lot to be grateful to him for. But one day we said that no matter what happens, whether he gets married or whatever, that we are going to continue being friends the way we are now."

I then ask him whether he thinks he could be happier in a city like Hermosillo, which is bigger. He just says, "No way. I do not like Hermosillo; it is so big; people are different. I feel lonely there. I feel much better in my town. I am from here, in spite of everything, I like people here better."

Manuel actually married a woman from his religious community, but even before that happened I tried to ask him about homosexuality and he just refused: "Why do you ask me about that," as if I were reproducing the same stigma.

Field Note, May 19, 1997

César told me today a part of his personal history that has impacted me very much. It says a lot about the types and levels of violence that can happen when this violence targets men who do not evidently conform to the ideal of manhood in these towns. And I had thought these towns seemed so peaceful and quiet.

After seeing each other in Tucson, César invited me to the town where he lives, El Edén, located about 120 kilometers from Los Corazones, in another region of the (Sonoran) mountains. It is true, as our friend Ignacio once suggested, that merely walking about with a person like César, who has gestures and a way of talking considered effeminate, can make people talk in a town such as this, a town that is well-known for being particularly conservative and religious. Yet this didn't matter to me. Furthermore, César, at forty-four, is quite important in that town, and he is involved in so many public projects that he is forever surrounded by people, including public officials and young people, women and men, seeking his help. In fact, it has been very difficult to find moments to converse with César. Sometimes he is with the local priest, who has been close to César since his arrival at El Edén. Sometimes he is at political rallies, because elections are coming up. Sometimes some young man asks him for assistance in getting through a bureaucratic procedure. But today we were finally able to talk.

César came to pick me up, took me to his house, and introduced me to his family as though I were somebody important. Although his father is rather distrustful and reserved, I was surprised to see the authority that César has over both the domestic and public spaces about him. And I was also surprised to see the sense of security with which he engages people. We then went to his "studio," a place where only he and people close to him enter. His family never enters this studio. In a joking tone César tells me, "If walls could talk you would hear that the entire town has passed through my hands, jajaja, well, not all the town, but I can assure you that three generations of men—belonging to the same family, jajaja. I am going to show you something. Look." César shows me an album containing pictures of men—some men are half naked, some are naked, others appear dressed and posing for him, some are from this town, and some from other nearby towns. "They are little friends," he jests. I can't help but be surprised about the comfort level (*soltura*) with which César speaks about his sexuality. I think that he wants to show me that this is his achievement: his personal conquest of respectability and trust. I ask him whether it was hard for him to reach this position in town. I also ask him whether he suffered aggression in "being how he is." I put it in these terms to avoid inserting my own categories.

César replies, "No, man, if I were to tell you. When I was a child, it was a different thing. I mean, not as a small child but a bit later, when I noticed that the 'little tone' (*quiebrecito*) in my voice was becoming noticeable and also the way I walked. Then my father started grumbling at me, he started on me. You know, people here are fanatical about religion. Of all the towns around here, this is the most fanatical. Yet the young people are changing. On the streets, well, yes, other children started saying things like 'you are a fairy,' or you 'look like a fairy,' and they use it as an excuse to begin pestering you. But I didn't give a damn [*me valía madre*]. I wasn't the only one and besides, they really liked following me and being with me, so it didn't matter that much to me. My brothers, to tell you the truth, have never said anything to me. But my dad started with 'we must discipline this boy and do it in a timely fashion. We must do it so that he won't become a fresh one'; *un fresco*, that is the expression they use here to denote fairy. They use it so that it won't sound as bad. I think it has to do more with a father's pride, no? What is at stake here is that the family must not feel embarrassed; that is all. For example, when siblings fight, a mother immediately runs and closes the curtains so that people won't know. That is what is important—keeping up the image. Otherwise, people might say that this is a family without principles, like the families at the edge of town, the so-called *gente de a tiro*, people of few means."

César continues: "It wasn't that we were rich. We were just regular folk. But I attribute all this to fanaticism, to ignorance, to pride, and also to machismo. So as I was saying, my dad started taking me with him to work, making me do hard things, evidently so that I would become a man. They were all things I did not like to do. He would make me get up at dawn in order to go work, and he even started making me shower with cold water real early in the morning. That did make me feel bad. It hurt me; it made me feel despised. He was very hard on me. [César pauses and I realize his eyes are full of tears.] One time he saw that I couldn't push the wheelbarrow (*no podía con la carrucha*) and that I dropped it. And then he said, 'That's enough. I hope you start losing this thing of being a fairy (*joto*), *cabrón*,' and he grabbed a whip and he whipped me all over until he got tired. Then he dipped me in freezing water and I would cry. But if I cried, he would whip me some more.

"Then, they started taking me to Hermosillo, to a doctor. It was in the middle of or toward the end of the sixties. I have no idea who recommended that to them but they started taking me to this doctor, and he said that it was evidently a hormonal problem, that I was low on masculine hormones. So they started giving me hormonal shots. They gave me lots of shots. What do you think of that? But, of course, it didn't work. I only got hairier [laughs]. I got hair before other kids. Yet that was it. Then the doctor said that there were treatments with electrical shocks. Did you know that? And they finally stopped taking me there. They never gave me the shocks. I felt very bad then, really bad. I felt like I had a bad sickness, that it was probably a bad one. I felt bad and, at the same time, I knew that I was not the only one in town. I even knew of other men that were not like me, I mean *kitchen* [a spatial term he uses to denote effeminate]. They were men who looked like men, yet they still did their wretched things (*leperadas*). That is, they played at measuring their penises, they masturbated, they did it with the female donkeys (*las burras*) between themselves, and nothing happened. How could this be? I thought. I respect people, I treat people nicely, I help out, and that is simply the way I am," César says.

"I guess in time my family got used to what I am, and they saw that people respected me. And now, my father, I just say hello to him, but that's it. Now that he is old I don't take or drive him here and there; I mean, it's just not in me. He lived according to his ideas and I live according to mine. And quite often I show him that I may be whatever but that people respect me whether it is because they need me or for whatever reason. But I have them in the palm of my hand. You know, what are they going to say about me if they themselves have had something to do with me? [laughs] And you know what's funny? Sometimes I end up being the man. Imagine that! They want me to fuck them. It is pure hypocrisy; they are all hypocrites."

He continues: "One time I was in another nearby town, and I had had a meeting with the mayor of that town. They wanted me to help them with economic matters that were not clear to them. So when we got out of the meeting, the municipal clerk from my own town walked by us. They had this thing against me because I belong to the other political party. So as he was walking by, he said something like 'what a fresh day we have today' (*qué fresco amaneció el día*) or something like that, but in a loud voice and looking at me. He was really trying to call me fairy (*fresco*). But then the mayor stopped him and told him, 'Listen, *cabrón*. César to us is a person who has always delivered and we respect him. If you were not taught to respect people, while you are in this town you are going to have to do it. If you don't, I am warning you, next time I will have you locked in jail.' The other just didn't say anything. He didn't say anything and then he left. That time, they even guarded me with another car until the next town. As you can see, not everything has been bad while living in these areas."

Field Note, March 23, 1998

Alberto comes from one of the town's distinguished families. He is blond, like everybody in his household and, although they are more middle class, they are considered highbrow. They hang out with the select group of "original" families, as they are given to calling themselves. They do so to denote that they are descendants of the old families who founded the town in the seventeenth century, the non-Indian families.

Over the last few years people have changed; according to Alberto, now everyone "behaves more evenly . . . they mingle at dances, they talk to each other more, they look at each other differently, they are friends. It didn't use to be this way. I've heard that through the 1970s there were dances where some people could not attend, and people would look at others as if they were precisely that, another thing."

Evidently, the economic crises of the 1980s, public education programs, as well as more accessible means of mass communication, have created this sense of social equity. Nonetheless, as even Sergio admitted, "They retain a certain aura [*cache*] that they continue to profit from." That aura is like a type of distinction in terms of customs, how they behave in public, or how they relate to each other in their homes. As one of the young men from such a family says, "It is something quite subtle; notice that we even walk in a different way, that is, in comparison with poorer people." I think of Bourdieu (1990) and his notion of habitus and social class. I also think of his arguments of hexis as it relates to social differentiation and the corporeal experience.

Anyway, Alberto is a friend of a family that I visit every day. I met him at one of the gatherings they have in order to play bridge or backgammon, games that are part of the distinction among these families. For a month now, we have been talking; each weekend when he returns from Hermosillo, we talk. He has been working there for three years. Alberto is thirty-six years old, fairskinned, green eyed, tall, and robust. He is a schoolteacher and worked in the town of Los Corazones from the time that he graduated until recently.

One thing that is immediately noticeable in Alberto is that he is a man who manifests self-assurance. When he arrives at a place, he greets people loudly with his deep and strong voice. He also engages people on the streets quite easily. And broadly speaking you can tell that Alberto has a slight elegance in his pace, a sort of refinement that could be considered a bit feminine by the town's standards. The same can be said for some of his gestures, his forms of reacting, and even his clothes: rather than wearing ranching, cowboy-type clothes, he wears city clothes; that is, sweaters and casual shirts, pants, and shoes. When he walks by Pedro's store, by the area where the men gather, Alberto sways by and with a strong voice says, "Good morning" or "provecho." The men, in turn, respond, "Thank you" or "good morning." They display a rougher side of masculinity. Their apparent moments of interaction with Alberto are limited to courteous statements that reaffirm the distance between them—not only of class but perhaps also of gender. I have never heard negative comments uttered by these men about Alberto.

This afternoon Alberto and I have a conversation at the town's plaza where a dance was taking place. After cordially greeting a person who is widely known as being a *joto* in town, Alberto initiates the conversation by asking me to guarantee him absolute discretion. He proceeds then to share experiences and information regarding some of the men in town. With the joy of having found a new accomplice, Alberto says that he is going to tell me "what gives" (*que ondas*) with the men walking about us. If Alberto would say "one" it would mean "he only likes dick," "two" would mean *jala como mayate* (he likes to be in charge), and "three" would indicate *cotorreo y es buena onda* (he likes to fool around and is a real good person). His proposal makes me laugh. Yet, I readily understand that this game is Alberto's way of sharing knowledge he possesses but has not been able to share with others. To my surprise, he mentions a lot of numbers and all in relationship to masculine men. Some of them cheerfully say hello to Alberto whether or not they are in the company of friends, girlfriends, or wives. At one point, a man of about twenty-seven years of age and dressed in ranching, cowboy-type clothes, approaches Alberto. I step aside in order to give them some privacy, but I am able to detect that there is some bantering going on between them. I also notice that Alberto is clearly, yet discretely, propositioning the man sexually but only to the point where his friend says, "Bad boy, bad boy, *malícia* . . . [malice], not here, we'll talk later." And then the friend leaves smiling. These words are very revealing.

As we sit on a bench, I ask Alberto whether it has been hard for him to live "the way he is" in this town or even at home. He replies, "No, not at all. Nobody has ever said anything about it at home, absolutely nothing. They don't ask; I don't say anything. Of course, they know or imagine it, but as I am telling you, not my siblings, not my parents. Have you noticed how we are with each other? My father is very affectionate and so is my mother. They still kiss each other in front of us. Maybe it's because of this, I don't know. In town my family is known for being this way; the children kiss Mom and Dad, and we kiss each other. We have always been very expressive, very relaxed, very lighthearted, and very demonstrative with each other. How can I put it? At home we don't live this *machista* ambiance."

Alberto continues: "And in terms of the town, nobody has ever said anything to me. I've made myself respectful and I've always been respected. I believe that as long as you respect people, they will respect you. They may talk; I suppose people talk or think things. Yet, don't people talk or think about just anyone? Moreover, if you are subtle and respectful, you will have no problems and you will have friends. The men who like you will have no problems in approaching you and talking to you in the streets. If you are going around creating havoc, being faggish, or simply making a spectacle of yourself, then people are going to shy away from you. Yet the truth of the matter is that they are embarrassed. I too would be embarrassed to be seen with someone like that. If they are married, nobody will get jealous or anything. They will consider you as simply being one of the townsfolk and they will say hello. Besides, how can I explain this to you? Around here, we are all relatives, compadres, or friends. We owe each other favors or whatever. So people cannot go about offending each other. Can you understand this? If we do so, we can be offending somebody else at the same time. That is, the offense can befall someone else in the family and nobody profits through such acts. I have always tried to be a helpful person. I've strived to help others in whatever which way I can. And I think that also works on my behalf because people are really very grateful."

I remain quiet for a while, pondering the things that Alberto has told me. It is true that the issue of class appears to weigh in Alberto's favor. Yet I also see another type of difference. I see how comfortable people seem about him. I also see the respect and love that adult men have for Alberto as well as the ways they manifest this affection in public. It is true also that he was married in Hermosillo, had a child, and then divorced on good terms. This does not erase his "difference." In terms of his gender presence, his refinement or slight femininity, Alberto is not the same as most of them.

Field Note, June 15, 2002

Francisco is a twenty-five-year-old man that I met two years ago as a result of hanging out in an area in Hermosillo known for its gay ambience (*de ambiente*). He is tall, of fair complexion, has an athletic body, masculine demeanor, and is good-looking. He is a factory worker employed in one of the many multinational assembly plants in Hermosillo. He was attending the university but was forced to leave after his widowed mother lost all their savings. She had invested their money in a type of savings plan that is popular among common folk. But then the plan went bankrupt.

On a number of occasions, we spoke superficially without really starting a friendship. Yet, in time, Francisco found out not only that I was very familiar with the town of La Grieta but also the type of work in which I was involved. His family still lives in La Grieta. It is under these circumstances that we began a closer relationship (*una relacion de confianza*).

Today, I ran into Francisco by the outskirts of Hermosillo. He was asking for a ride to his hometown, and it was then that we had the opportunity to converse more fully. Francisco said that he "doesn't want to frequent gay areas in Hermosillo anymore." He then explained that it had been a long time since he had gone to this part of town. He said that the last time he was there it had dawned on him that this is not what he wants. I asked him what is it that he wants, and he seemed confused.

Francisco said, "I don't know. Sometimes I wish I were like everybody else—marry, have a family—and so I feel bad when I go to a place like that, like the bar. But then, I go back again. You know, I feel disillusioned. I feel that this stuff is not going to do me any good. How can I explain this? I don't think I am going to find anybody worthwhile. I don't know. Do you remember that guy you saw me dancing with at The Secret [the only gay disco in Hermosillo]? Well, that time I was completely drunk, for real. And I thought that this guy was different. I really liked him (*me caia a toda madre*). We would fool around really nice (*bien machin*). We would go out and everything, but then, some of his other friends started meddling and saying shit and stuff, so I said, fuck it, I'm done with this. It's all gossip. It's all people that you can't trust. That's why I say I don't want to be part of this stuff. And yet, I tell myself, what if I force myself to marry even if I am not in love?"

"Well, maybe you will meet someone you will fall in love with," I said.

"The truth of the matter is that I like women a lot. But I like them sexually, not in a way that I would fall in love with them. I don't know. I don't feel the same with a guy; it's like I have a much better fit with a guy. But this is the problem. When I have a sexual fling with a guy, I feel like this isn't getting me anywhere and then I feel bad."

"Does your family know?"

Francisco continued: "No, and they will never know. Never. What for? That is, I am going to tell you something. I was always a gentle child, rather quiet, but I was always just like this, like you see me here. That is, I was not a *joto* sort of kid. None of that. Nobody ever called me any name. When I grew older I remained the same, although I went to church a lot. I helped the priest; Mom even thought that I was going to be a priest myself [laughs]. What do you think? And look at what I'm doing now—although there are many priests who like to fuck. As I was saying, I was a very calm person. I never did *joto* things. I don't like that. People who are like that, I do respect them but you are not going to see me with them. And of all places, not in my hometown. No, man, no, no; it's just not worth it. That is, I will say hello to them but they are not my friends. Your reputation will be burned and then you're fucked. People will then go around saying that you are like them or that you are fucking them. I have known guys that you can't even tell and then this has happened to them. And it's fucking worse in a small town. That's because people talk.

"I feel like my mom has an idea but then I say to myself, no, it can't be. Yet, doesn't it strike you funny that sometimes she asks, 'Don't you have a girlfriend?' And, 'Don't you plan to get married?' So, the other day I told her, 'You want me to get married? Because if you want me to get married, I'll just find somebody. It's not that big a deal, and then I'll be married, if that's what you want.' So she said, 'No, no, but don't become an old bachelor; you don't want to end up being alone.' Then I rubbed it in and told her, 'No, I am not going to get married.' To which she said, 'What, are you going to be a priest?' If you do not marry, they start thinking that maybe, just maybe, you like, you know . . . men. I am going to be sincere with you, but this is just between us, yes? The truth is that I don't talk to anyone about this, to no one. You never know if you can trust someone, but the truth of the matter is that sometimes I really get down and then I drink for days. Just drink like that until I fall asleep. There are times when I need to drink because I feel very sad deep inside. I don't know, I think a fucking whole lot about fucking. And sometimes I say, 'Why am I like this, God?'"

Franciso went on: "A friend of mine told me one time that the problem is that you don't accept yourself; that is, I don't accept who I am. He came up with stuff like that. Maybe, but I don't think so. I don't feel bad if I have a little fuck; I have no problem with that. Because everybody, at one time or another, has a little fuck with another man. Yet sometimes I meet someone and I like him, and then I do it with him and I feel bad.

"Another pal told me, 'You know what is the problem with you? That you don't let yourself be loved.' He told me this and sometimes I think about this. That is, when I am looking at men, and I think that I would feel real good with a mate and all, but I wouldn't like for him to be effeminate. And I wouldn't like for him to be participating in the *ambiance* or any of that shit. I wouldn't want him to go about in *joto* things, or for him to have *joto* friends. I would want him to be discreet and for us to be good pals. That is, I would want for us to treat each other as friends, none of this jealousy or arguments, none of that. And maybe down the line he will get married and maybe I will get married, but we can still have our thing because nobody is going to know. Yet I do feel that I have a hard time opening up to someone. I have a hard time falling in love. Because I cannot trust someone, then I cannot say what it is that I feel. I am not *machista*, definitely not *machista*, but you don't go about saying what you feel. You are embarrassed, you feel ridiculous, and then you are going to say these things to a guy? I don't know, even if I felt it, I am not like that."

"Yeah, I understand what you are saying," I responded. "Do you think that it is that we are unaccustomed to seeing two men caring for each other, to see them living as a couple?"

"Maybe, yes, it could be."

"Maybe things will change with time and society will be more accepting of things like this, no?" I asked.

"Like it is done in other parts of the world, no? Where is it? In France or somewhere, they can even get married. But in Mexico, well, we are a long way from that."

The Discourse of Homophobia

The term *homophobia* was coined in the United Stated by a researcher named Kenneth T. Smith. The term appeared for the first time in an article published in the journal *Psychological Reports* in 1971. A similar term, *homoerotophobia*, had been previously coined by Wainwright Churchill, an activist and intellectual, in his book dealing with homosexual behavior between males of different species (1967). Nonetheless, the term *homophobia* was made popular by George Weinberg who, in his book *Society and the Healthy Homosexual* (1973), defined it as "the fear of being with a homosexual in an enclosed space; the hate expressed by homosexuals against themselves."

The term *homophobia*, through its two components, *homo* and *phobia*, has been widely discussed and debated. These commentaries and debates point not only to theoretical differences but also to political positionings. In terms of the prefix *homo*, many discussions have centered on whether the prefix should be used as a short form for the term *homosexual* or whether the etymological meaning of *homo*, "similar," should be recaptured and emphasized. If we take the prefix *homo* as a short form of *homosexual*, then we have a definition similar to Weinberg's first notion. Yet, if we take the position of recapturing the true meaning of the prefix *homo* as "similar," we then encounter more of a psychoanalytical concept, one in which the other is the object of the phobia because he or she is similar to the self. That is, the "other one," the one who passes as a homosexual, reminds the self of its own repressed homosexuality. Weinberg's broader definition (1973), in fact, does not exclude this psychoanalytical focus.

Regarding the term *phobia*, discussions center on both its restrictive and broader uses. That is, one the one hand, the term can be used to denote an irrational fear, a fundamentally personal pathology. On the other hand, the term can also be used to characterize all the kinds of behaviors, attitudes, notions, stigmas, and violence that usually correlate to actual deeds.

Within these discussions a number of terms have risen in order to differentiate various aspects of this phenomenon. Among them are the following: *general homophobia, particular homophobia, collective homophobia, institutional homophobia, individual homophobia, cognitive homophobia, emotional homophobia, psychological homophobia,* and *homo-negativity* (see, for example, Borrillo 2000; Welzer-Lang 1994). These terms have managed to unveil the social and individual, the emotional, as well as the cognitive aspects of the violence and rejection practiced against homosexuality and homosexuals.

Despite deficiencies and criticisms within the debates, the enormous importance of the term cannot be ignored. The term *homophobia* has managed to turn around an important aspect of the oppression exercised within the field of sex and gender: "the homosexual is not the sick person. The sick person is the individual who thinks that a homosexual is sick." Or, as the French homosexual movement has upheld, the term *homophobia* points to the fact that "it is necessary to cure those who think it is necessary to cure homosexuals" (Dutey 1994, 177).

The term *homophobia* is now integrated into the sexual politics in Mexico, where it appears to be gaining more and more space both within means of mass communication and among individuals. The concept of homophobia has become important in the fight against oppression, segregation, and discrimination exercised against men and women who have expressed a homosexual orientation. More and more, members of the gay population in Mexico (those who define themselves as gay), along with the press and television stations, are using the term *homophobia*; in doing so, a social movement is being generated—one aimed at changing the social and sexual fields of power. The change and efficacy in the continuing use of the term can be detected through activities such as the establishment of the Citizens Commission against Hate Crimes due to Homophobia shaped during the 1990s. This commission was instrumental in the reform of Article One of the federal Constitution as well as the creation and adoption of a national law in 2003 against discrimination that includes discrimination due to sexual orientation. Although the national constitution in Mexico explicitly forbids discrimination for "sexual preference" (among other distinctions), many states, such as Sonora, do not penalize discrimination. In some cities, such as Hermosillo, Sonora, we have been able to reform the *Bando de Policía y Buen Gobierno* (the City Code) of the municipality to explicitly forbid discriminatory acts. Nevertheless, much more has to be done, in so far as homophobic crimes and violence persist all across the county. Maybe the only differences we have been able to introduce in the last two decades are the legal reforms aforementioned and an increased public awareness and condemnation.[3]

Although I recognize the important role that the concept and the use of the term have played at a political level, I also acknowledge the absence of academic debates on homophobia within the field of anthropology in Latin America and particularly in Mexico. This academic silence contrasts the significant body of knowledge produced since the 1970s that deals with the diverse ways in which people think and socially organize homosexual relationships. It seems to me that, because anthropology has shown a cultural sensitivity toward recognizing various sexual cultures, it should also acknowledge the cultural diversity in the construction of the forms of violence traversing the sexual field. If we take the anthropological assertion that the homosexual or gay identity and identification does not refer to a universal subject, how can the notion of homophobia as defined by Weinberg (1973) be applied universally? How can we imagine the existence of a universal fear of the homosexual or even a universal hatred of homosexuals against themselves if this type of identification is in fact a particular social and historical construction? Are there common elements in homophobic violence that allow for generalizations? And if there are, what are they and where is the evidence?

In Mexico, outside the academic realm, the use of the term *homophobia* has coupled the restricted definition of the term *phobia*, an irrational fear, with the use of *homo*, a short form of *homosexual*. While ignoring the aspect of the prefix *homo* that means "similar" or "likeness," the term *homophobia* has then evolved with a meaning attached to "the physical or verbal violence manifested against homosexuals." At its best, homophobia has been used to represent biased beliefs, attitudes, behaviors, and overall prejudices against homosexuals. It seems to me that the restrictive reading of homophobia not only is inadequate but also veils the complexity of the violence that is attached to a generic and/or sexual dissent. And although the dissent can be encapsulated in a term such as *homosexual*, it is much wider and more complex than the term itself. I believe it is necessary to analyze the complexities of power constructed in relationship to the stigmatized referent homosexual. Moreover, this analysis needs to incorporate the politicized sexual and gendered contexts as lived within the specific society as well as the lived homoerotic realities that go beyond the limits of the heterosexual–homosexual dichotomy. This dichotomy lies at the root of the original Anglo notion and term *homophobia*.

Weinberg's definition of homophobia pretends to stabilize and provide clarity and coherence to homosexual, while at the same time reducing the diversity of the homoerotic reality and the violence traversing it. Given the homoerotic realities in Mexico—that is, the fact that actual homoerotic experience is not reduced to the homosexual identity—the question remains what does the prefix *homo* in the word *homophobia* refer to? And if you take the *phobia* portion of the term, which homo" realities are the object of the negative constellation of beliefs, prejudices, attitudes, and behaviors in Mexico—or at least in the northern communities of Mexico under consideration? I believe that taking steps in understanding the mechanisms for sexual violence will also help us gain knowledge about the forms of resistance and transgression created by the subjects themselves. Furthermore, the knowledge will help us understand how these subjects have acquired ways to survive their dissidence, their resubjectification processes, their reverse discourses, as Foucault (2001) puts it. This knowledge can then help us imagine diverse ways for localized political action.

Getting Inside the Bowels of the "Monster"

My fieldwork experiences attested to the homophobic fence (*cerco homo-fobico*) described by the Mexican author Carlos Monsiváis (1995). In Mexico, this fence is a complex system of power relations between the following: (1) the terms used to construct otherness, (2) the meanings associated with such terms, (3) the applications of the terms, (4) the conduct that mobilizes violence, (5) the types of violence, (6) the forms used to resist violence, (7) the distribution of the social capabilities for resistance, and (8) the social regulation of the activities that promote the stigmatization of the parties involved.

However, the stories in this chapter attest not only to the fact that other issues are at the root of the formation of this type of violence but also of the possibilities for resistance to such violence. These other issues include the following: (9) age, (10) class or social status, (11) family type as an internal regulator of gender, and (12) religious beliefs or the forms through which religion is lived. Other elements that assuredly condition the number of power relationships traversing the homoerotic body and deed and that need to be further researched include: (13) the urban or rural living conditions, (14) the ethnic group, and (15) the sensitivity and ethics of the police force as it relates to the different forms of homophobic aggression. The reflections that follow are an attempt to contribute to this body of knowledge, although by no means do I pretend to encompass all factors or discuss all possibilities. Nonetheless, these reflections are based on my fieldwork experiences and particularly on the fieldnotes already presented.

In the first place, it is important to note that my fieldnotes denote the fact that being treated as or being suspected of being "less of a man" or being the object of the fairy stigma was prevalent among all the men I encountered, regardless of their gender identity or sexual orientation. The characterization is usually assigned if one does not dare, does not show valor, shows doubt in making a decision, does not show temerity, and so on. And these experiences are particularly prevalent during an individual's childhood. Seldom, and mostly in jest, do they occur in adult life. Yet, as described in previous chapters, to be accused of seeming faggish may be an everyday experience in the masculine socialization of children, one that is powerful enough to cause fear and reiterate adherence to the project of becoming a man. This childish fear to be characterized as or disqualified for being a fairy then appears to be a long-lasting fear of many men. Like the masculinization process itself, the fear is not brought to

conscious levels; it is neither talked about nor is it an object of social reflection. It is a silence only understandable through a patriarchal ideology
that naturalizes gender identities while erasing histories and experience.
Some of the men I interviewed had forgotten they had been subjected to
these experiences as children. They had even forgotten that these experiences had caused them pain and that they eventually became a constant
challenge in their childhood. It was through the interviewing process that
these men were able to recall the pressure they had experienced in childhood and adolescence to cover or suppress attitudes and expressions
deemed as "weak, painful, tender, amiable, cheerful, fearful, cautious,
generous, or compassionate." Any of these behaviors would have characterized them as faggish.

It seems to me that this use of stigmatization and violence for being or
seeming faggish or less of a man needs to be conceptualized as the basis or
the backdrop of the homophobic violence observed in the communities I
engaged while doing my fieldwork. I would venture to say that this stigmatization is also a backdrop to the homophobic violence experienced
throughout Mexico. This violence is directed to all male children, pubes-
cent boys, and adolescent males. In order to enter into young adulthood or
adult life, an individual has to go through the transformation of this mas-
culinizing violence. Now, although this homophobic violence tied to the
masculinization process is directed to all male individuals, it finds a particular target in the children, pubescents, and adolescents deemed effeminate because of particular visions of gender. The verbal violence of one's
mates from similar age groups, whether at school or during neighborhood
play, stigmatizes those who may deviate from the virile model.

As attested to in my fieldwork observations, beginning at a certain age
when one's "soft" manners are not confused anymore with childish behavior, the father of a boy assumes the principal role of masculinizer. The
mother in these instances then plays, for the most part, a passive role, one
of complicity at times, of resistance at other times. The pedagogy of masculinity used by the father consists of a series of practices that carry the
body as its principal focus. The objective is for the child to abandon his
sensitivity and for him to acquire another one, one that manifests gestures
and attitudes of a man. Getting up early, taking cold showers, and working
at hard chores are all strategies of virile "orthopedics." The verbal and
physical violence produced by whippings achieve the dual function of
punishing the transgression and of inducing behavior change because of
the fear of further pain. Emotional rejection is another form of violence
that runs parallel to physical violence; this rejection may be expressed

through the father's gestures of disdain or the gestures of peers; in the use of the stigmatized word *fag* assigned in desperation because of the lesser physical abilities or appearance; or in the exclusion from peers and games.

The violence against effeminates or "lesser men" becomes a telling example for other children, siblings, or acquaintances. This public exercise of violence is socially tolerated and sends a threatening message to those who dare to transgress the order of gender identity. And although this violence is directed to all children, the effeminates or lesser men are its target. Nonetheless, this emotional violence additionally touches the other children, the "non-effeminates." As a result of this particular pedagogy of masculine socialization, children learn to harass other children, and they learn that the violence and stigma of faggishness is a mechanism to exercise power and to differentiate men. They also learn that its use can bring punishments or rewards. And they are further taught that the culprits of this violence are the children themselves: because they are "like they are," they deserve punishment. Children also learn to become the tormentors of the others. They themselves become vigilant of one another in their own process of masculine socialization using the term *fairy* to threaten and punish. It becomes obvious then that the child who is the tormentor of other children has already been a tormentor of himself, of his own human expressive possibilities.

Homophobic violence during childhood is, above all, a form of gender violence. It is not a violence that emanates from dissidence, from a sexual orientation, or much less from homosexuality. The fact is that children tend to engage in a diversity of homoerotic games during infancy and puberty without these activities calling for the disciplinary gender violence. What worries adults during childhood and puberty is the presence of the effeminate child, the lesser man, the weak child. This dissidence from the ideal of manhood generates anxiety, not only among the victims but also among the victimizers, children or adults, men or women. Nevertheless, it is important to address another issue: not all families practice gender disciplinary violence against effeminate children. This is an issue that needs to be understood before any further generalizations can be made.

As we can glean through the testimonies presented earlier, Manuel's brothers opt first for the insult of the effeminate child. Later, and with the complicity of the mother and father, they opt for isolation, perhaps as a protective measure. Nevertheless, at a given moment, the father, drunk and sick as he was, even thinks of the ultimate punishment: death. Manuel's parents have very little formal education and have very few means; but above all, they possess a dynamic of domestic violence that emanates from a father-husband with severe mental problems and a strong anxiety due to his incapacity to construct himself according to his ideal of manhood.

On the other hand, Alberto's family reacts in a very different manner. His brothers don't insult him. The father doesn't submit the son to disciplinary violence. And everything appears to be resolved in a silence toward his sexual/gender dissidence that is interpreted as respect for Alberto. This is an educated family of median income but good community standing, well regarded and recognized. I believe that the fundamental difference in the families' reactions is the result of the internal dynamics of gender, mainly the deportment of Alberto's father: this is a family where affection is easily expressed in a physical manner. The father is an affectionate man, physically accessible, loving toward his mate, sons, and daughters. A common trait among them is their Catholic upbringing, although I don't have much information about the manner in which they practice Catholicism.

Between these two extremes, we can place the experience of César, who lives in a traditional Catholic town, within a family and community that place great value on appearances. In this case, whereas the brothers remain at the margin of verbal or physical violence, the father appears intolerant of and anxious about his son's effeminate deportment. The mother appears as a silent figure in the story and as an accomplice of the father. The preponderance of the father in this brutal masculinization and exemplary punishment reflects his dominance in the familial setting and the existence of orthodox gender ideologies in this agro-pastoral family. The middle-class status, with its access to education and health services, provides access to other modern forms of violence when the traditional techniques to form manliness through corporal punishment don't yield results: the intervention on the body to transform it through hormonal therapy. If the soul resists turning masculine, the possibility to submit the body of the boy to electroshock shines in the horizon of this modern and urban vision (of the 1960s and early 1970s).

In the configuration of violence, the ideologies and gender practices of family, education, class, and social status play an important role. The rural–urban differences in the infancy of these individuals yielded different technologies of promoting manhood and different types of physical and emotional violence. Yet, age is another element that is important to highlight in our understanding of homophobic violence. As previously discussed, puberty and adolescence suggest the possibility that the subject may engage in sexual experiences. This is the visualization of the subject with sexual desire. This transformation of the sexual status of the subject brings altogether the possibility of new forms of vigilance and violence linked to his erotic desires. The history of Manuel and, indirectly, that of César show us that expressions of sexual activity with other men—deemed passive because of the individual's effeminate ways—generate major forms of anxiety and violence, especially for the father. The uncertainty and anxiety become larger because the femininity displayed during childhood becomes complicated through sexual behaviors deemed scandalous. The individual then becomes "a young man who people say goes with other men." Fear gives way to anger, to rabid violence, and even to the possibility of subjecting the rebellious body to death.

The complexity of the homophobic fence can also be observed by looking at the transformation of violence in its adult manifestations. During adolescence and adulthood, the violence aimed at socialization tends to disappear. The insult *joto* aimed at transforming the subject disappears; but the term *joto*, as a pedagogical tool for others, remains. The implementation of verbal and physical violence acquires other characteristics during youth and adulthood due to different reasons: (1) Youth and adulthood mark the end of the socialization effort and the beginning of the social right to autonomy and individual liberty. Society as a whole acknowledges a basic right to being an adult and, with some ambiguity, the right to be a male (in the sense of biological male). (2) By this time, the individual has constructed his own status: a profession, an economic capital, a social capital of friendships and influences that, in many instances, need to be understood within their specific strategic initiatives of resistance and accommodation. (3) The attainment of adulthood makes the subject less of a victim and less immune to threats or physical aggression because the victimizer can now easily become the victim. (4) Adulthood also signals the possibility of receiving the "respect" accorded to citizens and the call for the authorities to intervene, all of which require the projection of an "image of respectability," an essential element in the integration of the subject to his community.

Adulthood involves another position within the homophobic machinery in these communities, and the term *respect* summarizes this position. Respect requires the observance of discretion, the appearance of normality as much as possible, and the effort not to scandalize. That is, respect implies not making public, to the eyes of others, personal preferences and what they consider scandalous transgressions of gender (e.g., transvestism). Respect also implies a tacit covenant between the subject and the community. The subject must disguise and keep to himself any dissenting actions, limiting them to the dark, the fields, or the bedroom. It is not by chance, then, that in this order of things, friendship and camaraderie become the social form adopted by this other type of relationship.

A term that sums up this community policy of gender and sexuality, of respect and discretion, is the one used by Alberto's friend: to use malice (*maliciar*). *Maliciar* means to have malice; to act with malice, with cleverness, intelligence, sensibility to the surroundings and its dangers; even with the awareness that the others have malice, that is, consciousness of the evil that actions can carry. Discretion reflects the awareness of malice. *Malicia* means then the consciousness of a gender and sexual order that limits the possibility of affective and sexual intimacy among males, through its violence. It is interesting to note that the individual who is respected can be the subject of continuous demands to demonstrate that he is still deserving of respectability: he must be more discrete than the common man, more amiable, more supportive, and so on. A way used by society to show respect and affection to those individuals considered different is to use diminutives when referring to them: for example, *Panchito, Toñito, Ricardito*, and the like. It isn't that all individuals who are given respect and affection are addressed with diminutives. Yet, many of them are, particularly those who are single, a little effeminate, and have taken their sexuality to the limit of concealment; even those who appear to live in abstinence. The diminutive can be interpreted not only as a form of caring, but also, I think, as a form of infantile characterization. To make the subject infantile is a manner of perceiving him as asexual or to veil his sexual desires. The diminutive is the expression of the politics of respect and discretion that pretends, through the use of a name, to symbolically erase the sexual life of an adult. This symbolic erasure, however, does not intend to necessarily erase the practice.

Another axis of significant distinction to understand the life possibilities of subjects with homoerotic desires is the gendered distinction of effeminate male. Non-effeminate men who during youth or adulthood experience the importance of their homoerotic desires, find themselves in a different situation than those subjects who from their infancy were labeled by their effeminateness or perceived lesser manhood. Although non-effeminate men were also targets of homophobic violence during their masculine socialization stages, as are all the boys, they will not be objects of the same distinction when they are adults, regardless of whether or not they participate in homoerotic relationships. Francisco's story is revealing in this sense. He did not endure cold water showers, whippings, or medical treatments or the threat of electroshock, although he did witness the violence imparted to others and, as such, he suffered the "violence of witnessing," the violence of threats, on top of the common masculinization violence applied to all men.

The violence of being a witness appears to show its most damaging effects precisely in the witness's distancing from the fairies, the effeminates, "the ones that show it," because of the fear of being socially burned (*quemarse*). The term *being socially burned* intimates that the person and his reputation are altered by the proximity to someone that, although respected, is the object of social distinction because of his supposed sexuality. The proximity to such a person could give the impression that the same sexual and maybe gender transgressions are shared. The individual fears being the object of distinction because of his real but hidden sexual desires toward other men. He enjoys the anonymity and the absence of the stigma, but he endures the fear of violence that he has seen applied to others. In contrast with the effeminate, he has not gone through the ritual that allows him to reach the covenant of respect. He may even reject this covenant.

On the other hand, the same violence experienced as a witness of the violence against other children and preadolescents who appeared effeminate—of witnessing such categorizations as sweet, delicate, tender, weak, compassionate, as well as his trajectories in becoming a man—can push an individual away from his own feelings and effeminate deportment. As we mentioned earlier, the child who witnesses violence against the effeminate is the victim of the emotional violence of threats and ends up canceling those elements of his personality that can arouse aggression and, in turn, also make him a victim. The emotional health of Francisco—his difficulties in matters of love with another man, his difficulties in accepting his own amorous desires, and his difficulties in expressing them—has as their background his socialization in the violence of the pedagogy of masculinization. Francisco doesn't want to be associated with effeminate deportment; he wants to be a masculine man, but he can't develop the relationship he desires because of his personal difficulties to accept his feelings, because they are deemed feminine. Francisco is embarrassed about this aspect of his self.

The condition of Francisco tells us of a history of violence and the effects of this violence in his adult life, which doesn't fit well in the most common definition of homophobia. It is not that Francisco is a homosexual who hates himself, to utilize Weinberg's (1973) terminology. His situation is more complex. Francisco is a man; he is *machín* (manly man), as he says. He even accepts his sexual desires toward women—which I was able to observe on several occasions in dances and nightclubs—as well as his desires toward men. But his emotional and social life is trapped in contradictions built by his journey in a particular sex/gender system and his position within it. It is not so much the erotic desire that he hates but a series of feelings, which he learned to consider effeminate or less virile. This issue is important to consider and value, the resubjectification work that men engaged in some kind of intimacy with other men have to realize in order to be able to create and sustain such intimacy. It is a process of partial resubjectification that involves a kind of "reverse discourse" against machismo, the dominant forms of masculinity, as well as the act of *rajarse*; especially in those cases where intimacy reaches love and/or erotic levels.

What about those other men, masculine men, married adults, or single young men, who engage in some form of affectionate and/or sexual intimacy with other men? What do we know about their homophobic experiences? Actually I think that we know very little simply because in as much as their intimacies are handled secretly, in-depth interview becomes much more difficult.

Nevertheless, we know some facts: (1) They know intimately how homophobic dynamics work, as every man does, as part of their masculinization process, although some of them may be more perceptive. (2) They know that they can pass by the homophobic violence because of their masculine identity (which may involve in some way a degree of heterosexual capacity or interest too) and, as much as possible, by keeping their desires secret. (3) They have to deal with and signify in harmless ways their sexual and love intimacies, in order to keep guilt and self-consciousness at bay. That is, they have to experience in some way or another a resubjectification process regarding sex and affective intimacy with other men, create reverse discourse to resist machismo or homophobia, and learn to negotiate, play, and resist dominant ideologies of manhood. This subjectification process, I should say, does not mean a full critique or consciousness of machismo or the sex/gender system (as it does not happen necessarily with gay or lesbian people either). Actually, many times, I think, it involves a practical mastery and exploitation of sexual and gender ideological contradictions, as well as the intricacies of homophobic terms, meanings, and playful and performative ways of resisting them. Certainly, there are those who may succumb to dominant ideologies and in spite of their own desires or deeds end up hating their homoerotic needs projected onto other people. Self-violence and violence toward others are in fact a possibility and a reality.

Homophobic Violence as a Regulator of Masculine Subjectivity

The expressions *rajarse* and *acá entre nos* index a complex cultural field of prohibitions, threats, stigma, violence, and prejudices as well as practices, transgressions, body contacts, and so on. Both terms refer to possibilities of expressions as well as social demands of repression; that is, possibilities to "open oneself to others" or to "close oneself to others" (*abrirse a otros o ser muy cerrado*). These terms index a social regulation and mandate· over subjectivities and bodies, according to their biological sex.

The term *rajarse*—as well as other words of stigma such as *puñal, loca, maricón, fresco, joto, culón, bizcocho*—takes part in a dominant conception and a social regulation of manhood. Nevertheless, it is important to consider that even though these terms are part of the regulation of masculine identity, they also highlight different perspectives and conjure diverse meanings and transgressions. Even when the terms maintain an underlying proximity, they are far from being synonymous or interchangeable. These words are immersed in a complex sexual and gender politics, and a better understanding of this field of regulation would allow us to better grasp the complexity of the violence we tend to associate with homophobia.

The words *bizcocho, culón,* and *rajón* are body metaphors of undesirable traits of subjectivity: ambiguity, weakness, vulnerability, lack of strength, exposure, fear, lack of self-confidence, borderless, and dependent. These metaphors convey a gender and sexual subtext associated with the absence of manhood or a diminished manhood. The term *joto* or *hombrecito a güevo* could also be used with the same meanings; nevertheless, the words *bizcocho, culón,* and *rajón* do not imply a homosexual desire or practice, as the word *joto* does. That is, considering that someone has a deficient masculinity does not necessarily suppose a homosexual desire or practice.

The words *puto, puñal,* and *maricón,* on the contrary, refer clearly to the idea that the man "likes" (*tiene el gusto,* or *le gusta*) other men and engages in homosexual practices. They are vulgar words, associated with images of being penetrated anally and with prostitution. The *puto, puñal,* or *maricón* in the cultural imaginary "likes" to be penetrated. This is particularly important in the definition of these words, because that is precisely what becomes despicable and rests so uneasily in the minds of those who use them.

These terms refer to a diminished manhood or a lack of manhood to the extent that to be attracted to another man's penis is considered to be submission to other men, to be at the service of other men, to lose control and power, to become "open" (through the body and the penetration) to other men. The sociocultural conception of the penis as a symbol of manhood and the act of penetration as an act of masculinization only add to the gender stigma of a lack of virility to the man who is penetrated (contrary to the one who penetrates). All these cultural readings render the terms *puto* and *puñal* the most aggressive and incisive in the homophobic discourse throughout Sonora and Mexico.

The words *maricón* and *loca* emphasize another aspect of this assumed lack or diminished manhood: effeminacy; that is, feminine behavior, gestures, ways of speaking, and attitudes on the part of those expected to behave, due to their biological sex, manly. In the Serrano communities and in Sonora, in general, contrary to the center of the nation or southern Mexico, the term *maricón* is not common. It is considered to have a strong emotional burden and to be too violent, because it designates sexual passivity as well as an unstable subjectivity, as in the term *loca* (crazy woman); that is, a feminine behavior, an explicit transgression of patriarchal gender order, specifically the masculine gender role.

The term *fresco* (fresh or cool) is more frequent in Sonora, and it comes from the Yaqui word *seeve*, which is applied to designate equally the temperature of things as well as those men who like to have sex with other men (Núñez 2013b). It is a less vulgar and not so aggressive term. However, its violent connotation depends on the intention, the tone of the voice, and the context. I used to hear this word many times as a joke among men as a way to challenge one another to exhibit a masculine performance at work.

The term *joto*, the most common of its type in Mexico, can be used to connote any of the stigma mentioned previously, although it is more frequently used to refer to effeminacy and, therefore, lack of or diminished manhood. Its emotional implication and violence varies according to the context of use. It is the term usually used to socialize children in the sex/gender regime.

The multiplicity of terms used regularly in Mexico to name the dissident sexuality of a man presumed "weak" (*puñal, loca, maricón, fresco, joto, culón, bizcocho*) should give grounds to suspicion. Why are so many terms used? Why the abundance of words? What is it so difficult to learn and describe with a single term? Why doesn't a single term, as is the case of *man*, exist to name the "other," a term that may be able to conjure up all the disgraces and fears of men, and at the same time, a term that can bring them to "order," to the display of the desired and socially expected manliness?[4] The explanation has to be found in the socially constructed character of being a man. The signs of manliness are social conventions with no fixed meanings, but established by differentiation and relatedness to other signs. In this context manliness is a contradictory fact, unstable, disputed, fragmented, and heterogeneous, always in process of "taking root" from multiple attempts, challenges, examples, and contexts of expression. There is no one term for otherness because unity is only a reflection, a cultural fiction created by difference. The function of the others is to serve as a mirror for a one always in formation, yet always paradoxically present. And the others are useful in order to establish the symbolic frontiers of manliness and the affiliation to an ideological project of being a man.[5]

Trapped between the grip of the demands for manliness and the impossibility of its complete, total, and absolute realization, the daily process of becoming a man covers the multiplicity of actions that permeate the life of the subject and that of many other subjects around him. As the ethnographic evidence suggests, one point that traverses the stigmatizing terms, as well as the diverse forms of violence previously discussed, is something that could be synthesized with the term *homophobia* but only if we understand this homophobia not merely as the hate and violence toward homosexuality and homosexuals. This homophobia would need to be understood as a technology of regulation of gender identity, specifically of masculine identity. This technology of regulation is just as ingrained in the social fabric as it is in the fabric of the subject: in his subjectivity and in his body in the form of ideas, values, and anxieties.

The concept of phobia is pertinent because it indexes an anxiety, a fear that embodies the masculine identity and experience. As discussed earlier, through the actions of the fathers of César and Manuel, homophobia implies an anxiety, a fear turned into violence, against what the diverse terms of the homophobic stigma designate: the transgression of gender identities and, in the case of men, the transgression of a dominant model of manliness.

Certainly, when we talk of violence we talk about actions. Homophobia also involves practices, socially regulated and validated, that to a greater or lesser degree intend to end this fear, this anxiety. Yet we must not forget that this anxiety has been previously created during a process of gender socialization. It is part of the socialization process common to all men, an element of culture that we have had to fight, attempt to resolve, confront, or assume in a number of ways.[6]

I believe the review of the concept presented here makes us consider that everyday homophobic violence should be understood in relation with the dominant (heterosexist and androcentric) ideologies of masculinity that permeate the social field, in which many men seem to be socialized, although these ideologies may be contested and resisted in many ways by men and women, specially in its extremist face: violence and murder. Certainly, as long as patriarchy is being contested in Mexico and everywhere, new forms of masculinity and heterosexuality, not linked to homophobia, are made possible. With this in mind, homophobia implies the actualization of a gender identity (particularly masculine, of the hegemonic ideal of masculinity) that feels its borders of identity threatened. A situation is perceived as threatening precisely because there is fear of the social effects of power that result when another subjective position in the sexual/gender field is assumed, a position of lesser value that socially is identified with the feminine, the lesser man, the lack, the "castration."

What then is the answer to anxiety? The joke, laugh, accusation, strike, disdain, mockery, sending away, silence, arrogance, and simple action of labeling correspond to different ways to suppress or project the anxieties of the psyche. And these processes of condensing or displacing account for processes of signification that are loaded with metaphors and metonymies. To call someone fag or tomboy, homosexual or lesbian, or heterosexual is to metonymize him or her. It is to take a part for the whole, to create an otherness and mark the frontiers of subjectivity (with its corporeal dimension). It is a desire to suppress what is fluid through its projection onto another or scapegoat, which—when it becomes the symbolic depository of the irrational, feminine, and incomplete—acts as a mirror that confers to the aggressor the spurious illusion of totality and completeness. There are metonymies that tend to confer power and others that tend to create situations of oppression.[7]

The daily practice of creating differences as in "they" (the homosexuals, fags, bisexuals, *putos*, *puñales*, *leandros*, *maricas*, tomboys, *machorras*, lesbians, *tortilleras*, etc.) versus "us" (the heterosexual men and women who are considered normal) is a homophobic practice that penetrates the anxiety to actualize the borders of subjectivity, conferring the illusion of unity and completeness according to a social ideal of masculinity. The most visible forms of violence and the most physical ones do not escape this logic. To strike the other previously constructed by society as vulnerable and undesirable is the result of a projection of internal threat found in the other: "the stranger," the "weird" one. The strike intends to suppress; it pretends to suppress the self before conceding and visualizing oneself as vulnerable, incoherent, dependent, wanting. The other reminds me of the artificiality of my construction. The other with a body who resembles mine, offers the possibility not only of a corporeal isomorphism but also of one that is wanting. The homophobic murder is the reification of an internal terror.[8]

When the object of violence is a family member or a loved one, similar processes occur, although they are more complex. It is not only the "individual I" who is confronted at the level of desire and at the level of other crucial dimensions of masculine and feminine subjectivity: the personal sense of honor, shame, dignity, or decency. It is also the "collective I"—the couple, friend, family, community, club, nation, region, and religion. The feeling of dishonor, shame, and damage inflicted by the homoerotic revelation of a member of the collective of his effeminacy or lack of manhood, is derived from this feeling of threat to the collective I from which we derive our power, and in relationship to which we organize our subjectivity. This is such because the collective I, to whom the individual I is affiliated in order to construct the self (Freud 1960), has a tremendous gender and ethnic underpinning.[9]

To understand the structural causes of gender and sexual violence is to understand that homophobia and misogynist actions are the product of the forms through which subjects are organized. It is understanding how gender identities are constructed and, above all, understanding that these are actions of a dominant model of masculinity based on the repression and disdain of the pleasant, affectionate, and amorous dimensions as well as other important emotional and aesthetic dimensions. These other repressed dimensions include the capacity to express fear, pain, or vulnerability; need, tenderness, compassion, sensitivity, and the like; and the privileging of values such as strength, invulnerability, emotional self-sufficiency, and rationality—and an institutional net that normalizes and supports this privileging.

Respect: The Social Regulation of the Public Homophobic Insult

Without undermining what has been previously stated, and particularly without pretending to take away the political importance of homophobia, we should not lose sight of the existence of individual and social forms of resistance to homophobic violence. After all, the anxiety and fear of being called a fag or a *puto*, as well as the resistance to the effects of the stigma of such terms, not only are part of the reality of men but also should be part of anthropological studies of homophobia and the politics of intimacy.

Field Note, February 4, 1998

This afternoon, after leaving the artisan shop of cowboy boots and having ordered a pair of boots and talked amply with Javier about his business, I stood next to three young men before crossing the road that cuts across Los Corazones, becoming its main street. One of them was older, about twenty-one years old, whereas the other two appeared to be approximately eighteen and fourteen years old. They were waiting for a ride to a nearby town. The youngest one asked for a ride from a car passing by, but the car did not stop. As the car moved away, he shouted, trying to be funny and venting his frustration, "fucking . . . faggish monkey" (*pinche chango joto*). The reaction of the adolescent surprised me, given the sobriety prevalent among the members of these communities, although at times it is "in jest," as the informants indicate. The older youth who was next to him told him in a serious tone: "You are not going to learn to respect until they bust your muzzle [*hocico*], *cabrón?* Until they bust your muzzle." The younger one retorted, "Why are they going to bust it, eh?" The middle young man advised, "Because of a lax mouth [*boca floja*]"; and the older one sarcastically challenged him to "keep on doing it and you will see."

The situation plays on the mobilization of the stigma *joto*, as well as on the value of respect when confronted with an insult. It is about a value, taught by the two oldest to the adolescent who does not practice it, because he doesn't know about it or because he doesn't abide by it in his desire to appear funny or maybe to express anger. The older boys lecture him about how the lack of this value in the adult world brings violence. Respect can also be learned through punches, by doing violence to the part of the body that emits the insult, the mouth. The older boys demonstrate that they are different from the younger one when they show him that they have incorporated the value of respect.

On this occasion, the insult fairy (*joto*), far from attributing to the one who emits it an aura of virility, brings a warning of possible violence and places him in a comparative position of moral inferiority and inappropriate manliness. The term *muzzle*, used to name the mouth of animals, indicates the antisocial, irrational, animal, and uncivilized nature of the youth's action. The term *lax mouth*, on the other hand, subtracts virility from the action: a lax mouth is someone "open, lax, without control of his boundaries." These terms stigmatize and index "an inadequate manliness." Respect and the everyday demonstration of this value are highly regarded by men and women in these communities. It is a value that in the case of adult males participates in the configuration of his moral personality and as a result in the configuration of his manliness. A "man-man," as Pedro says, "is someone that respects and is respected." The lack of this value translates into being less of a man: in being a talker (*mitotero*), or someone with an inadequate manliness, animal, savage, antisocial—in effect, a big muzzle.

Field Note, December 5, 1999

During these festive days there are a lot of people in the street, townsfolk as well as visitors. This morning an interesting situation arose in Pedro's store. As usual, there were many men, about six eating, standing, and chatting about various topics. Suddenly we noticed the approach of a man about twenty-seven years old. He walked with a certain cadence and effeminate gestures. His city dressing also distanced him from the virile cowboy model of the town. He had an earring in one ear and several silver rings on his fingers. The truth is that when I saw him arrive I thought immediately of the reaction he would cause. I sensed a form of silence, common among these men when an unknown person penetrates their circle. The man approached the shop and Pedro to place an order. He spoke in a soft tone of voice and a soft intonation; that is, in a way that would be considered delicate or feminine by the standards of the town. Pedro treated him like any other client. While he was being helped, the young man asked for directions to a little area in the region known for its beauty but seldom sought out by tourists. Pedro gave him directions on how to get there. Immediately another one of the men that hung around the place added details and suggestions to avoid getting lost. He asked him whether he was traveling with family, maybe to see whether he needed to warn him about possible dangers, and the young man answered, "No, I come with my friend," in the same soft tone of voice, calm, effeminate, but at the same time serious.

Pedro gave him the purchase, the young man paid, and as he does with all clients, Pedro thanked him. Also, as Pedro does with all of those foreign to the area, he said: "Best wishes . . . have a good trip." This expression is used by people from these parts and I have perceived it as very caring, particularly because I can sense its sincerity. I believe these good wishes for the trip say much about a community history in which journeys were long, difficult, and dangerous. Among close friends and family members, it is not unusual to hear the men even say: "God bless you."

As the young man went away, I waited for the start of comments and jokes about his effeminate demeanor. To my surprise, no one said anything.

The silence was prolonged. While the young man walked away, another man originally from the town, but who lives in Hermosillo, passed him, came into the store, and asked, "What about this guy?" Pedro, serious and laconic, answered without giving much importance to the question: "Some guy that comes to the festivities." No more comments. To my surprise, respect rules.

I believe this field note reveals the everyday practice of the value of respect vis-à-vis the other in terms of his presence and gender. The young man is not the object of a different treatment; on the contrary, he is the object of the cordiality given to visitors and foreigners. The respect to the other is part of the masculine values that undeniably not all men abide by, but that mobilize both the practices and the politics of gender. Besides this value, other values of manliness work toward this respect: courtesy, hospitality to strangers, and not talking badly behind people backs (i.e., to tell others in their face, "like men do").

Sometimes an extreme value that is sought after is "not to say anything about anyone unless it can be proven." The value of the proof is also something that is considered masculine. For example, Sergio told me that they had told him in the factory that one of the cousins of El Cabezón had talked about him, called him a fag, that they had seen him and a friend "together." He told me that he had gone looking for him so that the man would face him and repeat in front of him what he had said. He sent notice to the cousin of El Cabezón saying: "The guy is a coward (*culón*) and if he sees me he hides, takes another route, he is embarrassed, but why is he talking if he is going to end up looking bad? Now I have told everyone that the guy avoids me and does not show his face." The paradox in this story is that, as Sergio says, it is partly real, because he and a friend used to "have fun" during their adolescence.

"Everyone Is the Owner of His Own Body": Body, Autonomy, and Resistance to Homophobia

Field Note, August 14, 2000

This morning something happened that illustrated the meaning of respect and the limits to homophobic violence in the community. I was among the group of men who meet at Pedro's business, listening as always to their comments and anecdotes. On this occasion, Ventura was also present, taking a break from the work he does in the plaza. As usual, Ventura ate and talked at the same time, making all those present laugh in response to his stories and harmless imitations of community members. At this time Ramón walked by, a guy I know little about, but whom Ventura has described as one who takes advantage of others and is envious of other men's status in the community. Ramón was walking on the other side of the street, and as he came near where we were gathered, he addressed Ventura and shouted: "Hey, Ventura, so you and Chalo are getting it on."

The statement took all those present by surprise. A grave silence filled the place. Pedro stopped working.

Disconcerted, Ventura asked, "What?"

"Don't pretend. You and Chalo are fucking (*están culiando*). No?"

I didn't know what to think. It is true that Ventura is very inclined to kid around and that his personality might invite similar embarrassing jokes. But it was also clear that I had never heard a joke like this in the town, and by the grave faces and silence of the other men, this was not being taken as a joke.

Ventura said, "Come here and repeat in front of me what you are saying. Come, because I am not sure if I heard you well," he said while walking toward Ramón, who at this point kept moving away.

The men in the group said: "Don't let him, Ventura; fuck him (*chíngatelo*); don't let him."

"Fuck him, Ventura; don't let him go."

Pedro told him: "Ventura, go after him, go after him; don't let him get away. Don't let him insult your respect (*que te falte al respeto*); fuck him."

Ventura then crossed the street toward the plaza, called one of the two police officers that were sitting on a parked patrol car, and told him: "Hey, grab Ramón and take him to the police station. I will wait for you there. Arrest him for injury and defamation." The police officer started the car and drove toward Ramón, who was walking fast. They called him and asked him to get in the car because they were going to take him to the police station due to a complaint. Ramón had no alternative but to get in the car.

In the meantime, Ventura walked toward the police station while the men in the group reassured him: "You are going to fuck him." "We are witnesses of what happened."

"If they need me, I will testify," said Pedro. "It is time that they give a lesson to that idiot (*pendejo*) so he shuts his big mouth."

Ventura walked toward the station and asked me to accompany him. Ramón was already sitting in the commander's office. Ventura went in and I waited outside, but I could hear everything that was being said.

The police commander is thirty-six years old, blond, with broad shoulders, and thick, strong arms and legs. "He is a bull," a friend told me once when describing him. He has blue eyes, a blond moustache, and a serious demeanor that is expressed by his choice of clothing: blue jeans, long-sleeve shirt, cowboy boots, and hat. The commander is a handsome man, with a reputation for honesty, peacefulness, being a good negotiator of town conflicts, but he is also decisive and *entrón*; that is, capable of engaging in a fistfight, if necessary. He has a good reputation in this region. In other words, he is highly respected because he is a man who represents the values of "adequate manliness in the town."

Calm and serious behind his desk, the commander asked Ventura to explain why he requested that Ramón be picked up. Ventura told him what had happened. Ramón attempted to interrupt, and the commander told him to be quiet and that in time he would have his turn to speak. Ventura finished his narration, stating that he had proof and witnesses of what had happened. The commander asked Ramón: "What do you have to say?"

Ramón offered an explanation that was a bit incoherent and attempted to minimize the importance of the event: "Oh, well, it was only a joke."

Ventura replied, "I am not your friend and I don't engage in jokes with you, and besides . . . a friend would not joke like that; nobody considered this is a joke. A friend would never tell me such things in front of others."

Ramón then retorted, "Shhh, so what can you do? It is true; don't pretend. Many people say you are a *puto* [promiscuous, sexually motivated, faggot]; I did not say anything that was not true . . . so why do you get upset?"

The commander then intervened and told him, "Look, the problem here is not whether Ventura is *puto* or not; the problem here is not Ventura's life, but you. The problem is that you are not respecting him. What the fuck do you care if Ventura is or isn't? Who in the hell are you to care how Ventura fucks? And why do you have to be talking about his life, be it true or not? Why do you have to go around talking, like a *mitotero*, shouting in the street?"

The commander spoke in an angry tone: "You'd better understand clearly that each one is the owner of his body, eh? Each one owns his own body, and can do as he wishes, as his damn desires want, is that clear? If he likes to be taken or he likes to take it; it is something that should mean prick to you. Do you understand me? Anyone can make of his own ass a kite if he wants to, and as long as they don't ask for yours or force you; it is not of your prick business, understood? Now, this is not the first time that you go around 'talking,' so I see that you need a scare. I am going to fine you, but it'd better be a warning; one more like this one and you are going to be locked up for a few days, eh? The fine is for lacking respect, for injuries, for damage to the morale and public order."

The commander gave him the ticket and told him that he had one day to pay the fine. And he warned him that any retaliation or later insult to Ventura would cost him a larger fine and incarceration.

Ramón left serious and overwhelmed. Ventura shook the hand of the commander, who told him: "We are here to help, you know," and in low tone of voice added, "I am so glad that you brought him here." Ventura left the office smiling and told me: "I fucked him."

This field note illustrates the existence of a series of values, attitudes, and practices, even of an institutional nature, that regulates the circulation of homophobic stigma in these small communities. The very men, as exemplified by the reaction of Pedro and the group of friends that meet in the store, who tend to present a harsh image of manliness demand that respect be upheld in public life independently of the fact that they also may speculate about Ventura's life. It is not a matter of truth, but a matter of public order, a matter of how relationships among adults are regulated.

Above Ventura's sexuality is his right to be respected, not to be abused and offended in front of the others. The right for his sexual life to be kept as a private matter, even when it is not approved of or is considered negatively, as long as he has not made it a public issue through scandal. The commander, on the other hand, makes explicit the values that regulate the life of adult males: the right to be respected, the right to individuality, the right to privacy, the right to one's own body. Transcending the veracity or falsehood of the identity of Ventura as a *puto* is his right to privacy. His right over his body makes him equal at least to the rest of the men: "each one owns his own body." It allows autonomy over practices: "he can do as he wishes, as his damn desires want." There is even a supreme affirmation of corporeal autonomy and desire that legitimates the right to sexual choice: "anyone can make of his own ass a kite." All this must be within the proper reservations: "as long as they don't ask you for yours or force you."

To respect in public the autonomy of the other over his body, his privacy, his right to sexuality as long as it is not scandalous, is a value that is encased in an image of self-control, tightness, and seriousness. Not to do this makes the other a talker, a *mitotero*, as the commander said. It makes him someone who is less of a man. This attitude of respect, that not necessarily means approval of the sexual life of the other, can become an important element in the masculine deportment. In front of the other, who is different, instead of being afraid, alarmed, and giving way to criticism, to the "talk," one has to remain calm, respectful, distant, and serious; this is being "in control of oneself," as a demonstration of supreme individuality and personal security. "It is his thing" is an expression that synthesizes this masculine value, which has the effect of democratic civility.

"It Is His Thing": Respect, Sexual Ambiguity, and the Performance of Masculinity

Although the literature doesn't account for it, many men develop an intuition, a knowledge that permits them to navigate ambiguities, contradictions, and instabilities of the patriarchal system and its ideologies in such a way that they are able to resist, evade, transgress, and accommodate to stigmas and their effects in different contexts of life. An eloquent manner of resisting is playing with the possibilities of applying or not applying the terms, exploiting the dissonance that exists between the profound equivalence and the concrete designation of different realities. The following field note is revealing in this sense.

Field Note

This afternoon I took my car to a radiator shop in Hermosillo. A man about thirty-one years old helped me. He was manly like all the mechanics whom I have known and quite friendly, talkative, and relaxed. There were very few customers, maybe because of the time of the day and the heat. Another two men who worked in the shop walked around the area, busy with their own duties, which did not impede them from interacting among themselves and with the two customers present.

While the mechanic assisting me works diligently with a hammer, the radio is tuned to a mariachi music station and begins to play a bolero sung by Alejandro Fernández, a young singer characterized by the refinement of his physique and educated voice, not very common traits among mariachi singers. The mechanic in question stops hammering and enthusiastically cries out [*grita*]: "Listen, play it louder; that's it."

The other mechanic, the younger one, does as he is told and asks: "Do you like this?" to which the first mechanic responds while concentrating on his job: "*Un chingo*" [a whole lot]. Then he addresses me in a virile and strong voice like his deportment: "Compa, to this guy, I'll give them to him . . . I don't give a fuck, I will give them to him" [*a este bato sí se las doy, vale madre, si se las doy*].

His young coworker asks, "What will you give him?"

"My rear end and whatever else he wants," answers the mechanic with a firm voice. He then smiles and begins to sing.

The incredulous young coworker asks, "Really?"

"I don't give a fuck," [*me vale madre*] he replies. "*El cabrón esta rete chulo* [the young prick is so damn cute]; he has everything, a good voice and he is handsome," he retorts without stopping his work with the hammer.

The young partner smiles and tells the other mechanic: "What do you think of this guy?" The other one, older, without much ado answers: "It is his thing, as the saying goes, anyone is free to make a kite of his ass." His last words were lost between the radio tune and the accompaniment that the admirer of Alejandro Fernández made.

His trade, cloth, mannerisms, the homosocial world in which this episode unfolds, the cry of enthusiasm, even his taste for the mariachi, everything in the mechanic speaks of his manliness, including the words that he uses to qualify his confession of wanting a man: not giving a fuck, *cabrón*—not to mention the gravity of his voice and tone.

The young man smiles and asks, all the while captive by the restlessness that a confession of such nature creates, and particularly when delivered in such a manly manner: direct, decisive, relaxed, self-assured, and frank. The dissonance between the content of the confession, the homosexual desire, and its virile form make him doubt: "Are you sure?" and to seek certainty, referents of judgment: "What do you think of this guy?"[10]

This anecdote portrays two different subjectivities confronting the confessed homosexual desire: restlessness in the young man, sign of his own anguish, the lack of worry in the other, older one, who also embodies a conception of the right to privacy in sexual matters and physical autonomy: "it is his thing" and "everyone can make a kite of his ass." The discretion and respect, as well as the absence of restlessness, also connote manliness. It is probable that the younger man thinks everything is a joke, and that the mechanic is kidding around, that he is not speaking seriously. It is probable that he is right, but the message is still the same: the masculinity assured in the field of gestures, public presence, and mobilized with dexterity can create the suspension of the terms of stigma, even in the case of transgression at the level of sexual desire. The comments of the older mechanic—"it is his thing"—is a performance of maleness that is on par with the performance of the subject. And the younger mechanic appears to learn the subtle aspects of the politics that regulate male identities and the confession of the desire of intimacy. In some way, this is a daring aspect of male socialization among certain groups of men: to learn to respect and not to have fear, or to keep quiet in the face of "unexpected or uncommon" events.

CHAPTER FIVE

Acknowledging Pleasures, Deconstructing Identities

Anthropology, Patriarchy, and Homoerotic Experience in Mexico

Introduction

In previous chapters, I have tried to present, through a variety of ethnographic notes, the rich and complex sexual/gender field in which erotic and affective intimacy among men take places in northern Mexico. It has been my intention to show the different ways of living and understanding the homoerotic experience beyond the already known and theoretically discussed homosexual or gay identity or subjectivity. Informants from the sierra villages and from the city of Hermosillo (most of them immigrants from the same villages) with their sexual/gender practices and subjectivities, complicate any homogeneous characterization of Mexican (or Western) homoerotic experience. I argue that this characterization has its own history as well as its own ideological implications for the sex/gender system.

In this chapter, I engage in a series of reflections on what I think is the dominant theoretical discourse on the Mexican homoerotic experience. I have termed it "the dominant model for understanding male homoerotic experience in Mexico" (DMUH). I refer to a dominant commonsense and anthropological discourse on homoerotic relations among men, a model that is based on binaries such as penetrator–penetrated, active–passive, man–fairy, and dominant–submissive. Even though this model makes sense in terms of understanding certain homoerotic relationships, it is inadequate for understanding many others; furthermore, it presents a theoretical and methodological obstacle to acknowledging the wide variety of pleasures, meanings, erotic explorations, and daring identity transgressions that occur as erotic events among men.

I believe it is necessary to open up debate on this topic in order to gain a theoretical and political understanding of the following: (1) the way our models of comprehension render aspects of reality invisible and become complicit in systems of domination, in this case patriarchy; (2) the political nature of erotic experience, which articulates intimate forms of knowledge and practices that challenge dominant ideologies of gender and sexuality; and (3) how we might usefully reenvision male homoerotic experience in terms of studies of masculinities, and in so doing deepen our insight into masculine subjectivities, the identity politics in which they participate, and their virtually always ambiguous and contradictory insertion into the sexual/gender regime.

From Homosexual Ethnocentrism to a Cultural Geography of Homoerotic Experience

At one time, the concepts of homosexual and homosexuality, as well as other classificatory categories of sexual existence,[1] constructed within the framework of modern 19th-century discourses on sexuality, were accepted as objective, scientific terms to refer to any individuals involved in homoerotic relationships, no matter their cultural differences. Men who engage in homoerotic practices on a ranch in the state of Michoacán, a New York suburb, or a hut in Java could all be designated as homosexual by academics, even though the culture to which they belong might interpret those practices in different ways.

Some decades ago, this type of interpretive procedure came under severe criticism and was rightly termed ethnocentric. Its ethnocentrism consisted of using concepts from a modern, Western medical discourse to study the homoerotic behavior of people from other cultures and periods in history, without considering how the meanings of homoerotic bodily pleasures have different implications in different societies. Studies of homoerotic experience took an important turn with the rise of a poststructuralist paradigm alert to the systems of signification by which social reality is constructed. Foucault's "archaeology" of modern discourses of sex and the modern construction of sexuality, provided a model for students of anthropology and sociology to begin examining the various concepts of homoerotic experience in other cultural settings. It became accepted in academe that the concepts homosexual and gay refer to different signifying fields than those connoted by Mexican terms such as *cochón* or *joto*, which are used to refer to males who enjoy sex with other males.

Having dispensed with the ethnocentrism of previous studies of homo-erotic experience, anthropologists anxiously seeking the exotic set out to uncover the particular social relationships and meanings that structure sexual experience among biological males. In a fascinating display of voy-eurism and logophilia, anthropologists and their readers have learned the following: that among the Sambia of New Guinea, fellatio among males of different ages is part of a ritual system of masculinization (Herdt 1981); that homoerotic relations in ancient Greece were stratified according to age and seen in a pedagogical and political context (Foucault 1976); that in some North American tribes, males with homoerotic or androgynous preferences are granted special status allowing them to "marry" another male and carry out important religious and ceremonial activities in society (Williams 1986); and that in Nicaragua, a man can have sex with another male without being stigmatized, as long as his role in anal sex is the active one of penetration (Lancaster 1992).

I find anthropological descriptions that are "sensitive to native catego-ries" more credible than the fantastic extrapolations that see gays in the Stone Age; however, I do not find them altogether convincing, even though their simplicity is appealing. When I read such accounts, I wonder whether the Sambia, once masculinized, might not continue exploring their desires outside official masculine rituals[2]; whether two adults in clas-sical Athens might not have "had a fling" under the shade of a figtree; whether there might not be two brave Navajo warriors who indulge in pleasuring each other while out hunting; or whether somewhere in Mana-gua two good-looking butchers might not fool around with each other from time to time, without identifying themselves as active or passive.

My goal in exploring this issue (regardless of whether it has the inciden-tal effect of stimulating the erotic imagination of the readers) is to stimu-late the anthropological imagination to reconceptualize the different forms of homoerotic experiences and our representations of them. I wish to focus on the anthropology of the homoerotic itself in order to question its tendency to privilege only the dominant discourse, a discourse that eventually silences other ways of understanding and engaging in such erotic events within a single culture.

The fundamental theoretical and methodological stance that I propose in this chapter is the following: the anthropology of homoerotic experi-ence should not merely register social convention, assuming that it ac-counts for homoerotic reality, but should aspire to examine the sex/gender system—that complex interplay of ideologies, identities, powers, and plea-sures that construct or are constructed by individual sexual existence. In Bourdieu's (2001) terms, anthropology should attempt to examine the field of sexuality and the power struggle between different agents in society over the "legitimate" representation of sexual existence.

The Anthropology of Homoerotic Experience in Mexico

In Mexico, the historical trajectory of studies on homoerotic experience is more or less the same as the one outlined above.[3] After a brief period of ethnocentric abuse of the term *homosexual* in works on the condition of Mexican men and machismo in Mexico, the 1970s saw the emer-gence of anthropological studies of homoerotic experiences that were more sensitive to local categories in the area of sexual existence. This heightened awareness did not necessarily mean that ethnocentric catego-ries and approaches were abandoned; although pioneers of homoerotic anthropology such as Carrier (1972, 1976, 1985, 1995), Taylor (1978a, 1978b, 1986), and later Alonso and Koreck (1993), Almaguer (1991), and Herdt (1981, 1997) acknowledged the need to pay attention to the local sexual system and avoid ethnocentrism, their texts show a rather lax use of terms such as *homosexual, homosexuality, gay,* and *heterosexuality.*[4] Car-rier, for example, frequently uses expressions such as "Mexican homosexu-ality," the "homosexual world" (Carrier 1995, xi), and he translates the word *ambiente* (scene) as "gay" (Carrier 1995, 47). Likewise, Taylor uses expressions such as the "social life of homosexual males" and "homosex-ual subculture" (Taylor 1978a, 1978b, 1986). The authors Carrier (1972), Alonso and Koreck (1993), and Almaguer (1991) speak of "heterosexual" men, an identity category that is virtually unknown in Mexican culture, and whose very inclusion in these studies betrays an inadequate problema-tization of sex/gender ideologies and identities in work on homoerotic ex-periences in Mexico.[5]

Despite these theoretical and methodological inconsistencies, anthro-pological studies of homoerotic experience in Mexico have refined the characterization of the "Mexican sexual system" in a way that is more at-tentive to cultural particularities. In general, authors coincide in contrast-ing the features of Mexican homoerotic experience with those of the Anglo/Northern European sexual system (which Almaguer terms western bourgeois; 1991), and placing the former into the context of the Latin American sexual system, with its Mediterranean influence.[6] This difference between the systems reproduces, in Almaguer's view, the Freudian distinction between the "choice of sexual object" and the "sexual objective," in which the former concerns the biological sex of the person who is the object of desire, and the latter the act that one wishes to perform with a person, regardless of either's biological sex (Almaguer 1993, 257).

There is broad consensus among anthropologists regarding the relevance of the following issues: (1) In Mexico, sexual intercourse among males is seen as being organized according to the role played by each partner in the relationship: one is either the "active penetrator" or the "passive receiver."[7] (2) Differences in erotic roles involve a "gender stratification," because the active role belongs to a masculine subject and the passive role to an effeminate or less masculine subject.[8] (3) Differences in erotic roles corresponding to different gender identities are learned through terms that designate different social types: the active partner receives no special name; he is simply a man (although the passive partner may covertly refer to him as a *mayate* (which can be translated as "trade," according to Chauncey's *Gay New York*; 1994). The passive partner, however, is given derogatory names such as *joto, maricón, puto* (fairy, pansy, fag), and other less common terms. (4) This nominative differentiation indicates that the active partner is not stigmatized (he may even gain prestige), whereas the passive one bears a heavy stigma and becomes a power object. Indeed, because erotic relationships are constructed by means of this series of dichotomies in terms of gender and stigmatization, homoerotic practice itself can be seen as a relationship of power–pleasure. In the erotic act, the fairy is dominated and the man empowered.[9]

This anthropological characterization of sexual relations among biological males is sometimes complemented by researchers' passing observations about the small but growing gay community in urban middle-class settings. However, there are different interpretations of this phenomenon. Whereas Almaguer points out that in the Mexican/Latin American context there is no cultural equivalent of the modern gay man (Almaguer 1993, 257), Carrier acknowledges the presence and influence of gay identity in sexual culture in Mexico when he mentions the existence of "internationals" (people who have no particular preference for active or passive erotic roles). According to Carrier, Mexican gays decided to be both active and passive in order to be "politically correct" (Carrier 1995, 193). He nevertheless declares that the majority of men who have sex with other men in Mexico have not been affected by the gay liberation movement because most of them still prefer anal sex, and many still prefer a particular sexual role (Carrier 1995, 194).[10] Prieur's study on transvestism points to the presence of a gay identity and community in Mexico City (Prieur 1998). Alonso and Koreck, responding to Carrier, comments that she found no internationals in her research on gender ideology and the Mexican Revolution in a rural community in Chihuahua. She merely found passive and active, machos and *jotos* (Alonso and Korek 1993, 119).

In the passing comments on gay identity, what is referred to as "the Mexican sexual system" is in reality a type of "dual homoerotic system": one of Hispanic (Mediterranean) origin, structured around the active–passive dichotomy, and the other of northern European and North American origin, based on the interchangeability of erotic roles and the notion of being gay. The first, "traditional," system is the dominant one; the second, "modern," one is said to be the product of foreign influence and limited to urban and middle-class settings.[11]

This notion of a unified Mexican sexual system is open to the charge of ethnocentrism. Might there not be men in the Huasteca region that have erotic encounters after dancing to the music of a son in the village, without penetration necessarily taking place? Or two macho cowboys from Chihuahua who enjoy each other's bodies after watching a rodeo? How can the old "active masculine/passive feminized" model account for the taxi driver who gets transvestites to penetrate him in some grungy hotel in the Colonia Guerrero, Mexico City?[12] How can it account for the forms of solidarity, confessions, emotional intimacy, and affection between males from Guadalajara, Monterrey, Durango, Xalapa, or Hermosillo, in and through their homoerotic relationships, regardless of gay or other identities, as I have been showing so far?

Phallocentrism, Patriarchy, and the "Other Homoerotic Experiences"

In the following section I propose a critique (which does not claim to be comprehensive and is intended to promote discussion) of the traditional sexual system in the dominant model of understanding of the homoerotic experience, from two angles: first, its failure to understand areas of homoerotic experience not included in its binary premises; and second, the way it becomes complicit in the sex/gender ideologies that structure the patriarchal system. I will limit myself to aspects of the traditional sexual system because it has received the most attention, although I realize that there is still much research to be done on the characteristics, meanings, and sociopolitical features of gay identity in Mexico.

Homoerotic relations are structured based on penetrator–receiver roles. There are three fundamental problems with the assumption that homoerotic relations are based on penetrator–receiver roles. First, this assumption envisages homoerotic relations as being exclusively about anal penetration, which is completely false, because there are innumerable examples of homoerotic relations without penetration (in fact, judging from my research, they constitute the majority). Second, it erases in one phallocentric stroke the kisses, nipple stimulation, comforting hugs, fondling, acts of tenderness, muscular mass, brushes, looks, genital stimulation, and fetishist games; in other words, forms of bodily contact (to say nothing of emotional and intellectual contact) that are of crucial importance to the organization of desire and the sensation of satisfaction and pleasure that individuals experience (whether or not there is penetration by one or both partners). Third, it renders invisible the fact that in cases where penetration occurs in homoerotic relations, it is not usually restricted to only one of the partners (and we are not talking about individuals identified as gay).

These three points are borne out in numerous narratives. The following is merely one of many I collected. The speaker is Martín (twenty-eight years old, a masculine-looking high school graduate who works as a line supervisor in an assembly plant), who sometimes has homoerotic relations, which he terms *cotorreos* (fooling around, having fun). Here he is describing his experience with a twenty-six-year-old man, also of rugged, masculine appearance, who works as a laborer after having dropped out of high school. Neither of them considers himself gay, just "men who like a bit of fun." The following interview took place in a public park in Hermosillo, at night.

I said to him, "You know what, if we don't do anything, I'd be just as happy, because I've had a great time talking to you." He told me about his wife, the fights they used to have, and I gave him my opinion. We had an amazing talk, really fantastic. He said he felt the same, that he would be cool with whatever happened, it would be OK if we didn't do anything. But then, you know when you really get to know someone you start wanting to touch them, well, that's what happened. At one point (this was the best part) he put his hand on my knee and then he took my hand. I don't know if he wanted me to touch him 'down there,' but I took his hand and kissed it. Then, because it was getting cold, we stayed in the car and I put my arm around his shoulders and we gave each other a hug. It felt so fucking good to be so close to him . . . man, his smell . . . his body, right there . . . well built, solid . . . [he says, as if remembering the pleasure]. I started kissing his ear and he put his head back. I kissed his neck and I could see he'd closed his eyes, he was loving it. . . . I thought: I bet your wife has never ever kissed him this way. After a bit I unbuttoned his shirt and kissed his nipples. We unzipped our pants. I stroked his penis and it was like he'd never done it before. . . . I don't know but I grabbed his hand and even though he resisted a bit, you know, I could feel the tension in his muscles, he gave in and touched me there too, and we carried on, it was incredible . . . we kept going for quite a while, like over an hour, I don't know . . . then after a while we got out of the car. We were up in the mountains, boy was it cold, but we couldn't feel it, we were hugging each other standing up. I asked him to turn around so I could see his ass (the guy thought it was hilarious I wanted to look at him from behind). It was gorgeous; he had really cute buns . . . [he says with a smile]. He never said anything about penetration and to tell you the truth I didn't either; sometimes you just don't feel like it, although I would have liked to do it with him. And then we were done. It was amazing. . . . Then on the way back, it was like nothing had ever happened. Neither of us said anything about what we'd just done; we talked about other stuff, but at one point I took his hand because I had this special feeling for him, and he let me, he even laced his fingers between mine, for a bit . . . and then we got back. I tell you, this guy was real macho, real manly . . . and when we said goodbye we were totally cool with it, like, "See you later, man, thanks," and I said, "Yeah, man, see ya, thanks again, bud."

I include this transcription of one of the many narratives I recorded during my fieldwork, not to appeal to some fantasy of the reader's, but to show how inadequate it is to categorize homoerotic experiences on the basis of the penetrator–receiver dichotomy, and how reductionist that kind of interpretation is in terms of representing the diversity of homoerotic experience.

Having pointed out the limitations of that dichotomy, I will move on to a discussion of its ideological implications. In the first place, I believe that the privileging of the phallus seen in the DMUH is more than a mere oversight that can be remedied by simply adding on these "other" homo-erotic experiences. We cannot remove this particular problem by simply extending or improving the description,[13] because it stems from a failure to really problematize either the ideological implications of these analytical categories, or the political field to which such hegemonic concepts of sexuality contribute. To privilege the penetrator–receiver dichotomy in or-der to characterize homoerotic experiences in Mexico is to collude with patriarchy by reproducing dominant ideologemes of sex and gender that envisage human sexuality as a genital and orgasmic event. I do not mean that these phallocentric concepts do not influence the attitudes of many people, whether they are involved in homoerotic activities or not; instead I mean that by categorizing homoerotic events in this way, we preempt any possibility of recognizing the complexity and diversity of bodies, subjectivi-ties, meanings, and politics.

Second, the classification of individuals according to their erotic roles metonymically reduces them to their sexual organs (the penetrator be-comes the penis, the receiver the anus), a metonymy that reproduces dom-inant ideologemes about bodies, desire, and sexist (homophobic) and pa-triarchal gender identities. When a homoerotic individual (the passive one, who is socially stigmatized as the fag) is reduced to an anal receptacle, the homoerotic body is apprehended as an orifice and homoerotic desire as the penile desire for the anus. As we know, a central ideologeme up-holding patriarchy's economy of desire is that "desire cannot be more than desire for the phallus"—the phallus being the supreme symbol of the sys-tem of gender distinction and the institution of masculine power.

Finally, we should point out that the penetrator–receiver binarism over-looks the homoerotic practices and relations that day by day (and night by night) exemplify the many modes of transgressive insertion into the order of sex and gender. It renders invisible the disputes, resistance, and con-stant subversion of the ideological and power claims of the patriarchal system.

Erotic differences imply gender stratification: the active role is performed by a masculine subject and the passive role by a feminine or less masculine subject. Another problematic concept is that of stratification by gender in homoerotic sexual acts, whereby the active role is carried out by a mascu-line individual and the passive role by an effeminate or less masculine one. There are several difficulties with this notion. First, it prevents us from seeing that there are numerous erotic relationships between totally masculine individuals that are not stratified by gender. Many individuals who participate in homoerotic exchanges are normally masculine in their mannerisms, walk, clothing, bodies, attitudes, and occupations. In my ethnographic work, I have interviewed people of traditionally masculine occupations—for example, butchers, truck drivers, laborers, bus drivers, police officers, prison guards, cowboys, construction workers, soldiers, garbage collectors, auto-body workers, mechanics, thieves, executives, extreme sports fanatics, soccer players, baseball players, farm workers, boxers, and soldiers. All of these typically masculine figures enjoy pleasure with other men without necessarily falling into either active or passive roles, a dichotomy that is based on phallocentric criteria. Therefore, their erotic role is not dictated by their gender identity, or vice versa.

Last, the assumption of gender stratification fails to mention that even in those cases that reproduce the penetrator–receiver, masculine–feminine dichotomy (I would never claim that such cases do not occur), individuals are not uncritical bearers of the binarisms of the symbolic order. Rather, they live out their relations with men through gestures, language, and erotic behavior that they experience in a different way. In fact, even in a relationship as polarized as the penetrator–receiver type, leadership during the encounter is usually in the hands of the individual that the DMUH calls passive, effeminate, or queer, and not the active one. The following quote from one of my interviewees reveals that the terms *active* and *passive* are not limited to one meaning:

> I don't know why they say we're passive, when we're the ones who do everything; we pick them up, we convince them, we get them to go with us, we seduce them, we fondle them, sometimes they just lean back or lie down, and we kiss them, we touch them, we take off their clothes, etc., we even make them come. I've never felt at all passive, just the opposite. (Iván, age thirty-one, effeminate single hairdresser in the city of Hermosillo. The interview took place in his home.)

It is important to note this speaker's understanding of what it means to be active or passive. It is significant in the configuration of the identity of both partners, because, as I will show later, his interpretation is a vehicle for notions of power that do not coincide with those contained in the active–passive dichotomy.

According to my ethnographic data, different masculine individuals do not limit themselves to acting out the prescriptions of the symbolic order in their erotic encounters; rather, they participate to a greater or lesser extent in a negotiation of bodily contacts in which they resist certain caresses and experiences and dare to experience others: they allow kissing, but not contact with the buttocks, or the reverse; or oral stimulation of the nipples and the buttocks, but no kissing. Such discriminations among forms of contact have to do not only with particular erotic preferences but also with ways of managing bodily pleasures, sensations, desires, and fantasies that are repressed in the framework of their sexual and gender identities. This view is supported by notes from the field like the following remarks from Javier (a single man of forty-four, a manual laborer of masculine appearance):

> This kind of thing happens a lot. You pick up a real macho-looking guy [*un batote*][14] in a bar, or on the street, or at a dance, the kind of guy that when you look at him you think no way, he's not out looking for a good time [*cotorreo*] like you are, but when it really comes down to it they'll let you do all sorts of things, like kissing their ass; some of them will let you kiss them on the mouth or they just see you as masculine and interesting because no matter how masculine and 'heterosexual' [he emphasizes this word] they seem, anybody can be attracted to or admire another man. So anyway, like I was saying, you're with them and they like you and they feel like doing stuff or having stuff done to them that they've never done. For example, the guy I told you about that I met on the street; he was half drunk, a tall guy, a construction worker. He had huge great hands [he demonstrates the size with his own hands] and bushy eyebrows. Real tall, like 6'4", square jawed, real good looking. Well we started fooling around, first I fondled him, we hugged each other, I kissed his *chichis* [tits, meaning here nipples], but he didn't want to kiss mine. He let me kiss his mouth but he kept his lips shut, but after awhile I realized that he was looking at my penis, pretending not to at first, but he was obviously curious and after a bit I took his hand and he started masturbating me, with me helping him at first and then all by himself, even when I wasn't masturbating him at the same time . . . you know, sometimes even when you don't actually penetrate them they just like to feel your body behind them, just have you right on the edge of entering them and then, well, sometimes, you know, curiosity killed the cat.

The active–passive dichotomy and its assumptions about gender stratification silence these kinds of encounters and erase the erotic experiences of so-called masculine subjects, experiences that far from ratifying a dichotomous gender stratification contravene the dominant ideological assumptions about masculine identity.[15]

We need to undertake a full examination of the complicity with patriarchal ideologies of sexuality and gender that this concept of homoerotic experience inadvertently reproduces. The principal form of complicity is that the gender dichotomy of active–passive, which also underlies the man–fairy dichotomy, imposes a siege of silence on characterizations of homoerotic practices that reveal the fragmentary, inconsistent, heterogeneous nature of masculinities, as well as obscuring the possibilities for desire between bodies and subjectivities, thereby safeguarding an important ideologeme (Jameson 1981) of patriarchy: namely, that masculinity is an expression of the male body's innate nature, and that it functions as a predictor or indicator of heterosexual, phallocentric desire. It safeguards the supposedly consistent nature of the trilogy of prestige: biological maleness, masculinity, and heterosexuality.[16]

Homoerotic practices often involve a disruption of this central ideologeme of patriarchy, installing ideological disorder in individual experiences of the body, pleasure, and desire—both newly discovered or rekindled.

The active partner receives no special label; he is simply a man, although the passive partner may call him a mayate *(trade). The passive partner is referred to by derogatory terms such as* joto, maricón, *or* puto *(fairy, pansy, or faggot).* The first problem with this division of homoerotics into men and fairy is that it is based on false phallocentric and gender assumptions and is thereby incapable of describing forms of homoerotic experience that do not fall into either of its categories.

The second flaw I see in this dichotomy is that it ignores the perceptions and meanings attributed by the individuals involved, notably their use of names and their strategies for resisting the dominant ideologies in which they have been socialized. Many individuals in practice choose either to resist any assigned identity, beginning with the one connoted by the word *joto* (fairy); or to redefine the terms *joto, hombre,* or *mayate* (fairy, man, or trade) used in the dominant ideology, thereby overcoming the symbolic dominance of the man–fairy dichotomy.

During my fieldwork, I noticed that in Sonora some men frequently use the term *cotorreo* (a good time), in expressions such as *tener un cotorreo* or *me gusta el cotorreo* (to have some fun; I like fooling around), to refer to their practices, themselves, other men with homoerotic tastes, or men who want to engage in such activities at that moment, without necessarily implying a preference and certainly not an identity. *Qué ondas, no tienes ganas de cotorrearla?* (Hey, man, wanna have some fun?) is used to invite someone to have a homoerotic experience. The term *cotorreo* functions to avoid the field of binary sexual identities and stigma, by putting homo-erotic practices in the realm of adventure, shared achievement, fun, even mischief. The significance of the practice is shifted from the realm of ho-mosexuality and the dichotomies to which it is constrained by patriarchy to a much less threatening and more manageable symbolic terrain, closer to masculine solidarity, friendship, and male bonding. Calling this desire *cotorreo* resists patriarchy's power to name and categorize it.

When I have asked some men who situate themselves within the field of *cotorreo* about their identity, they respond with questions, blank looks, and a certain irritation at breaching the tacit agreement that "you don't ask that sort of thing; you don't talk about it, because silence protects us from the stigma of classification." When I insisted on the daring question, "Do you consider yourself a fairy (*joto*)? Gay?" Saúl (married, forty years old, engineer, and masculine in appearance, interviewed in his car outside a park in the city of Hermosillo) replied: "I never label myself. I do what I do, whether I do it with a woman or a man. You're the same person, pe-riod." Another interviewee, Noé (twenty-seven years old, married, in ad-ministrative work, goalie on a soccer team, masculine demeanor, inter-viewed in a park in Hermosillo at night), responded: "A fairy (*joto*)? No . . . I like women too . . . but I also like men" [smiles]. No, it's just kidding around (*el pedo es tranquilo*); it's just for fun (*cotorreo*). . . . Everybody does it, man [. . .] I do it because I like it; if I didn't, if it made me feel bad, I wouldn't do it. . . . There's no reason for anyone to know."

In these cases, the term *joto* is used in such a way that individuals are beyond the reach of its nominative power, and thus of the effects of its power over them. For example, only effeminate individuals are defined as *joto*, not masculine ones, even if the latter have homoerotic relations, which might or might not involve anal penetration. But also the terms *man* or *mayate* (trade) can be resignified in such a way that individuals can use them to describe themselves or homoerotic practices that, strictly speaking, subvert the dominant ideology. Let us return to Saúl's narrative:

> My friend's friend was my friend too. We used to fool around at parties and work meetings. I was going home the next day and so they had thrown a party for me. I'd had a few beers, maybe six or so. The guy is about my age, he must be roughly thirty-five. He says to me: "So you're leaving . . . , and so is the hottest ass in Guaymas." I answered him back: "And the longest prick too." "I'd have to see it to believe it," he replied;

jokingly, of course, just fooling around, like buddies, but I sensed something. At other times, I had sensed something as well, but that was it. The guy was married like me, and *desmadroso* (not a troublemaker). After the party was over I drove everyone back home. I deliberately went a certain way so that I could drop him off last. He was sitting up front, next to the driver's seat. Then he said: "So, you're leaving then . . . I'm going to miss you."

Up till then nothing was clear, it was just word play, but there was something underneath it all. We were getting close to his home and I said, "What now? Shall I drop you off or carry on?" I was looking sideways at him and driving at the same time. "Oh, you fuckin' shit . . . go on then," he said. I headed outside the city and pulled over on the side of the highway, but he said: "Not here, they might see us; carry on, I'll tell you where."

We got there, got out of the car, and not a fucking thing, neither of us did anything. "Screw this," I thought. "I'm leaving tomorrow." I took off my shirt and unzipped my fly. "Hey asshole, I didn't know that about you," he said. "Know what, asshole?" I said. "Either say yes or no, but don't make me feel bad." So then the guy takes off his shirt, pants, hat, and boots. When I saw that, I did the same. We stood face to face and neither of us made a move. . . . The guy had had quite a bit to drink too. "Screw this," I said. I grabbed the back of his neck and we kissed. We both penetrated each other, but not too far because we couldn't do it . . . but we did feel each other up (*cachoreamos*) a good while. The next day I left Guaymas. (Núñez 1994, 217–18)

This ambiguity and negotiation of erotic identities in the terrain of homoerotic experiences is used to manage desire and sexual pleasure with persons of the same sex. Javier, one of the interviewees previously quoted, put it this way:

No way, man, trade [*mayates*] don't exist, those guys who pretend to be macho . . . we all know that's just a way for them to do something they like and get away with it without being called anything; that's why they pose as *mayates*.

Actually "trade" does exist, but in an ambiguous and contested way. The resignification of the concept man can exploit the term's intrinsic ambiguities and contradictions in order to include homoerotic practices, that can even be seen as "very masculine." This kind of resignification can be seen in the following conversation with Francisco, resident of a town in the mountains of Sonora (forty-five years old, married with children, masculine looking, an extrovert whose work history includes being a cowboy, mining, and construction work. The interview took place at his home in a town in the mountains of Sonora in the afternoon). Francisco has a history of homoerotic relationships.

When I asked whether he considered himself homosexual or a fairy, he immediately rejected the terms and stated firmly, "Absolutely not, because I'm married, I like women, and as you can see, I don't act like a fairy." I repeated my question. "So, what do you consider yourself to be?" He looked blank and said, "I don't understand you." I explained that some people use certain categories such heterosexual, bisexual, and homosexual to classify people's sexual behavior. He had never heard of the words *heterosexual* and *bisexual*. After explaining them to him, I asked whether he thought one of them "made sense" in his life. He paused, smiled, and said, "Maybe I'm. . . . What did you call it? . . . Bisexual?" I smiled too, because strictly speaking it was true. Then he said in a serious, firm, and forthright tone, "Listen, Guillermo, I'm a man, very much a man." "How do you mean?" I asked. "What does being a man mean to you?"

After a silence, Francisco explained: "Listen, for example, like I said, I'm a real man, a real man, Guillermo. I know how to be a good friend. We could have a great time together, no problem, but if you invited me to do something, doesn't matter what. . . , and I felt like doing it, I'd go along with it. . . . No kidding, I'm not scared of anything, I'd stick with you to the death, I wouldn't rat on you . . . , but whatever we did together stays strictly between you and me. If you go blabbing about it, I'll kill you."

"No matter what the proposition is? Even sex?" I asked, intuiting his intention.

Franciso smiled again and said: "You know, one time I was out with a guy, having a few drinks near the river, and got to talking about being open-minded, broad-minded, about respect and loyalty to friends. Gradually we opened up and eventually he made this indirect hint about having a bit of fun. Then I told him what I just told you: I'm a real man, a real man, and if we do anything, don't forget I'm trusting you. It's got to stay between the two of us, OK? Cause if you go telling anyone, I'll kill you. I said several times, 'I'm a real man,' and the guy, well, by that point he was my buddy, goes, 'Hey . . . I'm a real man too, bud, and I like having friends like you.' And then we went ahead and did it" [he says smiling, indicating that they had had sexual relations].

The characterization of homoerotic experiences in Mexico by means of the dichotomy man–fairy (or trade–faggot) effectively overlooks the complex processes of negotiation, accommodation, resistance, and subversion that individuals undertake in order to account for their homoerotic practices and their meaning in their lives. What is overlooked in this dichotomized DMUH remains absent from the symbolic order. This absence has important political and ideological consequences that uphold patriarchal technologies of power, because on the one hand it silences the fact that there is a real struggle for the power to represent social reality in the field of sexuality and gender relations; and on the other hand, it silences the cultural and political nature of the definition and assignation of identities.

From the point of view of academic politics, it is problematic that anthropological studies should reproduce rather than question the categories of hegemonic discourse, thereby becoming complicit with patriarchy. The theory that erotic relations among men involve a hidden power–pleasure dynamic contains various flaws. First, it is based on inadequate, dichotomous characterizations of existent homoerotic experiences. Thereby, it overlooks innumerable relationships that are based on egalitarianism and generosity, relationships from which individuals derive experiences not of domination or humiliation but rather of pleasure, affection, self-esteem, happiness, camaraderie—experiences that in my opinion function as emotional empowerment and a source of personal growth. As we saw in the narratives included earlier, homoerotic encounters tend to be preceded by conversations, emotional closeness, and revelations about each other's (often dissimilar) lives, confessions that involve a degree of trust and a certain level of emotional intimacy in each partner, but above all complicity about the pleasure and desire that both of them are pursuing.

Second, it ignores the fact that power is not unequivocally derived from a predetermined position in the social order, but is a social relationship constructed by individuals by means of a complex interaction involving desires, meanings, material, and social resources, and so on. There are many elements in individual relationships that could give rise to domination, as well as to generosity. But power circulates in an ambiguous and contradictory way, just like pleasure, and it is inadequate to see the power–pleasure dichotomy as stratified by erotic and gender roles.

Last, even in the case of dichotomies such as penetrator–penetrated, active–passive, man–fairy, individuals tend to interpret power relations in a completely different way than the symbolic order. Passive individuals usually derive a sense of power that does not coincide with the phallocentric vision of power. Their reading is not that of the symbolic order, "I was acted on by the phallus," but a very different one: "I managed by dint of my persistence, my attractiveness, my powers of seduction, my capacity for persuasion, my 'powers,' to get the other man to confess his homoerotic desire for me by means of something very visible: his erection or ejaculation."

It is not coincidental that some individuals who are seen as fairy or passive from the dominant viewpoint describe their sexual activity using a verb that expresses their power: "I picked him up" (*echárselo*). Picking someone up involves making that person participate in your desire, extracting a confession from him about his homoerotic propensities, despite the assumed disinterest demanded by patriarchal ideologies of masculinity. Of course, the active individual could read things in a different, phallocentric way, assuming that he was the one who humiliated or dominated the other by erotic action, but it is worth asking why we should only take the active partner's reading into account.

The characterization of homoerotic relations as relations of power–pleasure in the DMUH has various important ideological implications that should be pointed out. In the first place, it represents the fag as an object of masculine power, whose position derives from his desire for anal penetration, and whose oppression is merely the consequence of his desire, because homoerotic desire is defined as an essentially masochistic desire, a desire for abjection. Regardless of whether masochistic desire is legitimate or whether it exists in homoerotic or other relationships, this representation reproduces a stigmatizing vision of homoerotic desire as unhealthy or sick, a move that in turn allows the individual stigmatized as a fairy to be held responsible for his oppression. Thus it is implied that his subordinate position in society derives from his body and his bodily desires and not from an arbitrary system of social distinction.

The interpretation of this desire is based on another ideological premise of patriarchy that is reproduced without question—namely, that the exercise of penetration by the penis expresses a position of power and a relation of domination. This assumption is usually backed up by references to sexual conceptions of power that exist in Mexican culture, as seen in the semantic studies of the verb *chingar* (to fuck). However, it is important to mention that the fact that dominant ideologies conceptualize power through metaphors of sexual penetration does not mean that all sexual relations are therefore necessarily power relations. The penis is indeed seen in certain dominant discourses as a power symbol, the supreme sign of gender difference, but that does not mean it is an instrument of power in and of itself. In other words, the penis is not the phallus. The link between them is more complex and has to do with the process by which an individual with a penis is socially constructed as possessing or claiming to possess the cultural signs of masculine power. The central drama of masculine identity arises precisely from the disparity between the corporeal and the social symbolic, between having a penis and having the phallus. The condition of masculinity is unstable, fragmented, contradictory, and ambiguous; yet society demands (and the individual wishes) that it be unified, consistent, and homogeneous.

The fact that the penis participates in a relation of power does not stem from its condition of being a penis and penetrating, but from its condition as part of the body of an individual with a masculine identity who makes sexuality an exercise of power, and who has a phallic, patriarchal vision of sexuality. But the penis can belong to bodies with gender identities that are capable of engaging in erotic relations of autogratification and generous gratification of other people.

This confusion of the penis with the phallus seen in concepts of homoerotic experience colludes with patriarchal ideologies that naturalize masculine power as deriving from the body. It also silences configurations of sexuality that reveal other nonoppressive visions of erotic relations and of power—ways of being a man and of living one's sexuality that resist or subvert the logic of phallic patriarchal power.

Nominative Forms and Sexual Diversity

I believe that the studies of native (including Mexican) homoerotic experiences, which have emerged in recent years to form a geographic encyclopedia of perversions, all suffer from a serious flaw: they privilege the "nominative form," the comprehensive model of the dominant discourse, and treat it as the one and only form of homoerotic relations in a given culture. The "nominative homoerotic form" is the predominant explanation given to "curious foreigners" who ask about relationships between people of the same sex (Murray 1997), but it completely fails to encompass the diversity of practices, meanings, and subject (or body) positions in which homoerotic experiences take place. This generalization of the nominative form is inappropriate, in my view, for several reasons: first, because it confuses social prescriptions with complex reality; second, because it accepts the dominant discourse without question and ignores the power games it constructs; and third, because by accepting the dominant discourse it draws a veil of normalcy that obscures the true nature of patriarchy as fractured, contradictory, and unstable.

I think this problem has to do with the concept of culture used by those authors in their theoretical approaches. Their studies, realized during the 1970s and 1980s, assumed a prescriptive and normative definition of culture. Thus, the study of sexual culture and sexual relationships between men was in fact the study of sexual scripts: the socially established and sanctioned sexual norms or the social conventions on sexuality. Gilbert Herdt, for example, defines sexual culture as a consensual model of cultural ideals about sexual behavior in a group (Herdt 1997, 17). This definition of culture does not allow registering the complex discursive relations of power and resistance in the sexual/gender social field, and on the contrary tends to privilege the norms and cultural ideals set out by dominant sexual discourse (Bourdieu 1988; Núñez 1994).

If we simply reproduce the dominant discourse on homoerotic experience in a culture, we fail to acknowledge the other homoerotic experiences present.[17] For the simple but profound reason that although the hegemonic discourse is onto formative (it tends to construct reality), the relationship between hegemonic and nonhegemonic elements is more ambiguous than we assume. As the popular saying goes, *del dicho al hecho hay mucho trecho* (there's a big gap between words and deeds), especially when what lies in that gap are bodies and nerve endings, unconscious desires, visual stimuli, unstable identities, and analytic, creative individuals capable of exploring, transgressing, and exploiting the contradictions of the dominant discourse.

I firmly believe that anthropologists of homoerotic experience must make the categories of the DMUH their object of study; it is important to attempt to understand anthropology's contribution to homophobic patriarchal technologies and its impact on the organization of intimate erotic encounters. Anthropologists today should also broaden the investigative horizon to acknowledge the diversity of pleasures, bodily encounters, organizational criteria of homoerotic practices, ways of constructing and deconstructing identities, personal meanings, and relations of pleasure and power. My critique of the DMUH, together with my ethnographic research and my discussion of different theoretical and conceptual models, shows that the multiple variants of homoerotic experience that fall outside the dominant model offer many lessons on men and on the following: (1) the various ways of positioning oneself in the field of gender and sexuality and of relating to hegemonic discourses on them; (2) the fragmentary, inconsistent, unstable, ambiguous, and heterogeneous nature of masculine subjectivities; (3) the processes of imposition, resistance, accommodation, and subversion that men undertake in the construction of their gender identities; (4) the importance of the body and its sensations—not only its meanings—in the processes of subject and identity construction; and (5) the importance of desire and pleasure for understanding masculine identities. It also allows us to see the field of homoerotic relations as a space in which patriarchal ideologemes of sex and gender are constantly being challenged; a space of human encounter that is open to the experience of bodily sensations, emotional intimacies, relations between different subject positions, desires and pleasures that promote the unlearning of dominant conventions of masculinity, and the formation of new ways of being a man.

Epilogue

History and a Photograph

When I first saw the picture of José Pedro and Francisco lightly holding hands, I felt I was in the presence of an intimate relationship between men that somehow continues to exist nowadays. This was something I intuited from my own personal and previous ethnographic experience with some people in the Serrano villages and in Hermosillo. Through this research, even if I had never known about any sexual encounter between José Pedro and Francisco, or any other couple of friends of the same period, I came to know that they had a privileged emotional and body intimacy that is not completely absent from the present. Nowadays in the Serrano villages of northern Mexico, and in urban Mexican areas such as Hermosillo, many men engage in intimate relationships with other men that take the cultural form of masculine comradeship or friendship, outside or resisting any stigmatized or vindicated identity category like those described as fairy, homosexual, or gay as well as the traditional, dominant conception of manhood. Certainly, young men in the present do not have the cultural license to have a graphic representation of themselves holding hands as a symbol of that intimacy, as José Pedro and Francisco had (although in some Serrano villages they can still dance, urinate, or sleep together). It is clear that to some extent a cultural transformation has taken place in the sex/gender regime over the last seventy years.

Although it was never my purpose in the present book to analyze the accuracy or intricacies of these historical transformations, we are aware of certain facts. First of all, we know that starting in the 1940s and 1950s the modern medical discourse on homosexuality has circulated among specialists in the cities, and later on, in the 1960s and 1970s, in popular culture directed to adults, through films, newspapers, and magazines. Since the 1980s and 1990s, the subject of homosexuality has been widely represented as a social and medical problem in Sonoran newspapers. In the late 1980s, 1990s, and nowadays, homosexuality has been much more openly discussed on TV talk shows, soap operas, reality shows, and educational programs. These discussions take the form of a liberal discourse under the rubrics of tolerance, acceptation, respect, diversity, and to a lesser degree sexual rights; or they sometimes emerge in the news through the debates over discrimination against homosexuals, homophobic violence, and same-sex marriage (Núñez 2000).

Second, after the Mexican Revolution, an important transformation of the heterosexual couple seemed to occur through the increasing circulation of the romantic ideal as the basis for marriage (and not only economic production, division of work, and reproduction). Domestic unity became transformed in the 1940s and 1950s in an increasingly industrialized and market economy, from a productive unit into a consumption unit. In the 1950s women reached political equality, and in the 1960s and 1970s they entered into higher education and paid employment in increasing numbers (Núñez 2013a). These changes put new pressures on men and their configurations of masculine identity, which became less and less dependent on exclusive labor realms, exclusive access to market economy, higher education, or political participation. At the same time, the women's movement began to change women's sexuality, making of pleasure and love a fair demand in heterosexual relations.

Following Katz's (1995, 2001) and Chauncey's (1994) arguments, I believe that in Mexico, the increasing diffusion of a new heterosexual ideal based on love and the sharing of emotions, and the increasing visibility of a public and stable homosexual or gay identity as a category to designate a sexual orientation (a slowly similar process that has also begun with heterosexual identity) that surpasses the traditional effeminate stereotype to include masculine looks, have brought about an increasing censorship or suspicion of homosexuality regarding intimate relations among men. In as much as masculinity in behavior or exclusivity in economic or social realms is not any more a solid base for masculine identity or being a "normal man" itself, heterosexual exclusivity tends to become a privilege element in the construction of normal manhood. Body contacts among men have particularly suffered from this new suspicion of homosexuality. As

romantic love became integrated into the heterosexual couple, men posing holding hands for a picture became a suspicious act containing a sexual interest, and became one of the first affective expressions to be cen-
sored among them. In recent years we have witnessed other regular forms
of body contacts in rural communities among men, like men sharing the
same horse, being taunted through jokes invoking the phantom of
homosexuality.

Nevertheless, upon concluding this research and the analysis I present
here, I am more convinced than ever of the persistence, although somehow changed, of earlier cultural forms, meanings, and values of intimacy
in many homoerotic relations among men, especially among lower classes
or rural origins. I must accept that this conviction is far from being scien-
tifically documented. This is not a historical research, but an anthropological one; and in this context, Sedgwick's commentary on the reap-
pearance of earlier categories and meanings of homosexuality and its
coexistence in the present with modern ones (1992) could not be more
adequate to frame and back up these feelings and intuitions. One thing is
clear: there is need for further investigation regarding the transformation
of these categories, meanings and subjectivities in relation to a larger sex/
gender system, and in the context of economic, social, and political
changes too. Some works, like those mentioned here by Chauncey (1994)
and Katz (2001) for the United States, are great examples of what could be
done. That kind of research project would certainly be the first historical
research of its genre in Mexico and Latin America. I hope to have contributed through this ethnography some insights and intuitions to stimulate
this type of historical research.

At the same time, I think that this ethnographic account of male intimacy in Serrano villages and in Hermosillo, may help anthropologists to
better understand or to raise questions on the historical account of past
forms, relations, and subjectivities. These include the trades, fairies, and
wolves described by Chauncey (1994), the love stories of friends and comrades described by Katz (2001), the studies on "erotic male friendship"
among cowboys by Packard (2005), and present forms existing in many
other societies and continents (see, for example, Murray and Roscoe
1998).

I hope to have contributed, through this research, to a better understanding of the sexual and gender values, meanings, subjectivities, and
practices (and their social contexts) of soldiers, peasants, cowboys, and
construction or manufacturer workers engaged in homoerotic relations in
varied ways (sometimes with intellectuals or artists, sometimes among

themselves), and that in the best of cases have been peripheral to literary or anthropological accounts of homosexuality. At the same time, I hope I have been able to prove through these cases, that the category of homosexual subjectivity is not adequate enough to understand all subjects engaged in homoerotic experiences. Their subjectification and resubjectification processes follow different paths, and for most of them, the same modern conception of sexual orientation or sexuality is not the major framework to understand their desires and erotic practices.

The Heterogeneous Homoerotic Present

The homoerotic present that I research in this work is a complex and heterogeneous reality with different meanings, identities, and ways of creating relations and integrating them into people's life. This heterogeneity that I have argued and substantiated cannot be contained in the single narrative of homosexual subjectivity or adequately accounted for by the narrative of a "double sexual system" of some anthropological accounts, and somehow reproduced by Latin American epidemiology and activists: the modern (of North European and American origins) gay system and the traditional (of Mediterranean origins) *joto–mayate* system. I tried to demonstrate here that these systems are in themselves far away from being completely reproduced in people's lives. On the one hand, the gay category and its meanings get appropriated and resignified by people under their own sexual traditions and understandings; on the other hand, partners tend to transgress and subvert constantly the supposed gender, sexual, and power binaries of the trade–fairy (*mayate–joto*) system, and with them, their patriarchal ideological assumptions about homoerotic experience in Mexico. Furthermore, I have also tried to demonstrate that there is a reality of homoerotic experience that resists, by resignifying, dominant conceptions of manhood and masculinity, as well as dominant conceptions of the homoerotic as always involving a homosexual, gay, fairy (*joto*), or trade (*mayate*) identity. It is a reality that has not achieved the same level of representation in historical, literary, or anthropological analysis. It is a reality that exists in the margins of representation not only of heterosexist discourses but also of major gay intellectuals and artists who have dared to write differently from homophobic discourses, about the homoerotic experience. Present homosexual liberation movements and gay culture, along with the widespread notion of gay or homosexual identity in big and midsize cities, seem to be adding to the oblivion or invisibility of this reality. Nevertheless, it is interesting to note, that in the experience of some people there is a kind of perception of this homoerotic reality, but it is very difficult to name and understand it, as some activists have confessed to me. Eribon, a contributor to a single homosexual narrative, seems to hint at this when he says in a footnote (in itself symptomatic of its uneasy character in the main text):

> To speak of "modern homosexuality," by which one understands "as we know it today," poses its own sets of problems, especially to the extent that it allows one to assume there to be some unique, unitary form of homosexuality and that we could take account of it by simply looking around us. But this would leave out, of course, all the forms that we do not "know," that we do not see, all the forms that do not fit within the "homosexual/heterosexual" duality. (Eribon 2004, 377)

To my understanding, what does not fit within that duality is precisely what does not even enter into modern common conception of sexuality and still lives in the present, not only in the homoerotic reality of "modern underdeveloped countries" but also in those very "modern Western countries," as Zeeland has tried to prove for the United States (1993, 1995).

The acknowledgment of a heterogeneous homoerotic reality, on the other hand, does not proceed without problems of its own. The notion of the heterogeneity of homoerotic experiences, subjectivities, categories, and meanings, strategically framed here under the concept of male intimacy, I argue, should not be understood as a social or political "equivalence" of all forms, meanings, subjectivities, and categories in the context of the sex/gender system or the social field; or just an "unstable and conflict cohabitation of ways of life, images, discourses that have no stability and no coherence either individually or among themselves" (Eribon 2004, 233).

Identity categories in the homoerotic field are more than labels to call "essentially the same acts and people." Instead, they express different sociohistorical trajectories of sexual discourses on the homoerotic experience; different positions in the social field along class, ethnic, and gender lines; and different personal and social histories of subjectification and resubjectification. Most important, they guard among themselves a different position in terms of their visibility, social recognition, ability to interpellate political forces, representation of their reality and interests, a different vulnerability vis-à-vis the heterosexist and homophobic technologies of power, and even a different vulnerability toward HIV/AIDS. (I have written extensively about this latter point in my book on indigenous men and homoerotic relations in Mexico and the multiple levels of vulnerability implicit, by class, ethnicity, sex/gender, and migration, to the epidemic. [See Núñez 2009]). Certainly, the coexistence of these differences and similarities is complex but still they create different regularities of meanings, ways of life, images, subjectivities, and experiences.

Although I frankly recognize that this research is far from providing a full historical and anthropological description account of this heterogeneous homoerotic reality (this was not my goal to begin with), I want to call readers' attention to what I would call a "homoerotic social formation" made up of many different discourses, subjectivities, categories, and ways of living linked in very complex way. This involves modern sexual categories such as homosexuality or gay as well. The meanings of these terms are far from being transparent; they have a history and a sociopolitical existence in every society, and that should be accounted for anthropologically, instead of presuming it from academic analysis of European literature. Behind these categories, there is a complex colonial, imperial, asymmetric or unequal economic, political, and cultural history. I think they should be analyzed in the complexities of their introduction, appropriations, re-elaborations, and cultural and political effects. Acknowledging the vast social and historical array of meaning and practices around male intimacy in different cultures and regions is just one step, but a necessary one.

Notes

Introduction

1. My English version from the original in French : "S'il y a une chose qui m'inté-
resse aujourd'hui, c'est le problème de l'amitié. Au cours des siècles qui ont suivi l'An-
tiquité, l'amitié a constitué un rapport social très important : un rapport social à l'inté-
rieur duquel les individus disposaient d'une certaine liberté . . . qui leur permettai
aussi de vivre des rapports affectifs très intenses. . . . Et l'une de mes hypothèses . . .
est que l'homosexualité (par quoi j'entends l'existence de rapports sexuels entre les
hommes) est devenue un problème à partir du XVIIIe siècle.. . .Tant que l'amitié a
représenté quelque chose d'important, tant qu'elle a été socialement acceptée, per-
sonne ne s'est aperçu que les hommes avaient, entre eux, des rapports sexuels. . . .
Qu'ils fassent l'amour ou qu'ils s'embrassent n'avait aucune importance . . . la dispari-
tion de l'amitié en tant que rapport social et le fait que l'homosexualité ait été déclarée
problème social, politique et médical font partie du même processus."
2. This image is identical in the posture to the one of Francisco and José Pedro.
Unfortunately, Don José died before I could ask for a copy and his family lost the photograph. The picture we present is of two men, friends, of the same time and from the
same Serrano region. I thank the family, Bojórquez López, for giving me permission to
use the picture in this book.
3. The term *gay* and others such as *joto* or *mayate* are going to be analyzed extensively in this text because they are involved in a politics of meaning in the Mexican
sexual/gender field. The term *gay* is used in this case and throughout this work to name
people who call themselves by this category, mostly those who are urban, middle class,
and young. In the last decade, however, this category of identity has been spreading
rapidly even in lower classes and rural settings.
4. In the dominant sexual discourse, *joto* is the most common Mexican term to call
a passive and effeminate partner in a homosexual encounter. In the same discourse,
the active and masculine partner is called *mayate*. The political character of this

discourse is widely analyzed in the chapters that follow. The English terms *fairy* and *trade*, as described by Chauncey in his study on homoerotic relations in New York City in the first decades of the twentieth century (1994), seem to better fit the Spanish terms.

5. The public expression of affection among friends in Mexico is by far more common and deeper than in the United States. Nevertheless, holding hands between men or between a man and a woman is seen as an expression of being in love. Nowadays, this is very common among young gay couples in Mexico City and in certain areas of urban centers such as Guadalajara or Morelia. Only in select indigenous communities did men used to hold hands as an expression of friendship. Contrary to the practice of men, everywhere in Mexico women usually express their friendship by holding hands.

6. I am assuming here Foucault's theoretical definitions on power and freedom. Power is a social relation that works to structure the possibility of action. Freedom involves, therefore, the possibility for choice. Power is only possible when choice is possible in human action. If human actions were the product of "natural necessity" or "instincts," it would be unnecessary to talk about power or freedom.

7. The term *sex/gender regime* is understood as a system—that is, a structure of relations—of social distinctions and power that has two major characteristics: it is androcentrist and heterosexist. The sex/gender regime produces different effects on people's bodies, desires, subjectivities, and relations. The term *patriarchy* is sometimes used here and by certain authors as a synonym, even though we know that it originally referred to a particular configuration of the sex/gender system—in which the father exerted the economic, political, and symbolic power over an extended agro-pastoral family (see Lamas 1996).

8. Chapter 5 fully explores this dichotomous characterization of Mexican homoerotic experience.

9. An enunciation is, according to Foucault, the smallest unit of discourse containing an object of discourse. An interviewee's expression "One has to be a real man and to have *muchos güevos* [big testicles] to do it" is an example of what I am trying to say.

10. The Spanish version from which I paraphrase into English reads: "¿Cómo se formó un tipo de gobierno de los hombres en el que no se exige simplemente obedecer, sino manifestar, comunicándolo, eso que uno es?" and it has been taken from *Michel Foucault. Tecnologías del yo y otros textos afines. Introducción de Miguel Morey* (1990). This quotation comes from archival documents existing in the *Centre Michel Foucault* and that are quoted by Miguel Morey.

11. In Freudian theory, polymorphous means that Eros may assume different objects of desire; perverse means that those objects of desire are mobilized for pleasure.

12. These are my translations from French.

13. In this regard I follow the path of the American anthropologist Mathew Gutmann, who did extensive research on machismo in a working-class neighborhood in Mexico City in the late 1990s (Gutmann 1996). In this book, I try to approach the concept hombre Mexicano from poststructural feminism and queer theory.

14. As a social organizer, I was a founder of the first formal lesbian and bisexual groups in Hermosillo and Sonora, Albures (Association of Lesbian and Bisexual Women United for Social Equality) in 2002. I facilitated the first workshops and supported the capacitation of its leadership too. The groups have taken part in the last two

out of three Marches for Sexual and Love Diversity organized since 2001. For the lesbian experience in Mexico, see Mogrovejo (2000) and Alfarache (2003).

Chapter 1

1. The term *vaquetón* defines a particular way of being a man and having a charismatic masculinity—one that involves a certain flexibility and transgression of the strictest Catholic morality. I analyze this term later in this chapter.

2. The meaning of this verb and its relation to masculine identity and men's intimacy is widely analyzed in chapter 3.

3. The adjective *serio* can be translated as "serious," but in as much as it refers to a regulation of speech with a gender context ("women speak unnecessarily or too much"), it connotes a whole range of values such as sincerity, truthfulness, capacity to keep one's word (see Núñez 2007b and 2013a). This dynamic is further explored in chapter 3.

4. This Opata word is almost never used in contemporary Sonora, except for old people.

5. If we understand power in the sense in which Michel Foucault discusses it—that is, as the structuration of the possibilities for action—then we can also understand transformations in the meaning of specific actions and the consequences for social action that follow from those meanings, as transformations per se in the relations of power that the sex/gender system holds over men in general in our society.

6. It is interesting to note that in today's society there are other gestures for expressing affection among men, such as putting one's arm across the other man's shoulders, that do not call into question the men's virility or manliness.

7. "Knowing about life" and "being worldly" are male experiences that are constructed from the time men are boys, through privileged and gendered opportunities for mobility in and around town and its outskirts. Some of these privileges exist in connection to male responsibilities as well as in the chores expected of boys—gathering firewood or fetching water. The woods (*monte*) are considered dangerous, not a fitting place for women. On the other hand, this knowledge of the world that boys acquire is plagued with religious connotations, insofar as the world is the site of sin in Catholic ideology. To be a man is to have a familiarity with worldly things that women—always pure and naïve—clearly lack. On this subject see Núñez 2013a.

8. Small groups or pairs of buddies are the quintessential sexual socialization space among male adolescents, particularly in rural areas. The diverse sexual practices engaged in by these groups have been known to include masturbation and sex with farm animals such as a young female ass or jenny, a female bull calf, chickens, turkeys, or female goats. Many urban people react negatively or are repulsed when they hear about such sexual practices. Although I will not pursue an analysis of these practices in this book, it is important to note that there are multiple references in the Western ethnographic record of such practices in different parts of the world. Bronfman and Minello found these sexual practices with animals and among children (between eight and twelve years old) in their study of the sexuality of rural Mexican immigrants to the United States (1995, 39). An anthropological study about sexual practices with animals in a rural setting in contemporary Greece also remarks pointedly on various homoerotic

exchanges among adolescents in that same country (Anest 1994). It is quite possible that the appearance of these teenage ritual practices in the sierra communities of northern Mexico may owe something to Mediterranean influences in the area, but this is not clear. For more on this subject see Núñez 2013a.

9. For a review of the concept and a study about its application in religious communities in North America, see Quinn (1996). The author introduces some additional interesting concepts, such as homo-emotional and homo-tactile. I define homosociality as the sociability among people of the same sex or the same gender. This sociability is the product of sexual and gender segregation through institutions and subjectivities.

10. A deeper account on the gender and sexual system and its transformation along three generations of men can be found in my book *Hombres Sonorenses: Un estudio de género de tres generaciones* (Núñez 2013a).

11. This invitation was not equivalent to the euphemism commonly used in the United States about "sleeping with" somebody to signify sexual activity. In fact, my point here is precisely to demonstrate how different the social constructions of intimacy and homosexuality are.

12. We have translated *joto* as "fairy" after Chauncey's study *Gay New York*. According to Chauncey, fairies were defined not by reason of "their same-sex desires or activities (their 'sexuality'), but rather the gender persona and status they assumed. . . . The fairies' sexual desire for men was not regarded as the singular characteristic that distinguished them from other men, as is generally the case for gay men today. That desire was seen as simply one aspect of a much more comprehensive gender role inversion (or reversal)" (1994, 47–48). *Mayate* was defined as "trade." According to Chauncey, the term "referred to any 'straight' man who responded to a gay man's advances" (1994, 70).

13. I found the use of the Yaqui word *seeve* in my research on sexuality and gender among Yaqui people of Sonora. The word *seeve* is used to refer to men "who like" other men and means cool. The temperature metaphor is applied to men (who are supposed to be hot) and to women (who are supposed to be cold), and is linked to a cosmogony: the sun and the moon. It is my hypothesis that the word *fresco* among Serrano people comes from the Opatas who inhabited this region and are the source of their *mestizaje*. Opatas were a Taracahita indigenous group, linked culturally and linguistically to other cahita people like Yaqui (Yoeme) and Mayos (Yoreme) of southern Sonora (see Núñez 2013b).

Chapter 2

1. The word *queer* has a translation into Spanish: "rarito" with similar connotations. The term *queer* has a long history in the English language, and according to Chauncey (1994), it was used in New York in relation to sexuality in the first decades of the twentieth century. According to Jagose, queer theory refers to those analytical models that dramatize the incoherence between sex, gender, and sexual desire and question the assumed patriarchal idea that gender derives naturally from biological sex and therefore predicts heterosexuality (Jagose 1996). In this chapter I explore the term "Mexican man" from this theoretical perspective and by using ethnographic data. My

aim is to show how people negotiate the meanings of manhood and masculinity in such a way that homoerotic practices can be made part of the masculine identity of many men.

2. The idea of a "sexual and gender field," using Bourdieu's social theory is mine, and was first used in my book *Sexo entre varones: Poder y resistencia en el campo sexual* (1994) to understand the sexual and gender field of Hermosillo and Sonora.

3. This peculiar double character of the values and qualities deemed masculine has been remarked upon in the ethnographic literature in relation to those cultures considered of Mediterranean origin. Peristiany, Pio Broja, and Bourdieu, among others, make reference to this duality to describe men in Greece, Spain, and Algeria. See the seminal work by Peristiany, *El concepto del honor en la sociedad mediterránea* (1968). Alonso (1995), in a related argument, reflects about the differences between natural and social dimensions of masculinity among the men of Namiquipa, Chihuahua.

Chapter 3

1. The word *ambiente* is hard to translate. It refers to a space frequented by men (and sometimes women) where there is a very important presence of men who like men. These men can call themselves gay, homosexual, bisexual, *jotos*, or just men who like or allow themselves a *cotorreo*; that is, to have fun (sexual fun). The term *ambiente* expresses the complex links between homosexual identities and practices in Mexico. See Núñez 2000, 193.

2. My first book, *Sexo entre varones: Poder y resistencia en el campo sexual*, can be seen as a research work on a particular kind of people with homosexual practices: those who come to identify themselves through a difficult process as homosexual or gay. In this later research, I expanded my field of vision through the category of male intimacy and its relationship to masculine identities. I consider, therefore, that affective and erotic practices can take place either within or outside gay identities.

3. I must confess that although I was very familiar with this song, and had even thought about the meanings of the word/concept *rajarse* for a course in linguistic anthropology with my mentor Dr. Jane Hill at The University of Arizona, all these implications for doing research with men had escaped me up to that moment.

4. I have many field notes about the instances of *rajarse*. I have decided to present the whole field note and not only the explicit sentence where it appears, because the whole note usually gives important ethnographic information about men's lives or society in general.

5. By referencial indexicality, Silverstein means the relationship of dependency, *de co-ocurrencia o existencia, implicada mutuamente entre signo y contexto* (Silverstein 1977, 146). Ochs means by direct indexicality: "a direct—that is, unmediated—relation between one or more linguistic forms and some contextual dimension. A particular particle in one language may be described as a direct index of the speaker's feeling" (Ochs 1990, 295).

6. Gilbert Herdt defines *idioms* as "characteristic expressions having particularities of cognitive and emotional meanings and style established in the ordinary interpersonal communications" (Herdt 1981, 14).

7. By "indirect indexicality," Ochs means the process by which "a feature of the communicative event is evoked indirectly through the indexing of some *other* feature of the communicative event. In these cases, the feature of the communicative event directly indexed is conventionally linked to and helps to constitute some second feature of the communicative context, such that the indexing of one evokes or indexes the other" (Ochs 1990, 295).

8. Irving, as did many other young men became familiar and adopted the word "gay," a novelty in their hometown by the late 1990s, when moving to Hermosillo. Nevertheless, the recent spreading of the word through media is making it possible for other people in rural communities to use it to refer to themselves or to others. I explore the use and meanings of this identity's categories in depth in the following chapters.

9. Irving's perception captures one of the points I want to make through this chapter: the diversity of the homosexual experience, not only in terms of the dichotomy "simply sexual act and love relationship" (as Foucault put it, and as Eribon repeats it to create its ontogenesis of the homosexual subjectivity)—a quite arbitrary dichotomy by the way, as I will show in later chapters—but also in terms of the way they are integrated to gender and sexual identities beyond the exclusiveness of the gay identity. But Irving raises another important issue: the different experiences of those taking part in the homosexual experience (*el hecho homosexual*), a diversity that put into a question any intention to make a homogeneous (and transhistorical and transcultural) narrative.

10. Up until this point in this chapter, I have limited discussion to the exemplified uses of *rajarse*. There are other uses and terms that refer to this fissure in a body, as when we say *rajas de chile*, especially green chile. The *rajas* of a green chile give the impression of a torn body. I thank Jane Hill for this commentary.

11. Pierre Bourdieu, in his famous study of Kabil society (see, for example, Bourdieu 1968) and in his later book *La Domination Masculine* (1998), refers to this sexual and sexist symbolic arrangement that structures society's cosmogony, too. Nevertheless, his references are in relation to men and women, without any mention of its implications for the politics of manhood and the politics of homophobia.

12. In his article "Le combat de la chasteté" (1982), as in other of his last works, Foucault insists on this relationship of subjectivity (as the product of a process of subjectification) as involving a relationship to oneself in the domain of sexuality and as well as an economy of acts.

13. Foucault describes the word *subjectification*: "le processus par lequel on obtient la constitution d'un sujet, plus exactement d'une subjectivité, qui n'est évidemment que l'une des possibilités données d'organisation d'une conscience de soi" (Foucault 2001, 1525).

14. Didier Eribon gives great importance to this notion in his book *Réflexions sur la question gay* (1999); his treatment of the subject matter brought my attention to this aspect of Foucault's theory.

15. I am connecting here, implicitly, the conception of silence as a poetic of manhood (as told by Herzfeld) and as an expression of an economy of desire (as set out by post-Lacanian psychoanalysis in Irigaray [1994] and McBride [1995]) with Judith Butler's reflections on the performative character of gender identity (1993).This is possible, because men's poetics, according to Herzfeld (1985), involve the performance of

an ideological project of masculinity. This ideological project as an ideal-ego takes part in the configuration of a psychic economy.

16. Drinking coffee, as shown by José Pedro, can play the same role.

Chapter 4

1. It is fair to say that things have been changing rapidly in the last ten years, since this interview was first conducted. In the decade of 2002–2012, gay identity and activism against discrimination made important inroads in Mexico, especially in Mexico City, with a strong impact on mass media. More and more gay characters (beyond stereotypes) and their acceptance on the part of parents (not only friends) are depicted in Mexican soap operas. The consequence has been a spread of the category and a certain familiarity with the term in many rural regions. It is not clear, however, the impact of this liberalization in the use of the category gay on the way people conceptualize and live homoerotic relations.

2. How might we talk about a person "in the closet" when the "homosexual experience" as affective and erotic intimacy is not always apprehended as a totalizing experience of a man's subjectivity or as the diacritic difference by which a man thinks himself homoerotic? Furthermore, how does one step "out of the closet" when the homosexual act is not always experienced from the position of stigma attributed to the term *joto*, *sodomite*, or even *homosexual*, but rather within the complex and disputed space of male identity, of being a man? Although sexual and genital experiences, and to a lesser extent also affective and corporeal experiences, may be kept secret, this secrecy does not necessarily translate into a secret about a truth of one's being or, in other words, into a "truth in itself lodged into one's sexuality." Even though the closet implies the notion of hiding something and of secrecy, not all secrets or hidden relationships involve the construction of a homosexual closet, as the term is commonly used. In order for that kind of secret to produce that kind of closet, the person must first be in a position to think of his or her life through the lens or the technology of the power-knowledge system that has constructed the subject position of a homosexual in the first instance, as Foucault has observed.

3. The egalitarian marriage law adopted in Mexico City on December 21, 2009, and the decision made by the Mexican Supreme Court in 2010 to make obligatory that all states recognize same-sex marriages realized in Mexico City, sent an important moral message to Mexican society in favor of equal rights and opened a path to normalization of homosexuality in daily life.

4. Borrillo suggests that behind this "linguistic disproportion lays an ideological activity that consists of naming in a number of ways that which seems problematic and sending to the realms of the implicit that which pretends to be natural or evident" (Borrillo 2000, 6).

5. This symbolic relationship between the self and the others is codified in the culture and language of Mexico through the expression "es de los otros" (he is one of the others). This expression is used to refer to one who is "not a man-man" but rather one *que se le hace agua la canoa, es puto, joto, maricón, choto, raro*; that is, "one who is considered as moving sensously, seeming faggish, effeminate, strange." This

expression was identified and used by Joseph Carrier in the title of his book *De los otros: Intimacy and Homosexuality Among Mexican Men* (1995), even though the author does not explore this symbolic order.

6. The topic of anxiety is central to psychoanalysis. Freud described it more as the unconscious, unfulfilled desire tied to an individual's primary anxiety: a fear of castration due to the unresolved Oedipus complex. It is the self's identification with the father that allows resolution of this fear. Lacan (1977) suggests that anxiety is lodged in the self through a sense of absence in the mirror stage. It is a sense of impotence. The desire is the desire of the other precisely because one expects a unity with the other, the image of completeness. Kardiner (1945), on the other hand, suggests that anxiety is a product of cultural activity in relationship to childhood activities, including threats, punishment, and so forth. This anxiety becomes a central element in the basic personality structure, which additionally contains a system of projection that includes social regulation. In this book, I have followed the reading of "group anxiety" elaborated in *Changing the Subject* (Henriques 1984), which posits that anxiety needs to be understood within the context of the social power relations in which it is lived. Furthermore, I argue that the management of anxiety continuously motivates the renegotiation of power relations. In other words, in dealing with anxiety, we are dealing with desire, cultural threat, loss of power, projection, and repression of desire, as well as renegotiation of power. See the article by Tony Jefferson (1994).

7. This reflection owes much to the theories of Kaja Silverman regarding the relationship between semiotics, subjectivity, and power expounded in the book *The Subject of Semiotics* (1983). Metonymy has been studied in its relationship to racism at its intersections with sexism in terms of cultural production, especially in literature. For an excellent essay that includes valuable theoretical sources relating to homoerotic experience and cultural production in Latin America, see Foster, *Cultural Production and Homoerotic Identities: Theory and Applications.*

8. Bibliographic references dealing with the construction of the other in its relationship with the construction of the modern self are abundant mainly because this process, I dare say, is one of the most important ones of our time. Some of the well-known authors dealing with this topic are Lacan (1977), Derrida (1976), Fanon (1965), Spivak (1988), Ferguson (1993), Irigaray (1994), Anzaldúa (1990), Butler (1990), Benhabib and Cornell (1987), and Said (1979).

9. The topics of gender, sexuality, and ethnicity in relationship to imagined communities such as the nation are briefly analyzed by Anderson (1983) and by anthropologists such as Alonso (1995). Yet they are profoundly elaborated on by so-called "third world feminists," among them Anzaldúa (1990), Mohanty (1984), Moraga (1983), and O'Malley (1986); and by scholars on masculinity such as Mosse (1996) and Bederman (1995). See also Mexican intellectuals such as Muñíz (2002) and Domínguez (2007).

10. On many other occasions during my fieldwork experiences, I was able to hear comments made by different men that mobilized the terms of stigma against them, thus suspending the negative charge of the term. For example, when I asked a man while we were watching a rodeo in Los Corazones whether he had ever participated as a rider, he answered me: "No way, I am too *bizcocho* [loosey goosey] for that." A friend of his challenged him: "Don't be a *culón*" (big ass), to which he answered laughing, "I am not *culón*; I am *very culón.*" The clear confession in an assured manner of what can

be understood as cowardice has the paradoxical effect of immobilizing its stigmatic connotations, and also its regulative effects of manliness.

Chapter 5

1. The term *sexual existence* is used differently here than the term *sexual identity*. The former allows us to see the subject's sexual life as being constantly defined and transformed. The term *sexual identity* establishes a narrative closure, constraining the subject's sexuality within certain parameters that essentialize and reify him or her. Sexual identity is a political fact (in a broader sense), the result of complex technologies of power operating on the subject's sexual existence. For a more detailed analysis, see Núñez 2000, 32.

2. Herdt explored in a later essay this possibility among the Sambia, as part of his study about the complex impact of the ritual of manhood in the organization of desire of Sambia men (Herdt, 1990).

3. I will limit myself here to the work of North American and European anthropologists who are widely known in academic circles around the world.

4. Annick Prier's study of transvestism and prostitution in Ciudad Nezahualcóyotl (1998) is an important exception.

5. I believe that what is needed is an ethnographic and historical study of the identity categories of homoerotic experience in Mexico—the uses and politics of meaning surrounding the terms *fairy, pansy, fag (joto, maricón, puto)*, and others; the appearance of the term *homosexual*, its popularization, the way it constructed new ways of representing homoerotic experiences, and its impact on the construction of new identities and life-styles; and the appearance and dissemination of discourses about gayness, especially from the 1980s on. The definition of heterosexuality is another topic that needs exploring. Heterosexuality as an identity does not exist in Mexico, or only, I would hazard, in a not very mainstream way. What does exist is the identity category "man," which signals a "naturalized" relationship with heterosexual desire and a more ambiguous one with regard to homoerotic experience. What is lacking is research that would allow us to recognize the diversity of positions of subjectivity and identity, as well as the contradictory and negotiated nature of their meanings.

6. Other anthropologists studying Latin American homoerotic experience whose work is relevant are Lancaster on Nicaragua (1992) and Parker (1991) on Brazil.

7. This criterion was first identified by Joseph Carrier (1972, 1976, 1985, 1995), although it was prefigured in Octavio Paz's famous work *El laberinto de la soledad* (1959), and in Ingham's study on culture and personality in a Mexican village (1968), cited by Carrier. Both authors based their conclusions on an analysis of colloquial speech: puns, insults, jokes, and wordplay. Carrier and subsequent authors such as Alonso and Koreck, Almaguer, and Prieur used these linguistic arguments to support their own studies. Carrier, however, attempts to go beyond the clichéd analysis of the meanings of the word *chingar* (to fuck) by referring to fieldwork data and data from several quantitative studies, which in my view do not support his conclusions but on the contrary demonstrate an ambiguity and fluidity for which the active–passive dichotomy cannot account.

8. On this point also, the difference between authors is merely one of emphasis and details. Carrier claims empirical proof of the correlation between passive–active and

femininity–masculinity. His work is questionable because of its biased selection of sources, but his actual data show such ambiguity and flexibility that it is surprising he failed to be aware of it.

9. In the case of Mexico, Alonso and Koreck (1993) and Prieur (1998) have stressed this aspect the most. Carrier holds that active–passive relationships (which supposedly coincide with the man–fairy dichotomy) are the product of lack of availability of women as sexual partners due to gender constraints (i.e., men have sex with fairies [*jotos*] because there are no women available). Alonso and Koreck, however, argue that fairies are also objects of masculine desire and suggest that penetration probably involves a particular intersection of power and pleasure for males, because emasculating another man becomes the supreme validation of masculinity. Lancaster also explores this "intimate aspect of power" (1992) for the case of Nicaragua and draws similar conclusions, which reinforce this view of the Mexican case.

10. It is worth mentioning that Carrier shows no convincing data to support these claims. Furthermore, I feel that it is extremely limiting for the study of gays (or homosexuals or fairies [*jotos*]) to focus on the existence or absence of anal penetration.

11. This dual characterization is particularly clear in Gilbert Herdt's work. For Herdt, Mexico is one of the "developing" countries, not only in economic but also in sexual terms, because it is changing from a traditional, unegalitarian model permeated by power dualities to another more modern, egalitarian, and nonhierarchical one.

12. Annick Prieur refers to this type of relationship (1998). I too have come across anecdotes of transvestites attesting to how frequent this behavior is.

13. Of course, we are still a long way from recognizing the diversity of homoerotic landscapes, as well as the meanings and identity processes in which they are inscribed. The ethnographic data currently available stress only certain groups: the urban, working-class transvestite sex worker studied by Prieur; the more or less effeminate, urban homosexual depicted by Carrier (who unlike Prieur does not delimit his subjects clearly and sometimes appears to suggest that they involve "men who seek out men"); and the "macho-joto" relations in a rural community in northern Mexico described by Alonso. For my part (Núñez 1994), I have studied homoerotic relations and the identity processes of those who come to identify themselves as homosexual or gay (although I insist that these definitely do not include all those who have homoerotic relationships).

14. *Bato* is a term used in northern Mexico and southwestern United States to mean "guy." The feminine counterpart would be *morra*. *Batote* means a big or impressive guy. The word seems to come from the Yaqui word *batoi*, which means "baptized" as a way to signal "being a person."

15. There is still a lot of work to be done on these assumptions governing the use of the body and the territorialization of desire in the body. I believe that they are assumptions rather than clear prescriptions and that they derive from discourses of masculinity and manliness: admonitions against blabbing; the "rear" as feminine; orifices as feminine; the masculine body as something closed and hard; manliness as control of emotions and desires; femininity as lack of control; the penis as a symbol of virility, and the like.

16. This trilogy of prestige (Núñez 2000, 57) functions, Judith Butler says, as a "cultural matrix" in which gender identities have become unintelligible, but at the

same time it means that other identities "do not exist" or "cannot be thought" (Butler 1990).

17. I feel that Prieur's work for the most part avoids merely reproducing the dominant discourse, and explores in some detail the game of significations in which the partners participate. However, Prieur studies a fairly unrepresentative homoerotic group (1988): one that has little formal education and is socially marginalized and self-destructive. Even homoerotic characterizations of these individuals tend to emphasize the dichotomies of the dominant discourse on what it means to be a fairy (*joto*). I believe this characteristic of her research population causes Prieur to fall back into aspects of what we have called the DMUH in describing it. This fact should lead us to question more deeply how our research subjects do not enunciate the "truth" of homoerotic relations, but only their particular way of interpreting such relations, which stems from their particular insertion in the field of social signifiers and distinctions, which in turn stems from their particular cultural, individual, and group history.

References

Acosta Félix, Andrés. 2003. *Lenguas en contacto: Un glosario de creatividad lingüística.* Hermosillo, Mexico: Author.

Alfarache, Ángela. 2003. *Identidades lésbicas y cultura feminist: Una investigación antropológica.* Mexico, D.F.: Universidad Nacional Autónoma de México, Plaza y Valdés.

Almaguer, Tomás. 1991. "Chicano Men: A Cartography of Homosexual Identity and Behavior." *Differences* 3(2): 75–100.

———. 1993. "Chicano Men: A Cartography of Homosexual Identity and Behavior." In *The Lesbian and Gay Studies Reader,* edited by Henry Abelove, Michele Aina Barale, and David M. Halperin, 255–73. New York: Routledge.

Alonso, Ana. 1995. *Thread of Blood: Colonialism, Revolution and Gender on Mexico's Northern Frontier.* Tucson: University of Arizona Press.

Alonso, Ana, and Maria Koreck. 1993. "Silences: 'Hispanics,' AIDS and Sexual Practices." In *The Lesbian and Gay Studies Reader,* edited by Henry Abelove, Michele Aina Barale, and David M. Halperin, 110–26. New York: Routledge.

Amuchástegui Herrera, Ana. 1998. "Virginidad e iniciación sexual en México: la sobrevivencia de saberes sexuales subyugados frente a la modernidad." *Debate Feminista* 18 (October): 131–51.

———. 2007. "Ética, deseo y masculinidad: la difícil relación entre lo sexual y lo reproductive." In *Sucede que me canso de ser hombre: Relatos y reflexiones sobre hombres y masculinidades en México,* edited by Ana Amuchástegui Herrera and Ivonne Szasz, 121–40. Mexico City, Mexico: El Colegio de México.

Anderson, Benedict. 1983. *Imagined Communities: Reflections on the Origin and Spread of Nationalism.* London: Verso/New Left Books.

Anest, Marie-Christine. 1994. *Zoophilie, homosexualité, rites de passage et initiation masculine dans la Gréce Contemporaine.* Paris: L'Harmattan.

Anzaldúa, Gloria. 1990. *Borderlands/LaFrontera: The New Mestiza.* San Francisco: Aunt Lute Books.

Badinter, Elizabeth. 1995. *On Masculine Identity*. New York: Columbia University Press.

Balbuena, Raúl. 2006. "Gays en el desierto: Paradojas de la manifestación pública en Mexicali." Tesis Doctoral en Ciencias Sociales, El Colegio de la Frontera Norte, Tijuana, Mexico.

Bauman, Richard. 1987. "The Descentering of Discourse." Paper presented in the annual meeting of the American Anthropological Association.

Bawin Bernadette, and Renée Dandurand. 2003. "Préssentation." *Sociologie et Sociétés. De l'intimité* 35 (2). Montreal, Canada: Les Presses de l'Université de Montréal.

Bederman, Gail. 1995. *Manliness and Civilization: A Cultural History of Gender and Race in the United States, 1889–1917*. Chicago and London: University of Chicago Press.

Benhabib, Seyla, and Drucilla Cornell. 1987. *Feminism as Critique*. Minneapolis: University of Minnesota Press.

Borrillo, Daniel. 2000. *L'Homophobie. Paris: Que sais-je?* Paris: Presses Universitaires de France.

Bourdieu, Pierre. 1968. "El sentimiento del honor en la sociedad de Cabilia." In *El concepto del honor en la sociedad mediterránea*, edited by John G. Peristiany. Barcelona, Spain: Editorial Labor.

———. 1988. *La Distinción*. Madrid: Taurus.

———. 1990. *Sociología y Cultura*. Mexico City, Mexico: CNCA-Grijalbo.

———. 1998. *La Domination Masculine*. Paris: Sage.

———. 2001. *La Science de la science et réflexivité: Cours du College de France 2000–2001*. Paris: Raison d'Agir.

Bronfman, Mario, and Nelson Minello. 1995. "Hábitos sexuales de los migrantes temporales mexicanos a los Estados Unidos de América: Prácticas de riesgo para la infección por VIH." In *SIDA en México: migración, adolescencia y género*, edited by Mario Bronfman et al. Mexico, D.F.: IPE.

Butler, Judith. 1990. *Gender Trouble: Feminism and the Subversion of Identity*. New York: Routledge.

———. 1993. "Imitation and Gender Insubordination." In *The Lesbian and Gay Studies Reader*, edited by Henry Abelove, Michele Aina Barale, and David M. Halperin, 307–20. New York and London: Routledge.

Cáceres, Carlos F., Mario Pecheny, and Veriano Tértor. 2002. *SIDA y sexo entre hombres en América Latina: Vulnerabilidades, Fortalezas, y propuestas para la acción. Perspectivas y reflexiones desde la salud pública, las ciencias sociales y el activismo*. Lima, Peru: Universidad Peruana Cayetano Heredia, Red de investigación en sexualidades y vih/sida en américa latina y ONUSIDA.

Calvario, Eduardo. 2003. "Masculinidad, padecimiento y accidentes de trabajo: El caso de jornaleros agrícolas del poblado Miguel Alemán, Costa de Hermosillo." Tesis de Maestría en Ciencias Sopciales, El Colegio de Sonora, Hermosillo, Mexico.

Carrier, Joseph. 1972. "Urban Mexican Male Homosexual Encounters: An Analysis of Participants and Coping Strategies." PhD diss., University of California, Irvine.

———. 1976. "Cultural Factors Affecting Urban Mexican Male Homosexual Behavior." *Archives of Sexual Behavior* 5:103–24.

———. 1985. "Mexican Male Bisexuality." In *Bisexualities: Theory and Research*, edited by Fred Klein and Timothy J. Wolf, 75–86. New York: Haworth Press.

————. 1995. *De los otros: Intimacy and Homosexuality Among Mexican Men.* New York: Columbia University Press.

Charmaz, Kathy. 2000. "Grounded Theory." In *Handbook of Qualitative Research,* edited by Norman K. Denzin and Yvonna S. Lincoln. Thousand Oaks, CA: Sage.

Chauncey, George. 1994. *Gay New York: Gender, Urban Culture, and the Making of the Gay Male World 1890–1940.* New York: BasicBooks.

Chodorow, Nancy. 1978. *The Reproduction of Mothering: Psychoanalysis and the Sociology of Gender.* Berkeley: University of California Press.

Churchill, Wainwright. 1967. *Homosexual Behavior Among Males: A Cross-Cultural and Cross-Species Investigation.* New York: Hawthorn Books.

Corrigan, Philip, and Derek Sayer. 1993. *The Great Arch: English State Formation as Cultural Revolution.* Oxford, England: Basil Blackwell.

Cosío Barroso, Izchel A. 2005. "Entre masculinidades y gayasidades: Tiríndaro, Michoacán. Un caso etnográfico." *Revista de Estudios de Antropología Sexual* 1(1): 127–40.

De Keijzer, Benno. 1988. "El varón como factor de riesgo: Masculinidad, salud mental y salud reproductive." In *Tuñón, Esperanza, Género y salud en el sureste de México,* 199–219. San Cristobal de las Casas, Mexico: Ecosur.

Derrida, Jacques. 1976. *Of Grammatology.* Baltimore, MD: Johns Hopkins University Press.

Domínguez, Héctor. 2007. *Modernity and the Nation in Mexican Representations of Masculinity: From Sensuality to Bloodshed.* New York: Palgrave Macmillan.

Dulac, Germain. 2003. "Masculinité et intimate." *Sociologie et Sociétés: De l'intimité* 35(2):9–34. Montreal: Les Presses de l'Université de Montréal.

Duranti, Alessandro. 1990. "Politics and Grammar: Agency in Samoan Political Discourse." *American Ethnologist* 17:646–66.

————. 1992. "Intentions, Self, and Responsibility: An Essay in Samoan Ethnopragmatics." In *Responsibility and Evidence in Oral Discourse,* edited by Jane H. Hill and Judith T. Irvine, 24–47. Cambridge, England: Cambridge University Press.

Dutey, Pierre. 1994. "Des mots aux maux. . . ." In *La peur de l'autre en soi: Du sexisme à l'homophobie,* edited by Daniel Welzer-Lang et al., 147–96. Montreal, Canada: VLB Éditeur.

Eribon, Didier. 1999. *Réflexions sur la question gay.* Paris: Fayard.

————. 2004. *Insult and the Making of the Gay Self.* Durham, NC, and London: Duke University Press.

Fanon, Franz. 1965. *The Wretched of the Earth.* New York: Grove Press.

Fausto-Sterling, Anne. 1992. *Myths of Gender: Biological Theories About Women and Men.* New York: Basic Books.

————. 1993. "The Five Sexes: Why Male and Female Are Not Enough." *The Sciences* 33 (2): 20–25.

Ferguson, Katy E. 1993. *The Man Question.* Berkeley: University of California Press.

Figueroa, Juan G. 2006. "¿Y si hablamos de derechos humanos en la reproducción, podríamos incluir a los varones?" In *Debates sobre masculinidades: Poder, desarrollo, políticas públicas y ciudadanía,* edited by Gloria Careaga and Salvador Cruz, 403–28. Mexico City, Mexico: Universidad Nacional Autónoma de México.

Foster David W. 1995. *Cultural Production and Homoerotic Identities: Theory and Applications.* Tempe: Arizona State University [edición de autor].

Foucault, Michel. 1969. *L'Archeologie du savoir*. Paris: Gallimard.

———. 1976. *Histoire de la sexualité, I: La Volonté de savoir*. Paris: Gallimard.

———. 1982. "Le combat de la chasteté." *Communications* 35: 15–25.

———. 1990. *Michel Foucault: Tecnologías del yo y otros textos afines. Introducción de Miguel Morey*. Barcelona, Spain: Paidós, I.C.E.-U.A.B.

———. 2001. *Dits et écrits II, 1976–1988*. Paris: Quarto Gallimard.

Freud, Sigmund. 1960. *Group Psychology and the Analysis of the Ego*. New York: Bantam Books.

———. 1962. *Three Essays on the Theory of Sexuality*. New York: Basic Books.

Fuss, Diane. 1991. *Inside/Out: Lesbian Theories, Gay Theories*. New York: Routledge.

Gal, Susan. 1991. "Between Speech and Silence: The Problematics of Research on Language and Gender." In *Gender at the Crossroads of Knowledge*, edited by Micaela di Leonardo, 175–203. Berkeley: University of California Press.

Garda, Roberto. 2007. "La construcción social de la violencia masculina: Ideas y pistas para apoyar a los hombres que desean dejar su violencia." In *Sucede que me canso de ser hombre: Relatos y reflexiones sobre hombres y masculinidades en México*, edited by Ana Amuchástegui Herrera and Ivonne Szasz, 635–81. Mexico City, Mexico: El Colegio de México.

Giddens, Anthony. 1992. *The Transformation of Intimacy: Sexuality, Love and Eroticism in Modern Societies*. Cambridge, England: Polity Press.

Glaser, Barney G., and Anselm Strauss. 1967. *The Discovery of Grounded Theory*. New York: Aldine.

Granados José A., and Guadalupe Delgado. 2007. *Salud mental y riesgo de VIH-SIDA en jóvenes homosexuales: Aprixmación cualitativa a la experiencia de la homofobia*. Mexico City, Mexico: Universidad Autónoma Metropolitana.

Guevara, Elsa. 2010. *Cuando el amor se instala en la modernidad: Intimidad, masculinidad y jóvenes en México*. Mexico City, Mexico: Universidad Autónoma de México.

Gutiérrez, Saúl. 1998. *Masculinidad y salud reproductiva*. Tesis de Sociología Política, Instituto de Investigaciones Dr. José María Luis Mora, Mexico.

Gutmann, Matthew C. 1996. *The Meanings of Macho: Being a Man in Mexico City*. Berkeley: University of California Press.

Henriques, Julian. 1984. *Changing the Subject: Psychology, Social Regulation and Subjectivity*. London and New York: Methuen.

Herdt, Gilbert. 1981. *Guardian of the Flutes. Idioms of Masculinity*. New York: McGraw-Hill.

———. 1990. "Developmental Continuity as a Dimension of Sexual Orientation Across Cultures." In *Homosexuality and Heterosexuality: The Kinsey Scale and Current Research*, edited by D. McWhirter, J. Reinsisch, and S. Sanders, 208–38. New York: Oxford University Press.

———. 1997. *Same Sex, Different Cultures: Exploring Gay and Lesbian Lives*. Oxford, England: Westview Press.

Hernández, Miguel P. 2002. "No nacimos ni nos hicimos, sólo lo decidimos: La construcción de la identidad gay en el grupo unigay y su relación con el movimiento lésbico, gay, bisexual y transgenérico de la ciudad de México." Tesis de Maestría en Antropología Social, ENAH, Mexico.

Hernández, Misael. 2004. "Hombres cabrones y responsables: Construcción y significados de las masculinidades en Ciudad Victoria, Tamaulipas." Tesis de Maestría, El Colegio de Michoacán, Zamora, Mexico.

Herzfeld, Michael. 1985. *The Poetics of Manhood: Contest and Identity in a Cretan Mountain Village*. Princeton, NJ: Princeton University Press.

Hill, Jane H., and Judith T. Irvine, eds. 1992. *Responsibility and Evidence in Oral Discourse*. Cambridge: Cambridge University Press.

Hocquenghem, Guy. 1972. *Le Désir homosexuel*. Paris: Éditions Universitaires.

Huerta, Fernando. 1999. *El juego del hombre: Deporte y masculinidad entre obreros*. Puebla, Mexico: Benemérita Universidad Autónoma de Puebla, Plaza y Valdés Editores.

Hymes, Dell. 1964. "Introduction: Toward Ethnographies of Communication." *American Anthropologist* 66(6), part 2: The Ethnography of Communication: 1–34.

———. 1971. "Sociolinguistics and the Ethnography of Speaking." In *Social Anthropology and Language*, edited by Edwin Ardener, 47–93. London: Tavistock Publications.

Ingham, John M. 1968. "Culture and Personality in a Mexican Village." PhD diss., University of California, Berkeley.

Irigaray, Luce. 1994. *Thinking the Difference: For a Peaceful Revolution*. New York: Routledge.

Irvine, Judith T. 1992. "Insult and Responsibility: Verbal Abuse in a Wolof Village." In *Responsibility and Evidence in Oral Discourse*, edited by Jane H. Hill and Judith T. Irvine, 105–34. Cambridge: Cambridge University Press.

Jagose, Annamarie. 1996. *Queer Theory*. New York: New York University Press.

Jameson, Fredric. 1981. *The Political Unconscious*. Ithaca, NY: Cornell University Press.

Jefferson, Tony. 1994. "Theorising Masculinity." In *Just Boys Doing Business? Men, Masculinities and Crime*, edited by Tim Newburn and Elizabeth A. Stanko, 10–31. London and New York: Routledge.

Jiménez, María L. 2003. *Dando voz a los varones: Sexualidad, reproducción y paternidad de algunos mexicanos*. Mexico City, Mexico: Universidad Nacional Autónoma de México.

Kardiner, Abram. 1945. *The Psychological Frontiers of Society*. New York: Columbia University Press.

Katz, Jonathan N. 1995. *The Invention of Heterosexuality*. New York: Penguin.

———. 2001. *Love Stories: Sex Between Men Before Homosexuality*. Chicago: University of Chicago Press.

Kimmel S. Michel, and Michel A. Messner. 1995. *Men's Lives*. Boston: Allyn &Bacon.

Kinsey, Alfred C. 1948. *Sexual Behavior in the Human Male*. Philadelphia: Saunders Company.

Lacan, Jacques. 1977. *Ecrits: A Selection*. New York: W.W. Norton.

Laclau, Ernest, and Chantal Mouffé. 1982. "Recasting Marxism: Hegemony and Socialist Strategy: Toward a Radical Democratic Politics." *Socialist Review* 6(12): 91–113.

Lamas, Marta, comp. 1996. *El género: la construcción cultural de la diferencia sexual*. Mexico, D.F.: Universidad Nacional Autónoma de México y Miguel Ángel Porrúa Casa Editorial.

Lancaster, Roger. 1992. *Life Is Hard: Machismo, Danger and the Intimacy of Power in Nicaragua.* Berkeley: University of California Press.

List, Mauricio. 2007. "Masculinidad e identidad gay en la Ciudad de México." In *Sucede que me canso de ser hombre: Relatos y reflexiones sobre hombres y masculinidades en México,* edited by Ana Amuchástegui Herrera and Ivonne Szasz, 433–78. Mexico City, Mexico: El Colegio de México.

López, Álvaro, and Rosaura Carmona. 2012. *El turismo sexual masculino en México.* Mexico City, Mexico: Universidad Nacional Autónoma de México.

López, Martín De la Cruz. 2010. *Hacerse hombres cabales: Masculinidad entre tojolabales.* Tuxtla Gutiérrez, Mexico: UNICACH.

Luciano, Lynne. 2001. *Looking Good: Male Body Image in Modern America.* New York: Hill and Wang.

Malinowsky, Bronislaw. 1922. *Argonauts of the Western Pacific: An Account of Native Enterprise and Adventure in the Archipelagoes of Melanesian New Guinea.* London: Routledge and Kegan Paul.

Marquet, Antonio. 2001. *Que se quede el infinito sin estrellas: La cultura gay al final del milenio.* Mexico City, Mexico: Universidad Autónoma Metropolitana.

———. 2006. *El crepúsculo de heterolandia: Master de jotería.* Mexico City, Mexico: Universidad Autónoma Metropolitana.

———. 2011. *El coloquio de las perras.* Mexico City, Mexico: Universidad Autónoma Metropolitana.

McBride, James. 1995. *War, Battering, and Other Sports: The Gulf Between American Men and Women.* Amherst, NY: Prometheus Books.

Miano, Marinella. 2002. *Hombre, mujer y muxe' en el Istmo de Tehuantepec.* Mexico, D.F.: CIESAS y Plaza y Valdés.

Mogrovejo, Norma. 2000. *Un amor que se atrevió a decir su nombre: La lucha de las lesbianas y su relación con los homosexuales y feministas en América Latina.* Mexico, D.F.: Plaza y Valdéz.

Mohanty, Chandra Talpade. 1984. "Under Western Eyes: Feminist Scholarship and Colonial Discourses." Boundary 2. 12:3–13:1. 333–58.

Monsiváis, Carlos. 1995. "Ortodoxia y heterodoxia en las alcohobas (hacia una crónica de las costumbres y creencias sexuales en México)." *Debate Feminista* 11:180–210.

———. 2010. *Que se abra esa puerta: Crónicas y ensayos sobre la diversidad sexual.* Mexico, D.F.: Paidós.

Moraga, Cherrie. 1983. *Loving in the War Years: Lo que nunca pasó por sus labios.* Boston: South End Press.

Mort, Frank. 1996. *Cultures of Consumption: Masculinities and Social Space in Late Twentieth-Century Britain.* London and New York: Routledge.

Mosse, George L. 1996. *The Image of Man: The Creation of Modern Masculinity.* New York and Oxford: Oxford University Press.

Muñiz, Elsa. 2002. *Cuerpo representación y poder: México en los albores de la reconstrucción nacional 1920–1934.* Mexico, D.F.: Miguel Ángel Porrúa.

Murray, Stephen. 1997. "Homosexuality." In *The Dictionary of Anthropology,* edited by Thomas Barfield. Oxford, England: Basil Blackwell.

Murray, Stephen, and Will Roscoe. 1998. *Boy Wives and Female Husbands: Studies in African Homosexualities.* New York: Palgrave.

Núñez Noriega, Guillermo. 1994. *Sexo entre varones: Poder y resistencia en el campo sexual.* Hermosillo, Sonora, Mexico: El Colegio de Sonora y Universidad de Sonora.

———. 1995. "La invención de Sonora: región, regionalismo y formación del estado en el México postcolonial del siglo XIX," In *Revista de El Colegio de Sonora* (Publicación semestral) 6 (9): 153–85. Hermosillo, Mexico: El Colegio de Sonora.

Núñez, Guillermo. 1998. "'Madres solteras,' 'madres adolescentes' y 'maquiladoras rurales,' Politicas de gènero y globalizaciòn en la sierra sonorense." *Estudios Sociales* 16. Hermosillo, Mexico: CIAD, AC-El Colegio de Sonora–Unison.

———. 2000. *Sexo entre varones: Poder y resistencia en el campo sexual.* Mexico, D.F.: El Colegio de Sonora, Porrúa, PUEG-UNAM.

———. 2004a. "Vínculo de pareja y hombría: atender y mantener en dultos mayores del Río Sonora México." In *Sucede que me canso de ser hombre: Relatos y reflexiones sobre hombres y masculinidades en México,* edited by Ana Amuchástegui Herrera and Ivonne Szasz. Mexico City, Mexico: El Colegio de México.

———. 2004b. "Los 'hombres' y el conocimiento: Reflexiones epistemológicas para el estudio de 'los hombres' como sujetos genéricos, en Desacatos." *Revista de Antropología Social* 15–16: 13–32. Masculinidades Diversas. Mexico, D.F.: CIESAS.

———. 2007a. *Masculinidad e intimidad: identidad, sexualidad y sida.* México, D.F.: El Colegio de Sonora, Miguel Ángel Porrúa y Universidad Nacional Autónoma de México.

———. 2007b. "Vínculo de pareja y hombría: 'atender y mantener' en adultos mayores del Río Sonora, México." In *Sucede que me canso de ser hombre. Relatos y reflexiones sobre hombres y masculinidades en México,* edited by Ana Amuchástegui Herrera and Ivonne Szasz, 141–81. Mexico City, Mexico: El Colegio de México.

———. 2009. *Vidas vulnerables hombres indígenas, diversidad sexual y VIH-Sida.* Mexico, D.F.: EDAMEX y CIAD, A.C.

———. 2010. "Reflexiones para una mesa de diálogo que a penas empieza: feminismos y estudios de género de los hombres en México." *Revista GénEros* 2(6): 35–54.

———. 2011. ¿Qué es la diversidad sexual? Reflexiones desde la academia y el movimiento ciudadano. Quito, Ecuador: Abya Yala, CIAD, A.C.

———. 2012. "Who Are the 'MSM'?" Sexual Identities, Social Class, and Strategies in the Fight against AIDS in Mexico. *Journal of the Southwest* vol. 54, no. 4 (Winter 2012): 635–82.

———. 2013a. *Hombres Sonorenses: Un Estudio de género de tres generaciones.* Mexico, D.F.: Universidad de Sonora y Pearson Educación.

———. 2013b. "Seeve/Frescos: sexualidad, género y etnicidad en los significados de las relaciones sexuales entre varones en comunidades yoeme (yaquis) de Sonora, Mexico," *Revista de Estudios de Antropología Sexual,* Primera época, volumen 1, número 4, 96–120.

Ochs, Elionor. 1990. "Indexicality and Socialization." In *Cultural Psychology,* edited by James Stigler, Gilbert Herdt, and Richard A. Shweder, 287–308. Cambridge: Cambridge University Press.

O'Malley, Ilene. 1986. *The Myth of the Revolution: Hero Cults and the Institutionalization of the Mexican State, 1930–1980.* Westport, CT: Greenwood Press.

Packard, Chris. 2005. *Queer Cowboys and Other Erotic Male Friendships in Nineteenth-Century American Literature.* New York: Palgrave Macmillan.

Parker, Richard. 1991. *Bodies, Pleasure and Passions: Sexual Culture in Contemporary Brazil.* Boston: Beacon Press.

Parrini, Rodrigo. 2007. *Panópticos laberintos: Subjetivación, deseo y corporalidad en una cárcel de hombres.* Mexico City, Mexico: El Colegio de México.

Paz, Octavio. 1959. *El laberinto de la soledad.* Mexico, D.F.: Fondo de Cultura Económica.

Peristiany, John G., ed. 1968. *El concepto del honor en la sociedad mediterránea.* Barcelona, Spain: Editorial Labor.

Ponce, Patricia. 2006. *Sexualidades costeñas: Un pueblo veracruzano entre el río y la mar.* Mexico, D.F.: CIESAS.

Prieur, Annick. 1998. *Mema's House, Mexico City: On Transvestites, Queens, and Machos.* Chicago: University of Chicago Press.

Quinn, Michael D. 1996. "Same-Sex Dynamics Among Nineteenth Century Americans: A Mormon Example." Urbana and Chicago: University of Illinois Press.

Ramírez, Juan C. 2005. *Madejas entreveradas: violencia, masculinidad y poder. Varones que ejercen violencia contra sus parejas.* Mexico, D.F.: Plaza y Valdés.

Rich, Adrienne. 1980. "Compulsory Heterosexuality and Lesbian Existence." *Signs* vol. 5, no. 4, *Women: Sex and Sexuality,* 631–60. Chicago: The University of Chicago Press.

Rivas, Eloy. 2005. "¿El varón como factor de riesgo? Masculinidad y mortalidad por accidents y otras causas violentas en la sierra de Sonora." *Estudios sociales. Revista de Investigación Científica* 13(26).

Rodríguez Gabriela y De Keijzer, Benno. 2002. *La noche se hizo para los hombres: Sexualidad en los procesos de cortejo entre jóvenes campesinas y campesinos.* Mexico, D.F.: EDAMEX.

Rosas, Carolina. 2007. "Migrar para proveer: *Cardaleños* desde Veracruz a Chicago: Un studio cualitativo con varones adultos." In *Reflexiones sobre masculinidad y empleo,* edited by María L. Jiménez and Olivia Tena, 473–506. Mexico City, Mexico: Universidad Nacional Autónoma de México.

Said, Edward. 1979. *Orientalism.* New York: Random House.

Salguero, María. 2007. "Preguntarse cómo ser padre es también preguntarse cómo ser hombre: reflexiones sobre algunos varoes." In *Sucede que me canso de ser hombre: Relatos y reflexiones sobre hombres y masculinidades en México,* edited by Ana Amuchástegui Herrera and Ivonne Szasz, 563–99. Mexico City, Mexico: El Colegio de México.

Salinas, Héctor. 2006. "Políticas públicas de disidencia sexual: apuntes para una agenda." In *Disidencia sexual e identidades sexuales y genéricas,* 21–30. Mexico, D.F.: CONAPRED.

Sattel, Jack W. 1983. "Men, In Expressivness and Power." In *Language, Gender and Society,* edited by Barrie Thorne, Cheris Kramarae, and Nancy Henley, 118–24. Rowley, MA: Newbury House.

Sedgwick, Eve K. 1990. *Epistemology of the Closet.* Berkeley: University of California Press.

———. 1992. *Between Men: English Literature and Male Homosocial Desire.* 2nd ed. New York: Columbia University Press.

Seidler, Victor. 1989. *Rediscovering Masculinity: Reason, Language and Sexuality.* London: Routledge.

Sherzel, Joel. 1987. "A Discourse-Centered Approach to the Study of Language and Culture." *American Anthropologist* (89): 295–309.

Silverman, Kaja. 1983. *The Subject of Semiotics*. New York and Oxford: Oxford University Press.

Silverstein, Michael. 1977. "Cultural Prerequisites to Grammatical Analysis." In *Linguistics and Anthropology: Georgetown University Round Table on Languages and Linguistics 1977*, edited by Muriel Saville-Troike, 139–52. Washington, DC: Georgetown University Press.

Simonelli, Jeanne M. 1987. "Defective Modernization and Health in Mexico." *Social Science & Medicine* 24(1): 23–36.

Smith, Kenneth T. 1971. "Homophobia a Tentative Personality Profile." *Psychological Reports* 29:1091–94.

Spivak, Chakravorty Gayatri. 1988. "Can the Subaltern Speak?" In *Marxism and the Interpretation of Culture*, edited by Cary Nelson and Lawrence Grossberg, 271–313. Urbana: University of Illinois Press.

Strauss, Anselm, and Juliet Corbin. 1990. *Basics in Qualitative Research*. Newbury Park, CA: Sage.

Taylor, Clark L. 1978a. "El Ambiente: Male Homosexual Social Life in Mexico City." PhD diss., University of California, Berkeley.

———. 1978b. "How Mexicans Define Male Homosexuality: Labeling and the Buga View." *Kroeber Anthropological Society Papers*, 53 and 54, 106–28. Berkeley: University of California.

———. 1986. "Mexican Male Homosexual Interaction in Public Contexts." In *The Many Faces of Homosexuality*, edited by Evelyn Blackwood, 117–36. New York: Harrington Park Press.

Trobst, Krista K., Rebecca L. Collins, and Jayne M. Embree. 1994. "The Role of Emotion in Social Support Provision: Gender, Empathy and Expression of Distress." *Journal of Social and Personal Relationships* 11(1):45–62.

Turner, Barry A. 1981. "Some Practical Aspects of Qualitative Data Analysis." *Quality and Quantity* 15: 225–47.

Weinberg, George. 1973. *Society and the Healthy Homosexual*. New York: Anchor Books.

Welzer-Lang, Daniel. 1994. "L'Homophobie: la face cachée du masculine." In *La peur de l'autre en soi: Du sexisme à l'homophobie*, edited by Daniel Welzer-Lang et al., 13–88. Montreal, Canada: vlb éditeur.

Williams, Walter L. 1986. *The Spirit and the Flesh: Sexual Diversity in American Indian Culture*. Boston: Beacon Press.

Whitman, Walt. 1973. *Leaves of Grass*. New York: W.W. Norton.

Zazueta, Edgar. 2008. "Las concepciones de género de los varones jóvenes adultos que han vivido en pareja heterosexual y su relación con el divorcio (Ciudad obregón y Hermosillo)." Tesis de Maestría en Desarrollo Regional, CIAD, A.C., Hermosillo, Mexico.

Zeeland, Steven. 1993. *Barrack Buddies and Soldier Lovers: Dialogues with Gay Young Men in the US Military*. New York: Harrington Park Press.

———. 1995. *Sailors and Sexual Identity: Crossing the Line Between "Straight" and "Gay" in the US Navy*. New York: Harrington Park Press.

Index

About the Author

Guillermo Núñez Noriega was born in Guaymas, Sonora, Mexico, in 1967. He studied sociology at the University of Sonora and holds a master's degree in humanities from Arizona State University and a PhD in anthropology from the University of Arizona. He has been a researcher at the Centro de Investigación en Alimentación y Desarrollo (CIAD) in Hermosillo, Sonora, Mexico, since 1997. He is the author of several books in Spanish: *Sexo entre varones: Poder y resistencia en el campo sexual* (1994, 1999, 2000), *Masculinidad e intimidad: identidad, sexualidad y sida* (2007), *Vidas vulnerables: hombres indígenas, diversidad sexual y VIH-Sida* (2009), *¿Qué es la diversidad sexual? Reflexiones desde la academia y el movimiento ciudadano* (2011), and *Hombres Sonorenses: un estudio de género de tres generaciones* (2013). He has published widely in scientific journals and books in Mexico and Latin America on the topics of sex and gender in northern Mexico, indigenous homosexualities, risk and health, regional culture of northern Mexico, and Chicana feminism. He is considered one of the leading authorities on the study of sexuality, masculinity, and gender in Latin America. He founded the scientific organization Academia Mexicana de Estudios de Género de los Hombres. When he was twenty years old, he organized the first grassroots educational campaign about HIV and AIDS in his home state, Sonora, and since then he has been a social organizer and activist in Mexico on issues of sexual freedom, gender equality, social justice, HIV and AIDS, and nondiscrimination. He is a frequent lecturer in many universities in Mexico and Latin America.

The Southwest Center Series

Joseph C. Wilder, Editor

Ignaz Pfefferkorn, *Sonora: A Description of the Province*

Carl Lumholtz, *New Trails in Mexico*

Buford Pickens, *The Missions of Northern Sonora: A 1935 Field Documentation*

Gary Paul Nabhan, editor, *Counting Sheep: Twenty Ways of Seeing Desert Bighorn*

Eileen Oktavec, *Answered Prayers: Miracles and Milagros Along the Border*

Curtis M. Hinsley and David R. Wilcox, editors, *Frank Hamilton Cushing and the Hemenway Southwestern Archaeological Expedition, 1886–1889*, volume 1: *The Southwest in the American Imagination: The Writings of Sylvester Baxter, 1881–1899*

Lawrence J. Taylor and Maeve Hickey, *The Road to Mexico*

Donna J. Guy and Thomas E. Sheridan, editors, *Contested Ground: Comparative Frontiers on the Northern and Southern Edges of the Spanish Empire*

Julian D. Hayden, *The Sierra Pinacate*

Paul S. Martin, David Yetman, Mark Fishbein, Phil Jenkins, Thomas R. Van Devender, and Rebecca K. Wilson, editors, *Gentry's Rio Mayo Plants: The Tropical Deciduous Forest and Environs of Northwest Mexico*

W J McGee, *Trails to Tiburón: The 1894 and 1895 Field Diaries of W J McGee*, transcribed by Hazel McFeely Fontana, annotated and with an introduction by Bernard L. Fontana

Richard Stephen Felger, *Flora of the Gran Desierto and Río Colorado of Northwestern Mexico*

Donald Bahr, editor, *O'odham Creation and Related Events: As Told to Ruth Benedict in 1927 in Prose, Oratory, and Song by the Pimas William Blackwater, Thomas Vanyiko, Clara Ahiel, William Stevens, Oliver Wellington, and Kisto*

Dan L. Fischer, *Early Southwest Ornithologists, 1528–1900*

Thomas Bowen, editor, *Backcountry Pilot: Flying Adventures with Ike Russell*

Federico José María Ronstadt, *Borderman: Memoirs of Federico José María Ronstadt*, edited by Edward F. Ronstadt

Curtis M. Hinsley and David R. Wilcox, editors, *Frank Hamilton Cushing and the Hemenway Southwestern Archaeological Expedition, 1886–1889*, volume 2: *The Lost Itinerary of Frank Hamilton Cushing*

Neil Goodwin, *Like a Brother: Grenville Goodwin's Apache Years, 1928–1939*

Katherine G. Morrissey and Kirsten Jensen, editors, *Picturing Arizona: The Photographic Record of the 1930s*

Bill Broyles and Michael Berman, *Sunshot: Peril and Wonder in the Gran Desierto*

David W. Lazaroff, Philip C. Rosen, and Charles H. Lowe Jr., *Amphibians, Reptiles, and Their Habitats at Sabino Canyon*

David Yetman, *The Organ Pipe Cactus*

Gloria Fraser Giffords, *Sanctuaries of Earth, Stone, and Light: The Churches of Northern New Spain, 1530–1821*

David Yetman, *The Great Cacti: Ethnobotany and Biogeography*

John Messina, *Álamos, Sonora: Architecture and Urbanism in the Dry Tropics*

Laura L. Cummings, *Pachucas and Pachucos in Tucson: Situated Border Lives*

Bernard L. Fontana and Edward McCain, *A Gift of Angels: The Art of Mission San Xavier del Bac*

David A. Yetman, *The Ópatas: In Search of a Sonoran People*

Julian D. Hayden, *Field Man: The Life of a Desert Archaeologist*, edited by Bill Broyles and Diane Boyer

Bill Broyles, Gayle Harrison Hartmann, Thomas E. Sheridan, Gary Paul Nabhan, and Mary Charlotte Thurtle, *Last Water on the Devil's Highway: A Cultural and Natural History of Tinajas Altas*

Thomas E. Sheridan, *Arizona: A History*, Revised Edition

Richard S. Felger and Benjamin Theodore Wilder, *Plant Life of a Desert Archipelago: Flora of the Sonoran Islands in the Gulf of California*

David Burckhalter, *Baja California Missions: In the Footsteps of the Padres*

Cathy Moser Marlett, *Shells on a Desert Shore: Mollusks in the Seri World*

Guillermo Núñez Noriega, *Just Between Us: An Ethnography on Male Identity and Intimacy in Rural Communities of Northern México*